Workbook/Laboratory Manual
to accompany

Yookoso!
Continuing with Contemporary Japanese

Second Edition

Suzuko Hamasaki
University of California, Irvine

Hifumi Ito
University of California, San Diego

Hiroko Kataoka
California State University, Long Beach

Akemi Morioka
University of California, Irvine

Yasu-Hiko Tohsaku
University of California, San Diego

McGraw Hill

Boston   Burr Ridge, IL   Dubuque, IA   Madison, WI   New York   San Francisco   St. Louis
Bangkok   Bogotá   Caracas   Lisbon   London   Madrid
Mexico City   Milan   New Delhi   Seoul   Singapore   Sydney   Taipei   Toronto

McGraw-Hill Higher Education

A Division of The McGraw-Hill Companies

This is an  book.

Workbook/Laboratory Manual to accompany
Yookoso! Continuing with Contemporary Japanese

6 7 8 9 0 QPD/QPD 9 0 9 8 7 6 5 4 3

ISBN 0-07-013698-X

http://www.mhhe.com

Contents

To the Instructor

This *Workbook/Laboratory Manual* is designed to accompany *Yookoso! Continuing with Contemporary Japanese, Second Edition.* It offers a variety of listening and writing exercises to reinforce the language functions, pronunciation, vocabulary, and structures that are presented in the main text. It also includes explanations, charts, and exercises for the newly introduced **kanji.** Each numbered chapter consists of four sections: *Listening Comprehension Activities, Kanji Practice and Exercises, Writing Activities,* and a *Chapter Review.*

The *Listening Comprehension Activities* and *Writing Activities* for each chapter are divided into subsections corresponding to those in the main textbook. After completing a given subsection in the main textbook, the instructor can assign the appropriate exercises in the *Workbook/Laboratory Manual.*

In the *Listening Comprehension Activities,* we have made every effort to provide students with authentic-sounding Japanese discourse, in both dialogues and monologues, but the questions and instructions are given in English so that the student can concentrate fully on the content of the recorded material without spending a lot of time decoding written Japanese. The activities in this section develop listening comprehension through dialogues, interviews, and narratives. A feature of this section is "Task Listening," a set of exercises requiring students to make decisions, solve problems, or synthesize information based on the content of spoken dialogues. All spoken material for the *Listening Comprehension Activities* is recorded in the Audio Program, and audioscripts are included in the *Instructor's Manual.*

The *Kanji Practice and Exercises* section consists of three parts. The first part is a chart of the active **kanji** presented in the chapter. The second presents exercises for both reading and writing those **kanji.** The third, "Kanji in Everyday Life," gives students practice in making intelligent guesses about unfamiliar combinations of familiar **kanji,** an important skill for reading signs and personal messages in Japan. Only those **kanji** previously presented for active mastery are used in the *Writing Activities* section, so we suggest that students finish the *Kanji Practice and Exercises* before moving on to the *Writing Activities.* The *Kanji Exercises* in *Do You Remember?* provide a game- and task-based review of the **hiragana, katakana,** and **kanji** introduced in Book 1.

In the *Writing Activities,* the exercises progress from controlled, mechanical exercises to those requiring dialogue completion or creative or personalized responses. Many activities are based on drawings, realia, or authentic materials. Any of these exercises may be done as group or pair activities in class or individually at home. In addition to topic- or function-based exercises, some chapters include opportunities for practicing specific grammatical structures presented in the *Language Notes* of the main text.

At the end of each chapter are several *Review* exercises that combine chapter material in new ways.

The cast of characters from the main text also appears throughout the *Workbook/Laboratory Manual.* The answers to all the exercises are included in the *Instructor's Manual.*

The authors would like to express their gratitude to Sachiko Fuji and Yumiko Shiotani for their contributions to this *Workbook/Laboratory Manual.* We also wish to extend our sincere appreciation to Thalia Dorwick, Vice President and Editor-in-Chief at McGraw-Hill, for her guidance, suggestions, and insightful comments, and to Peggy Potter and Pat Murray for their superb editing. Finally, we must note the invaluable assistance of Natalie Durbin and the rest of the capable production staff at McGraw-Hill.

Suzuko Hamasaki
Hifumi Ito
Hiroko Kataoka
Akemi Morioko
Yasu-Hiko Tohsaku

To the Student

The format of the *Workbook/Laboratory Manual* follows that of the main textbook. Each of the numbered chapters consists of four sections: *Listening Comprehension Activities, Kanji Practice and Exercises, Writing Activities,* and *Chapter Review.*

The *Listening Comprehension Activities* section contains questions and activities based on the dialogues and narratives recorded in the accompanying Audio Program. The recordings provide you with opportunities to listen to spoken Japanese in a variety of contexts and to practice and test your listening skills outside the classroom.

The *Listening Comprehension Activities* include open-ended, multiple-choice, and true/false questions, and fill-in-the-blank exercises for you to work on while listening to the recordings. The written instructions explain the task, provide you with a general idea of the context, and identify the speakers of the dialogues or narratives. All instructions and questions are in English so that you can practice listening to spoken Japanese without worrying about understanding written Japanese.

We suggest that you follow these steps when you do the *Listening Comprehension Activities.*

1. Read the instructions carefully so that you understand the topic and context of the recording and who the speakers are. If possible, guess what vocabulary might be used, and figure out how much of it you already know in Japanese.
2. Study any new vocabulary that is provided after the instructions.
3. Before reading the questions in the exercise, listen to the recording once. Think about whether or not you have understood the gist of the passage and how much specific information you have been able to comprehend.
4. Read through the questions. Figure out what information you need to answer them.
5. Listen to the recording again, concentrating on finding the information you need.
6. Listen to the recordings as many times as necessary. Do not, however, stop the recording in the middle of the dialogues or narratives. (In real-life situations, no one will stop talking for your convenience unless, perhaps, you are engaged in a personal conversation.) If necessary, review the vocabulary, expressions, and structures in the corresponding sections of the main textbook before repeating this process.

In most of the listening activities, you can answer the questions without understanding everything in the recording. Even when listening to spoken English in everyday life you can often get the gist of a conversation or the specific information you want without understanding every word. You will find that the same strategy works for Japanese.

In the "Task Listening" exercises, you will make decisions, solve problems, or gather information based on the content of a dialogue or narrative.

One effective way to develop your listening skills is to listen to your Japanese recordings as much as possible. You can listen to them while exercising, doing household chores, riding public transportation, or just relaxing. Or you can listen to them in the car while driving around town or while stuck in traffic. At any rate, try to pay attention to the general content of the recordings. You will find that the more you listen to them, the more you will understand, and the better your listening skills will become.

You can also use the audio program for improving your pronunciation. After you are able to comprehend the gist of a recorded segment, pay attention to the speakers' intonation and rhythm. Try to repeat their words after them and mimic their delivery.

The *Kanji Practice and Exercises* are designed to provide you with practice in writing the active **kanji** presented in the main chapters. (The *Kanji Exercises* section in *Do You Remember?* reintroduces you to **hiragana, katakana,** and the **kanji** presented in Book 1.) The **kanji** charts are organized in the following way:

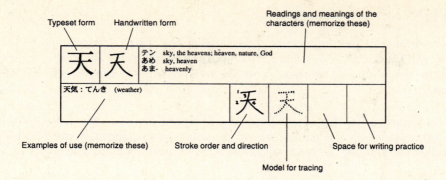

The Latin alphabet has no set stroke order, so many English-speaking students tend to ignore the rules for writing **kanji** and develop bad habits that result in misshapen characters. You must follow the set stroke order and direction. Your characters will look better, and practicing the correct way of writing will help imprint the shape of the character in your memory. These charts have only two spaces for practicing each character, so for additional practice use engineering graph paper. Better yet is the special "**kanji**-ruled" paper, called **genkooyooshi** in Japanese, that can often be found in Japanese and Chinese import stores.

It is always a good idea to learn a new **kanji** along with its most commonly occurring compounds or with its **okurigana** (**hiragana** endings) instead of as an isolated symbol. For this reason, we have provided exercises in which you either transcribe the pronunciation of a **kanji** or compound in **hiragana** or insert **kanji** into sentences. The more you see and write the new **kanji** in meaningful contexts, the better you will remember them.

A feature of the **kanji** section in this *Workbook/Laboratory Manual* is called "Kanji in Everyday Life." If you ever go to Japan, and especially if you ever live there, you will frequently need to read unfamiliar combinations of familiar **kanji** and make intelligent guesses about material that you do not understand entirely. This section gives you practice in those important skills.

The *Writing Activities* give you the opportunity to use the vocabulary, expressions, and structures presented in the main text in their written forms as you practice expressing your ideas and thoughts in Japanese. Like the *Listening Comprehension Activities,* the *Writing Activities* are divided into the same subsections as the main textbook, so refer to the relevant section if you have any questions. Only **kanji** presented before or in the current chapter are used in the *Writing Activities.* We recommend that you work with the *Kanji Practice and Exercises* first. Then the *Writing Activities* will provide extra reinforcement for the **kanji** you have just learned.

At the end of each chapter are several *Review* exercises that combine chapter material in new ways.

The cast of characters from the main text also appears throughout the *Workbook/Laboratory Manual.* The students use Japanese in their language class and as a means of communication with each other. As you hear and read about these characters and work through the exercises and activities in this manual, you will learn to talk and write about your own life and concerns as an English-speaking student of Japanese.

About the Authors

Suzuko Hamasaki has been a lecturer in Japanese at the Department of East Asian Languages and Literatures, University of California, Irvine, since 1991. For the past few years, she has been in charge of teaching and developing the advanced Japanese course. She holds an M.A. in linguistics from California State University, Fullerton.

Hifumi Ito has been a lecturer in Japanese at the Program in Japanese Studies, University of California, San Diego since 1989. Currently, she is coordinating the second-year Japanese language course and is in charge of Japanese TA supervision and training. She received her M.A. in Japanese from the University of Minnesota.

Hiroko C. Kataoka is associate professor in the Department of Asian and Asian-American Studies at California State University, Long Beach, and chief academic specialist at the Japan Foundation & Language Center in Los Angeles. In addition to the Japanese language, she has been teaching Japanese language pedagogy courses. She received her Ph.D. in education at the University of Illinois, Urbana-Champaign. She has written numerous books, articles, and conference reports on teaching Japanese. She has also given a number of workshops on language pedagogy.

Akemi Morioka has been academic coordinator of the Japanese program in the Department of East Asian Languages and Literatures at the University of California, Irvine, since 1989. She is an author of 日本について考えよう *Let's Think about Japan* (McGraw-Hill), a Japanese textbook for intermediate to advanced learners. She holds an M.A. in linguistics from California State University, Long Beach.

Yasu-Hiko Tohsaku is a full professor at the University of California, San Diego, where he is the director of the language program at the graduate school of International Relations and Pacific Studies and the coordinator of the undergraduate Japanese language program. He received his Ph.D. in linguistics from the University of California, San Diego. He is the author of numerous papers on second-language acquisition and Japanese language pedagogy. He is also the author of the main text of *Yookoso!*

DO YOU REMEMBER?

Listening Comprehension Activities

A. Classmates. Listen to three young men, who have just enrolled in a summer English class, as they talk about themselves. Then fill in the blanks with the initial of the person described by each sentence.

(K: きむら   N: のぐち   S: さとう)

1. _____ is from Kyoto.

2. _____ is from Kobe.

3. _____ studies in Osaka.

4. _____ studies in Tokyo.

5. _____ has not decided on a major yet.

6. _____ is a junior at a university.

7. _____ does not go to a university.

8. _____ is majoring in engineering.

9. _____ likes sports.

10. _____ likes to study.

11. _____ detests studying.

12. _____ studies guitar at a music school.

13. _____ works on Thursdays and Fridays.

Which bachelor do you like the most? And why? In English, explain why you like that bachelor the most.

_____

_____

B. My Town. Heather Gibson is in Tokyo, and has sent an e-mail to her former Japanese teacher in California. Listen to what she wrote and insert in the squares provided the correct names of the buildings on the following map, and add descriptions in the parentheses.

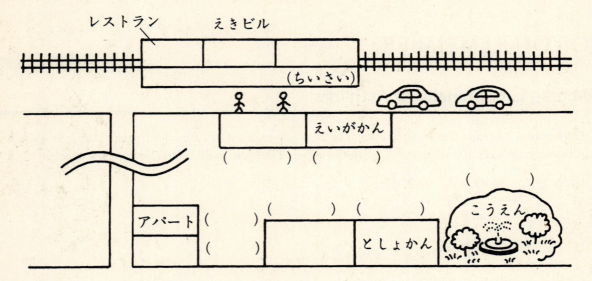

C. Everyday Life. Listen to Takako Matsui talk about her life. Then fill out the chart showing her weekly schedule in English, and answer the questions by choosing the most appropriate answer from a, b, and c.

	7 A.M.	8	10	12 NOON	2 P.M.	4	6	8
Monday/ Wednesday								
Tuesday/ Thursday								
Friday								
Saturday								

1. How well can Takako Matsui speak English and French?
    a. very well   b. not very well   c. very badly

2. What kind of part-time job(s) does she do?
    a. working at the office   b. working at a coffee shop   c. both a and b

3. What instrument does she play?
    a. piano   b. flute   c. guitar

4. What nationalities are the students in the karate class?
    a. Japanese   b. American and Chinese   c. both a and b

5. What day of the week does she like the most?
    a. Monday   b. Wednesday   c. Saturday

D. Weather and Climate. Listen to the monologue and choose the best answer for each question from among a, b, and c.

1. The speaker came to Tokyo
    a. this summer.   b. last summer.   c. last spring.

2. The speaker studies Japanese every day because
    a. there is a lot of homework.   b. she has a lot of spare time.   c. the teacher is strict.

3. Summer in Tokyo is
    a. as hot as in Tifton.
    b. hotter than in Tifton, but less humid.
    c. hotter and more humid than in Tifton.

4. Last summer, the speaker went to the beach and the beach was
    a. crowded.   b. pretty.   c. quiet.

5. Tokyo Disneyland was
    a. more fun than its American counterpart.
    b. not so much fun as its American counterpart.
    c. as much fun as its American counterpart.

6. During winter in Tokyo, it is
    a. warm but very windy.   b. cold but not so windy.   c. cold and very windy.

7. The speaker likes winter
    a. in Tifton more than in Tokyo.
    b. in Tokyo more than in Tifton.
    c. in Tokyo as much as in Tifton.

8. In winter, it snows
    a. only in Tokyo.   b. only in Tifton.   c. both in Tifton and in Tokyo.

9. On Christmas day, the speaker and her boyfriend
    a. stayed home all day.   b. went to a cafe.   c. went walking in the park.

10. The speaker is going back to Tifton
    a. in January.   b. in April.   c. in July.

E. Hobbies and Leisure Activities. Listen to John Kawamura asking Hitomi Machida about sports, and mark each statement true (T) or false (F).

1. _____ Machida can swim about five kilometers.

2. _____ Machida used to swim with her brothers every day.

3. _____ Of the three siblings, Machida's older brother can swim the farthest.

4. _____ Machida often goes swimming even though she is busy.

5. _____ Kawamura likes basketball more than swimming.

6. _____ Kawamura does not play basketball because he is busy.

7. _____ Machida would love to play basketball with Kawamura.

F. Food. John Kawamura has been in Tokyo since last summer, and he writes to his former teacher in California occasionally. Listen to his message, and then answer each question briefly.

Useful Vocabulary: からだ *body, health,* しんせん（な）*fresh, new*

In the letter:

1. What does he say about the weather in Tokyo now? _____

2. Where did he go with his host family? _____

3. How did the fish taste at the restaurant? _____

4. What are the fish he was used to eating? _____

5. What did he try for the first time at the restaurant? _____

6. Has he eaten raw beef? _____

7. What does he say about natto for breakfast? _____

G. Shopping. Listen to Ms. Yamaguchi's experience with a sales clerk in a store. Then choose the best answer to each question.

1. Ms. Yamaguchi asked a sales clerk to help her because
   a. she did not know if it was the right store.
   b. she did not know what to get.
   c. she wanted to know whether they would accept credit cards.
   d. she wanted to know if they were having a sale.

2. Ms. Yamaguchi wanted to buy a present for
   a. her mother.   b. her father.   c. her grandmother.   d. her boyfriend's mother.

3. Ms. Yamaguchi was asked by the sales clerk about
   a. her budget.
   b. the size of the person receiving the gift.
   c. the favorite colors of the recipient.
   d. the age of the recipient.

4. Ms. Yamaguchi did not like the first sweater because
   a. it looked small.   b. it was too gaudy.   c. the color was not pretty.   d. it was over her budget.

5. The next sweater suggested to Ms. Yamaguchi was
   a. red.   b. blue.   c. yellow.   d. black.

6. Ms. Yamaguchi did not like the sweater that was on sale because
    a. it was too flashy.   b. it looked cheap.   c. it was too small.   d. it was still too expensive.

7. Ms. Yamaguchi did not want to get a hat because
    a. she knows the recipient does not like hats.
    b. she has given a hat to the recipient before.
    c. she herself does not like hats.
    d. she has never seen the recipient wearing hats.

8. The sales clerk's next suggestions were a hat and
    a. other clothes.   b. other accessories.   c. cosmetics.   d. designer-brand bags.

9. The sales clerk suggested one of their necklaces because they
    a. were designed by a famous designer.   b. sold well.   c. were exotic.   d. both a and b.

10. The item that Ms. Yamaguchi bought was
    a. earrings.   b. a necklace.   c. a hat.   d. nothing.

H. Interview. You are working for the personnel department of a language school in Japan. Today your supervisor is going to interview a Japanese person who is applying for a job as a French teacher, so the supervisor has asked you to take notes as you listen to their conversation. Fill in the memo below, and state your opinion about the candidate. Can you think of any important question or questions that the supervisor forgot to ask? You may write in English.

   Useful Vocabulary: おしえる *to teach*

Name _____ (Female/Male)

Date of birth _____ Birthplace _____

Residence _____

_____

Education _____

_____ Major _____

Qualifications/Skills

Hobbies

Work experience

What do you think of this applicant?

_____

What important question(s) did your supervisor forget to ask?

_____

Kanji and Kana Exercises

This section is longer than the kanji exercise sections in the other chapters, because you may need to review nearly everything you learned last year. But don't worry. The hiragana, katakana, and kanji will all come back to you with a little practice.

A. Do you remember your hiragana? The following chart has some hiragana missing. Can you fill them in? (Keep in mind that not all the possible syllable combinations are used in modern Japanese.)

a-	k-	s-	t-	n-	h-	m-	y-	r-	w-
	か		た		は				わ
い	き	し		に		み		り	
	く		つ		ふ		ゆ		
え		せ		ね		め		れ	
			と		ほ				ん

B. Let's play しりとり! English speaking people sometimes play a game in which one person thinks of a word, for example, *cat;* the next person must think of a word beginning with *t*, such as *time;* the third person must think of a word beginning with *e;* and so on. The Japanese version of this game is called しりとり— literally, *taking the hips*—and is based not on letters of the alphabet but on the hiragana. Thus if the first person says ねこ (*cat*), the next person has to say a word beginning with こ, such as こども.

Each of the hiragana in the spiral, except the に at the outer edge and the ん at the center, is the beginning of one word and the end of another. Can you fill in the gaps? There are 33 clues, one for each word in the spiral. Can you continue the series of words until the final ん?

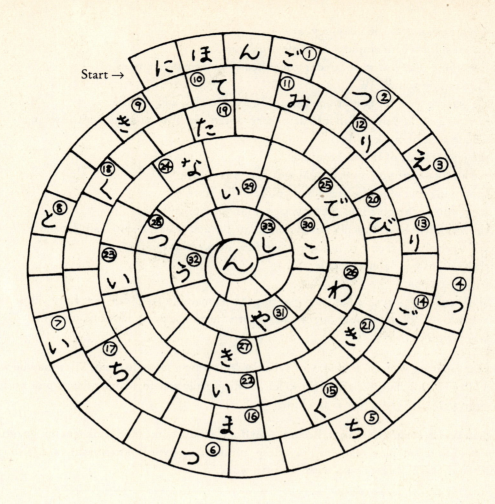

Start →

Clues:

[例] the language spoken in Japan → (Answer) にほんご

1. one of the twelve months (ご □ つ)
2. a piece of furniture found in classrooms and offices
3. something you write with when you want to be able to erase easily
4. the first day of the month
5. public transportation that runs underground
6. the opposite of interesting
7. not your older sister
8. not always, not never, but . . .
9. something you buy at the post office
10. something that comes in the mail
11. the color of grass
12. what you do when you slave over a hot stove all day
13. a fruit that is made into pie, sauce, and cider
14. one hundred, two hundred, three hundred, four hundred . . .
15. a vehicle that you can't drive without a license

16. seven days a week, 365 days a year
17. the meal for which employed people usually go out
18. something that you wear "under your shoes," as the name implies
19. the day you were born
20. the generic term for conditions like colds, flu, measles, and malaria
21. how you could describe an instructor who doesn't let you get away with anything
22. having a lot of work to do
23. the Japanese art of flower arranging
24. the kind of shirt you wear in cold weather
25. something that tends to ring when you're in the shower
26. what you wish you could get on your tuition (dream on!)
27. the room where you gather with your instructor and classmates to learn Japanese
28. what people are trying to become when they do weight training
29. the child of your aunt or uncle
30. today, after dark
31. an American sport that has been played professionally in Japan for over sixty years
32. something a clothing store might have before the new season's fashions come in
33. where you're from

C. Find the Japanese verbs in the array of syllables following and circle them. They may be written top to bottom, bottom to top, left to right, right to left, or diagonally starting from either top or bottom. Their English equivalents are given below as a hint.

(animate) exist, (inanimate) exist, become, can do, clear up, come, do, drink, get up, go, go out, leave (home), look, open, play, read, rest, say, sleep, speak, start, swim, take (a bath), take (a shower), take off, understand, wash, wear (a hat), wear (a shirt), work, write

ひ	ぐ	う	は	い	る	ね	る	く	い
ぬ	よ	れ	な	じ	く	か	は	な	う
る	お	そ	す	お	め	ぶ	た	み	る
け	き	よ	む	の	そ	る	ら	れ	ゆ
あ	る	は	す	あ	で	わ	く	い	る
ら	び	れ	や	め	か	お	る	き	す
う	た	る	は	る	け	か	で	く	ろ

D. You are attending an art exhibit featuring drawings by elementary school children from all over Japan. You have heard that the son of your friends the Matsumuras won a prize for first-graders. As you walk around the gallery, you see that one section is reserved for the top ten drawings in each division, and the children have written their names and home towns in hiragana on their drawings. Look at the list of winners, and answer the following questions.

1. いけだ　みか、おおさか
2. ぬまだ　ひろし、よこはま
3. まつむら　けんいち、とうきょう
4. とがわ　みなえ、こうべ
5. そめかわ　ちあき、よこはま
6. うちだ　しゅんじ、ひめじ
7. ゆざわ　りえ、あきた
8. さいとう　ようた、さっぽろ
9. すずき　りえ、ふくおか
10. さいとう　まゆみ、なごや

a. What prize did the Matsumuras' son win? _____

b. Where are the Matsumuras from? _____

c. What is the son's given name? _____

d. Which city produced more than one winner? What are their names?

_____

e. Which two winners have the same family name? Are they twins? How do you know?

_____

f. Which two winners have the same given name?

_____

E. Do you remember your katakana? The following chart has katakana missing. See if you can fill in the gaps.

a-	k-	s-	t-	n-	h-	m-	y-	r-	w-
ア		サ		ナ			ヤ		ワ
	キ		チ		ヒ			リ	
ウ		ス		ヌ		ム	ユ		
	ケ		テ		ヘ			レ	
		ソ		ノ		モ			ン

F. Read the following words aloud and write their English equivalents. If you have trouble guessing the English equivalent of a katakana word, try saying it fast.

1. アスレチック _____

2. アマチュア _____

3. アレルギー _____

4. イエロー _____

5. イブニングドレス _____

6. エグゼクティブ _____

7. エネルギー _____

8. エレベーター _____

9. カムバック _____

10. キャリアウーマン _____

11. クレジットカード _____

12. コンビニエンスストア _____

13. サンキュー _____

14. セロハンテープ _____

15. トランジスタラジオ _____

16. ネービーブルー _____

17. パトロールカー _____

18. ビタミン _____

19. フォーマルウェア _____

20. ベテラン _____

21. ポピュラーミュージック _____

22. マヨネーズ _____

23. ヨーグルト _____

24. リバーシブルジャケット _____

25. レバー _____

G. Find the katakana words in the array of syllables and circle them. They may be written top to bottom, bottom to top, left to right, right to left, or diagonally starting from either top or bottom. Their English equivalents are given below as a hint.

beer, classic, coffee, curtain, drum, game, gas station ("gasoline stand" in Japanese English), glass (cup), ice cream, iron, print, radar, restaurant, shirt, skate, skirt, soccer, soda, sports, super, table, word processor (contracted form)

ツ	ー	ポ	ス	カ	ー	ト	ド	ク	ゲ
ャ	カ	ア	ケ	ム	サ	ン	ハ	ラ	ー
シ	ッ	イ	ー	ン	タ	ノ	コ	シ	ム
ハ	サ	ス	ト	ス	ー	パ	ー	ッ	ナ
エ	ー	ク	ン	ロ	イ	ア	ヒ	ク	プ
ツ	ビ	リ	プ	ビ	ン	テ	ー	カ	リ
ラ	ソ	ー	ダ	ー	レ	ス	ト	ラ	ン
ガ	ワ	ム	ル	ブ	ー	テ	パ	ー	ト

H. These kanji represent numbers. Arrange them in order, from the smallest to the largest:

一、五、十、三、七、九、八、二、万、六、百、千、四

_____

I. Himiko's agent has arranged a world concert tour for her. Here is the concert schedule, along with some notes on other things Himiko will do in some of the cities. Look over the schedule, and answer the questions in English.

ホノルル　　　　　　　　　九月一日
（サーフィンをしてみる。）
ロサンゼルス　　　　　　　九月三日
（コンサートの後でハリウッドのパーティーに行って、有名なスターに会う。）
バンクーバー　　　　　　　九月七日
デンバー　　　　　　　　　九月九日
ヒューストン　　　　　　　九月十一日
シカゴ　　　　　　　　　　九月十三日
トロント　　　　　　　　　九月十五日
アトランタ　　　　　　　　九月十七日
マイアミ　　　　　　　　　九月十九日
（フロリダで一週間休む。）
ワシントン　　　　　　　　九月二十六日
（ホワイトハウスでのコンサート）
ニューヨーク　　　　　　　九月二十七日
（エンパイアーステートビルを見てから、そのロビーでミニ・コンサート）
モントリオール　　　　　　十月一日
ロンドン　　　　　　　　　十月三日
（バッキンガムきゅうでんでのコンサート）
パリ　　　　　　　　　　　十月五日
（パリで一週間買い物をする。フランス料理もたくさん食べる。）
ローマ　　　　　　　　　　十月十三日
（ローマで一週間買い物をする。イタリア料理もたくさん食べる。）
シンガポール　　　　　　　十月二十二日
メルボルン　　　　　　　　十月二十四日
シドニー　　　　　　　　　十月二十六日
ホンコン　　　　　　　　　十月二十八日
（ホンコンで一週間くらい買い物をする。中国料理もたくさん食べる。）
日本に着く　　　　　　　　十一月六日

1. How long is the entire concert tour? _____

2. In which country will Himiko spend the most time? _____

3. How many times will she go to Canada? _____

4. In what three famous buildings will she perform? Under what circumstances will she give a mini-concert?

_____

5.   What will be the longest leg of the trip? _____

6.   There are four weeklong breaks scheduled into the tour. Where will they take place, and what will Himiko do during each of them?

_____

_____

_____

7.   Is her tour confined to the Northern Hemisphere? _____

8.   Will the tour bring her to your area? If not, what is the concert site closest to where you are now?

_____

J.   Which of the following kanji or compounds refer to people? Which refer to foods and beverages? Weather and geographic features? Colors? Actions? Measurements of time and dates? Directions and locations? Write each kanji or compound under its correct category along with at least one of its meanings. You may use the same kanji more than once.

学生、一月、人、話、上、時、山、下、朝、来、今、来週、飲、午後、土曜日、冬、東、女、勉強、赤、魚、風、見、入、雨、黄色、先生、酒、書、母、白、雪、父、茶、夕方、中、春、売、姉、野、青、南、黒、米

people: _____

foods and beverages: _____

weather and geographic features: _____

colors: _____

actions: _____

measurements of time and dates: _____

directions and locations: _____

K. Write the antonym (word having the opposite meaning) of each kanji below.

[例] 大 – _____ → 大 – __小__

1. 強 – _____
2. 和 – _____
3. 前 – _____
4. 買 – _____
5. 行 – _____
6. 男 – _____
7. 明 – _____
8. 近 – _____
9. 多 – _____
10. 外 – _____
11. 入 – _____
12. 始 – _____
13. 黒 – _____
14. 日 – _____
15. 上 – _____
16. 右 – _____
17. 朝 – _____
18. 暑 – _____
19. 父 – _____

L. Match the kanji compounds with their pronunciations by writing the letters of the correct pronunciations in the blanks.

1. _____ 一番
2. _____ 運動
3. _____ 家族
4. _____ 兄弟
5. _____ 牛肉
6. _____ 食事
7. _____ 出口
8. _____ 主人
9. _____ 千円
10. _____ 昨日
11. _____ 台風
12. _____ 大学
13. _____ 店員
14. _____ 天気
15. _____ 北風
16. _____ 電話
17. _____ 本屋
18. _____ 下手
19. _____ 夕方
20. _____ 洋服

a. かぞく
b. たいふう
c. しゅじん
d. いちばん
e. てんいん
f. しょくじ
g. てんき
h. きのう
i. ようふく
j. きたかぜ
k. でんわ
l. ほんや
m. ゆうがた
n. へた
o. せんえん
p. きょうだい
q. うんどう
r. だいがく
s. でぐち
t. ぎゅうにく

M. You might call this exercise しりとり with kanji. For example, the compound 上手 ends with 手. The word 手がみ begins with 手, even though the kanji 手 is pronounced differently than in 上手. Thus if you see 上____がみ、then the correct answer is 上手がみ、じょうず and てがみ.

1. 午 _____ ろ、_____ and _____

2. 勉 _____ い、_____ and _____

3. 音 _____ しい、 _____ and _____

4. 大 _____ 生、 _____ and _____

5. 有 _____ 前、 _____ and _____

6. 先 _____ 曜日、 _____ and _____

7. 上 _____ 物、 _____ and _____

8. 朝 _____ べる、 _____ and _____

9. 読 _____ く、 _____ and _____

10. 今 _____ 食、 _____ and _____

11. 全 _____ 屋、 _____ and _____

N. You are signing up for a class at a culture center in Japan, and the clerk has asked you to fill out the following form. What information would you put in each of the numbered blanks? (You do not need to fill out the application blank yourself, and you will not know all the kanji, but you will be able to figure out what should be written in each blank or which choice should be circled.)

1. 氏名		2. 性別　　男　　女
3. 生年月日	年　　　　月　　　　日生まれ	
4. 現住所	市　　　区　　　町	
5. 電話番号	―　　　　―	
6. 職業	公務員　会社員　自営業　学生　その他	

1. _____

2. _____

3. _____

4. _____

5. _____

6. _____

O. You have a very bad sore throat, and your doctor has prescribed some medication for you. The directions on the package read: 「このカプセルは、一日三回食後に二錠ずつ十日間お飲みください。」 Even if you don't know all the kanji, you should be able to figure out how many times per day, how many days, and at what time of the day you need to take the capsules. You should also be able to figure out how many capsules you need to take each time.

_____

_____

P. The basement of a Japanese department store is usually devoted to food, featuring many of the items you find in a Western supermarket but also including gift-wrapped gourmet foods, baked goods, coffee beans, tea leaves, expensive cuts of meat, endless varieties of traditional Japanese ingredients such as _みそ_ (_fermented bean paste_) or _かまぼこ_ (_fish sausage_), and take-out meals of both Japanese and Western cuisine. The food vendors offer free samples at the 「試食コーナー」. Meanwhile, on the upper floors of the department store you will find a number of 試着室. If 教室 means _classroom_ and 寝室 means _bedroom,_ what do you think people do in the 試着室?

_____

_____

Q. You have seen the signs 「外出中」 and 「ミーティング中」 on the closed doors of people's offices. Now you have seen the sign 「使用中」 on the closed door of a public toilet stall. What is the meaning of each of these signs, and what does 「…中」 mean by itself?

1. 外出中:_____

2. ミーティング中:_____

3. 使用中:_____

4. …中:_____

If you are still having trouble remembering last year's kanji, even after completing these exercises, set yourself on a program of reviewing gradually while learning new material. Every night when you study Japanese, go over the kanji and vocabulary of one of the lessons of Book 1. Soon you'll be back up to speed.

Writing Activities

A. In Japanese society, people are expected to introduce themselves whenever they join a new group. John Kawamura is about to join the university's film appreciation club, and he is nervous about his self-introduction, so he has asked you to help him. Using the information on the following card, write a self-introduction for him.

> **Name:** John Kawamura
>
> **Age:** 20
>
> **Birthplace:** California, USA
>
> **Nationality:** USA
>
> **Major:** Economics, Japanese
>
> **Courses currently enrolled in:** Japanese (third year), Japanese history
>
> **Japanese language:** started studying in California, took second-year courses in Tokyo last year
>
> **Residence:** homestay with Mr. and Mrs. Yamaguchi in Setagaya, Tokyo
>
> **Hobbies:** jogging, watching movies

わたしは_____1と言います。20_____2です。出しんは_____3です。せんこうは_____4と_____5です。今年は_____6と_____7を勉強しています。日本語の勉強は_____8で始めました。今は、

_____9ホーム・ステイをしています。しゅ味は_____10と_____11です。どうぞよろしくおねがいします。

B. Now write your own self-introduction, similar to the one you helped John Kawamura write. You may, of course, add any additional information you want.

わたしは_____ と言います。_____

_____

_____

_____

_____

_____

_____

C. One of your neighbors was murdered sometime between Thursday afternoon and Friday noon last week. A police detective has come to your apartment to ask some questions. Answer them as completely as possible in Japanese to prove that you had nothing to do with the murder. Here is your appointment book for Thursday and Friday of last week. You might need to provide some more information if the detective asks you about details that are not filled in.

Useful Vocabulary: けいじ _police detective_

JULY 7, THURSDAY		JULY 8, FRIDAY	
8:00	Japanese class	8:00	Japanese class
9:00		9:00	help session with Professor Yokoi (two hours)
10:00		10:00	
11:00		11:00	
12:00		12:00	lunch with Heather and Masao
1:00	tennis class	1:00	
2:00		2:00	
3:00		3:00	
4:00	Japanese history class	4:00	
5:00		5:00	tennis with Mei Lin
6:00	Linda and Hitomi coming over for dinner	6:00	
7:00		7:00	go to movie with Takeshi, John, Daisuke, and Satomi
Evening	study Japanese with John and Henry at John's house until 11:00 p.m.	Evening	

けいじ：先週の木曜日は学こうへ行きましたか。

あなた：はい。_____[1]

けいじ：何時ごろアパートへかえってきましたか。

あなた：_____

けいじ：その後は。

あなた：_____ 3

けいじ：夜はうちにいましたか。

あなた：いいえ、_____ 4

けいじ：どこで勉強したんですか。

あなた：_____ 5

けいじ：何時までそこにいましたか。

あなた：_____ 6

けいじ：何時にねましたか。

あなた：_____ 7

けいじ：しつれいですが、一人ぐらし (living alone) ですか。

あなた：_____ 8

けいじ：金曜日にもがっこうへ行きましたか。

あなた：はい。_____ 9

けいじ：何時にうちを出たんですか。

あなた：_____ 10

けいじ：どうしてそんなに早く出たんですか。じゅぎょう (class session) があったんですか。

あなた：_____ 11

けいじ：それから。

あなた：_____ 12

けいじ：一人で昼ごはんを食べましたか。

あなた：_____ 13

けいじ：そうですか。どうもいろいろありがとうございました。

あなた：いいえ、_____ 14

D. Use the information in this chart of tomorrow's weather to complete the three parts of this exercise.

CITY	WEATHER	HIGH TEMPERATURE	WIND	NOTES
Sapporo	Snow (20 cm)	–3C	North, 25 km/h	Snow until Friday
Tokyo	Cloudy	8C	No wind	Rain in the early afternoon
Osaka	Clear	10C	South, 8 km/h	Colder in the morning
Kagoshima	Rain	20C	East, 5 km/h	Cloudy in the afternoon
Naha	Clear	25C	West, 20 km/h	Clear until Sunday

1. Fill in the blanks using the information from the chart.

   a. 東きょうの明日のお天気は＿＿＿＿＿＿＿＿で、＿＿＿＿＿＿＿＿＿は
      ８度です。風は＿＿＿＿＿＿＿＿。午後は＿＿＿＿＿＿＿＿かもしれま
      せん。

   b. なはのお天気は＿＿＿＿＿＿＿＿です。きおんは＿＿＿＿＿＿＿＿で、
      暑いでしょう。＿＿＿＿＿＿＿＿の風が強いでしょう。しゅうまつまで
      ＿＿＿＿＿＿＿＿でしょう。

   c. さっぽろは、明日は＿＿＿＿＿＿＿＿でしょう。きおんはマイナス
      ＿＿＿＿＿＿＿＿度で、強い北の風が＿＿＿＿＿＿＿＿。

   d. かごしまは、明日は＿＿＿＿＿＿＿＿。＿＿＿＿＿＿＿＿で、
      ＿＿＿＿＿＿＿＿風がふくでしょう。午後は＿＿＿＿＿＿＿＿。

   e. おおさかの明日のお天気は、＿＿＿＿＿＿＿＿です。きおんは
      ＿＿＿＿＿＿＿＿ですが、午前中は、すこし＿＿＿＿＿＿＿＿でしょう。
      ＿＿＿＿＿＿＿＿ふくでしょう。

2. Fill in the blanks.

   a. 東きょうは_____ よりきおんが高いです。

   b. なはは_____ より風が弱いです。

   c. かごしまより_____ の方があたたかいでしょう。

   d. 東きょうより_____ の方が天気がいいでしょう。

   e. さっぽろと東きょうとおおさかの中で、一番寒いのは、_____
   です。

   f. さっぽろとおおさかとかごしまの中で、一番風が弱いのは、

   _____ です。

3. Each of the following people is wondering what cities in Japan to visit. Using the information on the weather chart, figure out which city would be the best destination for each person, assuming that everyone will be traveling this week.

   a. わたしはハワイのしゅっしんですが、まだスキーをしたことがありませんから、冬はぜひ一度スキーをしたいです。

   _____

   b. 暑いのはいやですが、寒いのもいやです。あたたかいところがいいですね。雨ですか。かまいませんよ。

   _____

   c. サーフィンが好きで、毎日うみ (ocean) に行きたいです。冬でもサーフィンをしたいんですが、ぜんぜん風がない時は、サーフィンはむずかしいです。

   _____

E. What would be a good birthday present for each of the following people? Be specific. Instead of stating only that you would buy a CD for a person who likes music, state what kind of CD you would buy.

1. 山田さんは、中国語を勉強しているので、中国へ行きたがっています。

   _____

2. 山田さんは、ミステリーを読むのが好きで、おもしろい本をほしがっています。

   _____

3. 山田さんのお母さんは来月ヨーロッパへ行くよていです。

   _____

4. 山田さんのお父さんは、かんこく料理をならいたいと言っています。お酒と、からい食べ物が好きです。

_____

5. 田中さんは、ハンサムでスポーツが何でも上手です。いつか、オーストラリアでゴルフをしようと思っています。

_____

6. 田中さんのお兄さんは、外国の映画を見るのがしゅみだそうです。

_____

7. 田中さんの妹さんは、うたがとくいで、イタリアへうたを勉強しに行きたがっています。

_____

8. 田中さんのおくさんは、いつもきれいな服を着ています。今は、あたらしいアクセサリーをほしがっているそうです。

_____

9. 田中さんのお子さんは、やきゅうが大好きです。大きくなったら、プロやきゅうのせんしゅ (player) になろうと思っています。

_____

10. 田中さんのいぬは、テレビを見ながらドッグ・フードを食べるのが好きです。へんないぬだと思いませんか。

_____

F. You intend to do the following activities, but you lack some of the things you need in order to do them. What things might you need to buy, and where would you go to buy them?

ACTIVITY	WHAT TO BUY	WHERE TO GO
てがみを書く	かみ、ペン、ふうとう	ぶんぼうぐ屋
サンドイッチを作る	1	2
「ようこそ」の ワークブックをする	3	4
ジョギングをする	5	6
すしを作る	7	8

G. Some people who have lost their jobs are attending an informational seminar about possible new careers. Today, eight sessions are scheduled. Match each attendee with the most appropriate session, based on his or her personal statement of interests and abilities.

1. _____ わたしは日本語とえい語が話せます。

2. _____ わたしはおいしいパンやスープが作れます。

3. _____ わたしはとても上手にオルガンがひけます。

4. _____ わたしはワープロが使えます。

5. _____ わたしはコンピュータのプログラミングができます。

6. _____ わたしはくるまのうんてんが上手にできます。

7. _____ わたしはすう学がとくいで、わかりやすくせつめい
(explanation) できます。

8. _____ わたしは上手にしゃしんがとれます。

    a. タクシーのうんてんしゅ
    b. ひしょ (secretary)
    c. 先生
    d. ツアーコンダクター
    e. コック
    f. コンピュータ　プログラマー
    g. きょう会のオルガニスト
    h. カメラマン

H. Fill in the blanks with the appropriate verbs for wearing clothes. Then draw a picture of John Kawamura and what he will be wearing as he goes out the door.

a. カワムラさんは、白いTシャツを＿＿＿＿＿＿＿＿＿¹います。今日は暑いので、青いショートパンツを＿＿＿＿＿＿＿＿＿²います。昨日デパートで買（か）ったあたらしいスニーカーを＿＿＿＿＿＿＿＿＿³います。とても安（やす）かったそうです。お父（とう）さんからのプレゼントの金（きん）のとけいを＿＿＿＿＿＿＿＿＿⁴います。外（そと）に行（い）く時（とき）は、サングラスを＿＿＿＿＿＿＿＿＿＿＿＿＿＿＿⁵。赤いぼうしも＿＿＿＿＿＿＿＿＿＿＿＿＿＿＿⁶。

b.

I. Fill in the blanks with the appropriate particles. You will be using the following particles: に、へ、から、の、まで、で、し、を、な、と、より、も、が、だ、か. You will need some of these particles more than once, but you will not need to use は at all. If no particle is necessary, write X in the blank.

1. ブラウンさんは、アメリカ＿＿＿＿¹しゅっしん＿＿＿＿²、きょねん＿＿＿＿³日本＿＿＿＿⁴勉強（べんきょう）し＿＿＿＿⁵来ました。今年（ことし）＿＿＿＿⁶20さい＿＿＿＿⁷なります。今、とうきょう＿＿＿＿⁸日本語＿＿＿＿⁹勉強（べんきょう）しています。毎日＿＿＿＿¹⁰しゅくだい＿＿＿＿¹¹する＿＿＿＿¹²、かんじもおぼえる＿＿＿＿¹³、まじめ＿＿＿＿¹⁴いい＿＿＿＿¹⁵学生です。きれい＿＿＿＿¹⁶アパート＿＿＿＿¹⁷すんでいます。一人＿＿＿＿¹⁸すんでいます。お父（とう）さん＿＿＿＿¹⁹お母（かあ）さんはアメリカ＿＿＿＿²⁰います。ブラウンさん

_____²¹ アパート _____²² がっこう _____²³ でんしゃ_____²⁴ 30分くらい

です。

2. しゅみは音楽です。ピアノ_____¹ ひけますし、うた_____² うたえます。

スポーツ_____³ 音楽_____⁴ 方_____⁵ 好きです。ともだち_____⁶ きっさてん

_____⁷ 話し_____⁸ するの_____⁹ 好きです。きっさてん _____¹⁰ 行った時は、

いつもコーヒー _____¹¹ 飲みます。あまい物_____¹² 中_____¹³、

チョコレート _____¹⁴ 一番好き _____¹⁵ そうです。

3. アメリカ_____¹ かえったら、大学いん _____² 入りたい_____³ 思っています。

大学いん _____⁴ 日本ぶんがく _____⁵ 勉強するつもりです。大学 _____⁶ 先生

_____⁷ なる _____⁸ どう _____⁹、まだわかりません。

CHAPTER **1**

TRAVEL

Listening Comprehension Activities

Vocabulary and Grammar 1A: Travel

A. Listen to the description of four trips, and indicate which country the person went to.

1. _____   3. _____

2. _____   4. _____

B. Listen to the descriptions by four people, and identify what kind of trip each one took.

1. _____   a. かんこう旅行
2. _____   b. だんたい (group) 旅行
3. _____   c. 海外旅行
4. _____   d. 出張

C. Daisuke Yamaguchi has just returned from a trip to New York. Listen to Yamaguchi tell Mei Lin Chin about his trip and then choose the most appropriate answers to the questions.

1. Why was Mr. Yamaguchi busy in N.Y.?
   a. Because it was a business trip
   b. Because he went to see many places
   c. Because it was a short stay

2. How much time did he have for sightseeing?
   a. A couple of days   b. One day   c. Half a day

3. What did he see in N.Y.?
   a. Many shops   b. A museum   c. A musical

4. What kind of hotel did he stay in?
   a. A hotel close to the international airport
   b. A hotel with many tourists
   c. A hotel which is old and famous

5. What kind of trip does he want to make to N.Y. next time?
   a. Group tour   b. Sightseeing   c. Business trip

D. John Kawamura has returned from a trip to Kyoto. Listen as he tells Professor Yokoi about his trip, and then answer the following questions.

What does Kawamura say about his experience about the following?

1. Shinkansen: _____

2. Inn: _____

3. Sleeping in futon: _____

4. Eating at the inn: _____

5. Tour bus: _____

6. Kinkakuji Temple: _____

E. Listen as Henry Curtis consults Professor Yokoi about his plan to visit Ensenada, Mexico, a city close to the California border. Then choose the best answer to complete the sentences.

Useful Vocabulary: しんぱい *worried*

Professor Yokoi suggested that Curtis:

1. go with _____.
   a. his parents   b. his best friend   c. someone who knows the place

2. go to _____ to purchase an airplane ticket.
   a. a travel agent   b. the airport   c. the front desk at a hotel

3. _____ for sightseeing information.
   a. buy a map   b. buy a tour book   c. check the website

4. stay at a big hotel, because _____.
   a. he can enjoy different cultures
   b. hotel employees can speak English
   c. there are better facilities

5. take _____ from the airport to the hotel.
   a. subway   b. bus   c. taxi

6. _____ Coronado before leaving for Mexico.
   a. learn Spanish from   b. write a letter to   c. get travel tips from

F. Listen to the following conversation between Mei Lin Chin and John Kawamura and then mark each of the following statements either true (T) or false (F).

Useful Vocabulary: すごす *to spend*

1. _____ Chin doesn't mind cold weather because she is used to it.

2. _____ Chin is good at skiing.

3. _____ Both Chin and Kawamura will be away from Tokyo during winter vacation.

4. _____ Kawamura goes home every winter.

5. _____ Both Kawamura and Chin will spend Christmas with their families.

G. Listen to Linda Brown talk about her family's Christmas traditions, and then circle all items that describe those traditions.

Useful Vocabulary: 飾る *to decorate*

1. go out to buy a Christmas tree

2. decorate the tree

3. go to church

4. open some presents before Christmas day

5. go to after-Christmas sales

6. make a snowman

7. have a big party on Christmas eve

8. sing at a karaoke bar

9. cook a big breakfast together

10. have a relaxed afternoon

Vocabulary and Grammar 1B: Transportation and Schedules

A. Takako Matsui is studying English in California. Today she visited the college where Bob Smith, Cody Smith's younger brother, is a student. Listen to her diary, and complete the sentences by writing what she did.

Useful Vocabulary: 車屋 *car dealer*

Takako looked at _____ before Smith came to her house. Smith arrived a little

_____ 10:00. After they parked the car, they first went to

_____. Students were studying and _____ there. In

the computer room, students were _____ websites and writing

_____. After they left the library, they went to

_____ to eat _____. After lunch, they went to a

_____, and saw _____.

After leaving the college and before going home, they went to a _____.

Takako wants to enjoy American student life, and she wants to _____ as the

first step.

B. Mei Lin Chin is asking John Kawamura about his trip to Hakata in Kyushu. Listen to the dialogue and choose the best answer for each sentence.

> **Useful Vocabulary:** ゴールデンウィーク *Golden Week (the series of holidays that fall between April 29 and May 5),* こむ *to be crowded*

1. According to Kawamura, it takes _____ hours from Tokyo to Hakata by Shinkansen.
   a. 3   b. 4   c. 6

2. Kawamura encourages Chin to buy a ticket right away, because it will be _____ during Golden Week.
   a. expensive   b. no offices open   c. crowded

3. Kawamura suggests that Chin make a hotel reservation at a _____.
   a. station   b. travel agency   c. hotel

4. As for a travel guide, Kawamura suggests that Chin _____.
   a. use pamphlets   b. buy books   c. get one at Tokyo Station

5. Kawamura wants to go to Nagasaki _____.
   a. during Golden Week   b. if he has time   c. if he has money

Vocabulary and Grammar 1C: Sightseeing and Travel Planning

A. Professor Yokoi is inviting her class to a party at her house. Listen as she gives directions and complete the summary by filling in the blanks.

Those coming by car should go _____ down the broad street in front of the university

for about _____ minutes. You will see a big _____ on your

_____. Turn _____ at the corner, and go straight for about

_____ kilometers. You will see the large Daiichi _____ building.

Turn _____ at the corner, and soon you will see a golf course on your

_____. Professor Yokoi's house is _____ from the club house. It will

take about _____ minutes by car.

Those coming by bus should get bus number 54 at the bus stop _____ the

university library. After riding for about _____ minutes, get off the bus

_____ the club house. From there it will take only _____ minutes on

foot.

B. Yoshiko Tanaka is going to California for the first time. Listen to the letter Yoshiko's mother writes, and for each item, circle the advice her mother offers.

Useful Vocabulary: 気をつける *to be careful*

1. About luggage:
    a. take one suitcase   b. take light cloth bags   c. take a backpack

2. About clothing:
    a. take just a few spare clothes   b. take lots of sweaters   c. take casual clothes

3. About carrying cash:
    a. take plenty of cash   b. not a good idea   c. use a credit card instead

4. About souvenirs:
    a. buy for all the family and friends   b. do not buy too much   c. do not buy at all

5. About eating:
    a. take many gourmet foods   b. try to cut off sweets   c. do not eat too much

6. About medicine:
    a. take some   b. buy some in California   c. do not take any

7. About going out at night
    a. do not go out at all
    b. take a taxi when going out
    c. go to good clubs and concerts as much as possible

8. About contacting home:
    a. write postcards   b. call home once or twice   c. call home every day

C. Henry Curtis is going to stay at a Japanese-style inn for the first time. Listen to Curtis asking Hitomi Machida about manners there. Fill in the blanks to complete the summary.

Useful Vocabulary: お湯 *hot water*

At the entrance of a ryokan, you will change from shoes to _____. A yukata, which is a

summer cotton kimono, will be provided, and you may wear it at the hotel _____, and

even when you _____. There is a bath in each room, but you _____

go to the bigger bath, also. First, you have to _____ before getting into the bathtub.

You have to be careful with the water _____. Japanese inns serve

_____ and _____. At night, you _____ prepare

the futon yourself.

D. Heather Gibson is giving a report to her class on youth hostels. Listen as she explains what youth hostels are like and what a person needs to know when staying there. Then circle the things you have to do at a youth hostel.

a. become a member

b. ask for room service

c. make beds

d. wash sheets

e. clean the room

f. cook

g. wash dishes

h. come back early at night

E. Masao Hayashi has just returned from Sapporo, and Hitomi Machida wants to know how his trip was. Listen to their conversation, and then list things that Hayashi originally planned to do, choosing from among a–f.

Useful Vocabulary: はくぶつかん *museum*

Things Hayashi originally planned to do are: _____

a. take a taxi to the airport

b. get on an 8:00 airplane

c. make a hotel reservation in Tokyo

d. stay at an inexpensive hotel

e. sightsee Sapporo on foot

f. spend a day in a museum

F. Professor Yokoi is planning a potluck party, and her students are asking what they should bring. Listen to their conversation and indicate who is going to bring what.

1. Kawamura _____

2. Gibson _____

3. Curtis _____

4. Chin _____

5. Yokoi _____

a. drinks
b. dessert
c. Chinese dish
d. rice dish
e. Italian dish
f. paper cups and plates
g. chicken dish

Kanji Practice and Exercises

1 私 私 | シ private
わたし／わたくし I, me, my

私：わたし／わたくし (I)
私の目：わたし／わたくしのめ (my eye)

2 京 京 | キョウ、ケイ capital, metropolis; Kyoto; Tokyo
みやこ capital, metropolis

東京：とうきょう (Tokyo)
上京：じょうきょう (going to Tokyo)

3 都 都 | ト、ツ、みやこ capital, metropolis

京都：きょうと (Kyoto)
東京都：とうきょうと (the Tokyo metropolitan
  area)

4 寺 寺 | ジ、てら temple

（お）寺：（お）てら (temple)

5 神 神 | シン、ジン、かみ、かん、こう- god, God

神：かみ (god)
神社：じんじゃ （[Shinto] shrine）
神道：しんとう (Shinto)
神風：かみかぜ (kamikaze)

6	社 社	シャ company: Shinto shrine やしろ Shinto shrine		
	神社：じんじゃ ([Shinto] shrine) 会社：かいしゃ (company, business) 会社員：かいしゃいん (company employee) 社会学：しゃかいがく (sociology)		社	社
7	内 内	ナイ、ダイ inside; within; between, among うち inside; house, one's home; within; between, among		
	国内：こくない (domestic, within the country) 家内：かない (one's own wife)		内	内
8	曲 曲	キョク curve; melody ま-がる bend, curve, be crooked, turn ま-げる bend something, distort		
	曲がる：まがる (turn, curve) その道を曲がって下さい：そのみちをまがって 　　ください (please turn at that corner)		曲	曲
9	目 目	モク、ボク eye; classification, order (in taxonomy) め eye (suffix for ordinals) ま eye		
	目：め (eye) 二本目の道：にほんめのみち (second street) 五つ目のかど：いつつめのかど (fifth corner)		目	目
10	所 所	ショ、ところ place		
	所：ところ (place) 場所：ばしょ (place) 近所：きんじょ (neighborhood) 名所：めいしょ (famous place)		所	所
11	予 予	ヨ previously, beforehand; I, myself あらかじめ previously, in advance かね-て previously, already		
	予約：よやく (reservation)		予	予

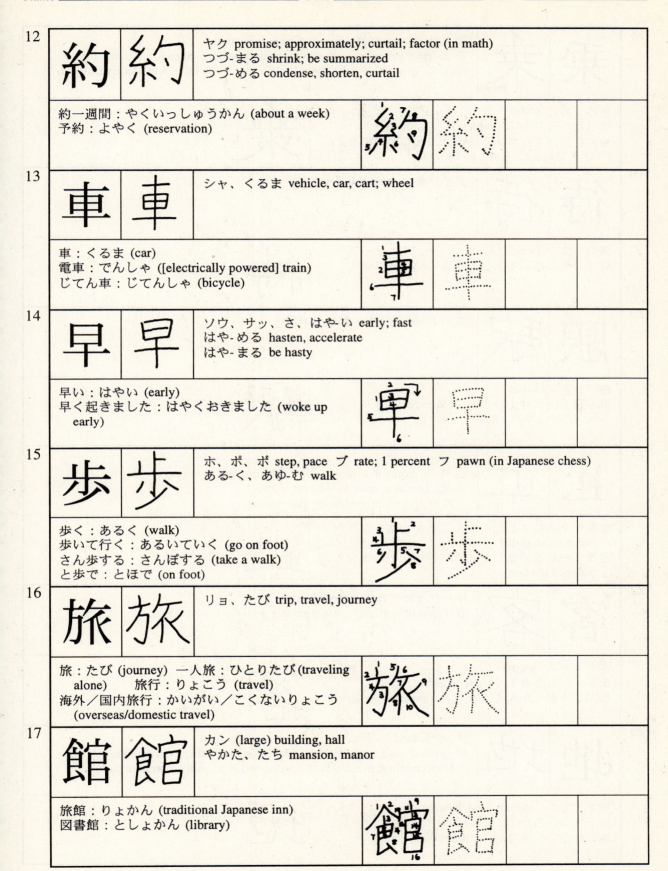

12 | 約 約 | ヤク promise; approximately; curtail; factor (in math)
つづ-まる shrink; be summarized
つづ-める condense, shorten, curtail

約一週間：やくいっしゅうかん (about a week)
予約：よやく (reservation)

13 | 車 車 | シャ、くるま vehicle, car, cart; wheel

車：くるま (car)
電車：でんしゃ ([electrically powered] train)
じてん車：じてんしゃ (bicycle)

14 | 早 早 | ソウ、サッ、さ、はや-い early; fast
はや-める hasten, accelerate
はや-まる be hasty

早い：はやい (early)
早く起きました：はやくおきました (woke up early)

15 | 歩 歩 | ホ、ポ、ボ step, pace ブ rate; 1 percent フ pawn (in Japanese chess)
ある-く、あゆ-む walk

歩く：あるく (walk)
歩いて行く：あるいていく (go on foot)
さん歩する：さんぽする (take a walk)
と歩で：とほで (on foot)

16 | 旅 旅 | リョ、たび trip, travel, journey

旅：たび (journey) 一人旅：ひとりたび(traveling alone) 旅行：りょこう (travel)
海外／国内旅行：かいがい／こくないりょこう (overseas/domestic travel)

17 | 館 館 | カン (large) building, hall
やかた、たち mansion, manor

旅館：りょかん (traditional Japanese inn)
図書館：としょかん (library)

18	乗 乗	ジョウ ride; multiply, raise to a power (in math) の-る ride; get on, mount; join in; be deceived, be taken in の-せる give a ride, take aboard; place, put, load; let join in; deceive, take in

乗る：のる (ride)
乗り物：のりもの (vehicle)
電車に乗って行きましょう：でんしゃにのって
　　いきましょう (Let's go by train)

19	待 待	タイ、まつ wait, wait for

待つ：まつ (wait)
待ってください：まって下さい (please wait)

20	駅 駅	エキ (train, bus, or subway) station

駅：えき (station)
東京駅：とうきょうえき (Tokyo Station)

21	止 止	シ stop と-まる (come to a) stop　と-める (bring/put to a) stop や-む (come to an) end, be over, stop やめる (put to an) end, stop, discontinue

電車が止まりました：でんしゃがとまりました
　(the train stopped)
タクシーを止めました：タクシーをとめました
　(stopped the taxi)

22	客 客	キャク guest; customer, passenger カク guest; customer, passenger; (as prefix) the past (year)

客：きゃく (guest)
乗客：じょうきゃく (passenger)
かんこう客：かんこうきゃく (tourist, sightseer)

23	地 地	チ earth, land ジ ground, land, earth; texture, fabric; field (of a flag), background; 　respectability; musical accompaniment, in actuality; narrative part

地下：ちか (underground, basement)
地下てつ：ちかてつ (subway)
地味な色：じみないろ (drab color)

24	図 図	ズ drawing, diagram, plan ト、はか-る plan				
	地図：ちず (map) 図書館：としょかん (library)		図	図		
25	海 海	カイ、うみ sea, ocean				
	海：うみ (sea, ocean) 海外旅行：かいがいりょこう (overseas travel) 北海道：ほっかいどう (Hokkaido)		海	海		

Kanji Exercises

A. Match each kanji or kanji compound with its closest English equivalent.

1. 駅 _____
2. 海 _____
3. 館 _____
4. 客 _____
5. 京都 _____
6. 曲 _____
7. 止 _____
8. 寺 _____
9. 社 _____

10. 車 _____
11. 所 _____
12. 乗 _____
13. 神 _____
14. 図 _____
15. 早 _____
16. 待 _____
17. 地 _____
18. 東京 _____

19. 内 _____
20. 歩 _____
21. 目 _____
22. 約 _____
23. 旅 _____
24. 予 _____
25. 私 _____

a. Kyoto   b. Tokyo   c. to stay overnight   d. inside   e. eye   f. place   g. to promise
h. previously   i. vehicle   j. early   k. to walk   l. to ride   m. (large) building   n. to wait
o. to stop   p. trip   q. sea   r. guest   s. temple   t. god   u. earth   v. to bend   w. drawing
x. station   y. map   z. Shinto shrine   aa. I

B. Write hurigana for each kanji or kanji compound. Pay special attention to the changes in pronunciation that may occur when kanji are compounded.

1. 歩く
   _____

2. 乗る
   _____

3. 止まる
   _____

4. 曲がる
   _____

5. 待つ
   _____

6. 予約
   _____

7. 所
   _____

8. 場所
   _____

9. 近所
   _____

10. 国内
    _____

11. 海外
    _____

12. 海
    _____

13. 一人旅
    _____

14. 旅行
    _____

15. 駅
    _____

16. 車
    _____

17. 電車
    _____

18. 客
    _____

19. 早い
    _____

20. 図書館
    _____

21. 地図
    _____

22. 京都
    _____

23. 東京
    _____

24. 寺
    _____

25. 会社
    _____

26. 私
    _____

27. 五つ目
    _____

28. 神社
    _____

C. Fill in each blank with the kanji for the word or phrase that is spelled out in hiragana under the line.

1. _____ から _____ までしんかんせんに _____ って _____ きました。
   とうきょう　　　　　　きょうと　　　　　　　　　　　　　の　　　　　い

2. ホテルの _____ に _____ い _____ があります。
   　　　　　まえ　　　くろ　　　くるま

3. _____ の _____ くの _____ に _____ しました。
   えき　　ちか　　　　　りょかん　　　　よやく

4. _____ を ____ ながら ____ くと ____ かりますよ。
　　　ちず　　　　　み　　　　　　い　　　　　わ

5. ____ つ ____ のかどを ____ に ____ がって ____ さい。
　　みっ　　め　　　　　　みぎ　　　ま　　　　　　くだ

6. _____ には、お ____ や _____ など _____ な ____ がたくさん
　　きょうと　　　　　てら　　　じんじゃ　　　　ゆうめい　　　ところ

あります。

7. _____ はどこに ____ ったらいいですか。
　　こくないりょこう　　　　　　　い

8. _____ で _____ しながら ____ ちます。
　　としょかん　　　　べんきょう　　　　　ま

9. ____ はおみやげを ____ う ____ でこんでいる。
　　みせ　　　　　　か　　　ひと

10. ____ はすぐそばです。 ____ いて ____ きましょう。
　　うみ　　　　　　　　　　ある　　　　い

11. ____ く ____ きないと _____ に ____ れませんよ。
　　はや　　お　　　　　　　でんしゃ　　　の

12. ____ に _____ を _____ するつもりです。
　　なつ　　　ほっかいどう　　　　りょこう

13. ____ は _____ の ____ から _____ です。
　　あに　　　ことし　　　はる　　　　かいしゃいん

Kanji in Everyday Life

1. You are mailing a birthday card in Tokyo, and you notice that there are two mail slots, one labeled 都内 and the other labeled 他府県. If the card is for your friend who also lives in Tokyo, which slot do you put the letter in?

   _____

2. You are reading a magazine article about an American who has been living in Japan for twenty years. The article refers to him as a 神父. What do you think that means? (Hint: It's not "godfather.")

   _____

3. There's a sign at the corner that says 止まれ. What should you do?

   _____

4. You're all set to do some research at the National Diet Library (similar to the U.S. Library of Congress) in Tokyo, but you notice a sign that says 本日休館. How does this affect your plans?

_____

5. You're watching a quiz show on television. When a new contestant comes onstage, the subtitles identify him as 寺田洋一, 30 さい, 駅員, 京都. What can you learn about the contestant from these subtitles?

_____

6. On the message board in a train station, you see the following handwritten message: 夏目さん：デパートの屋上のビヤガーデンで待っています。—青木 Whom is the message for? Whom is it from? What is the message about?

_____

7. You are working for a Japanese company. While reading some legal documents, you learn that your employer made a 口約束 with another business. What do you think that is?

_____

Writing Activities

Vocabulary and Grammar 1A: Travel

A. Think up a detailed plan for a trip you would like to take someday. Then answer the following questions about the plans you have made.

1. かんこう旅行がしたいですか。

_____

2. どこに行きたいですか。

_____

3. 何が見物したいですか。

_____

4. 何日、旅行したいですか。

_____

5. 乗り物は、何に乗りたいですか。{バス／車／電車／しんかんせん／ふね／ひこうき／タクシー}

_____

6. どこに、とまりたいですか。{旅館／ホテル／ユースホステル}

　　_____

7. だれと旅行したいですか。

　　_____

B. Change the following sentences into suggestions using 〜たらいかがですか or 〜たらどうですか or 〜たらいいと思います.

　　[例] ワンピースを着る → ワンピースを着たらどうですか。

1. ぎゅうにゅう (milk) をもっとたくさん飲む

　　_____

2. やさいを食べる

　　_____

3. 先生に聞く

　　_____

4. 図書館へ行ってみる

　　_____

5. めがねをかける

　　_____

6. コートをぬぐ

　　_____

7. プールでおよぐ

　　_____

8. ぼうしをかぶる

　　_____

9. もう少し待つ

　　_____

10. バスで見物する

　　_____

C. Make the following suggestions using the でも construction.

[例] Suggest going to see a movie or something like that.
…えいがでも見に行ったらどうですか。

Suggest going to the ocean or somewhere like that on Sunday.
…日曜日に海へでも行ったらどうですか。

1. Suggest coming to your house on Saturday or some other time.

_____

2. Suggest sightseeing Nara or someplace like that.

_____

3. Suggest riding the train or something like that.

_____

4. Suggest wearing a sweater or something like that.

_____

5. Suggest drinking juice or something like that.

_____

6. Suggest asking Mrs. Yamamoto or someone like that.

_____

7. Suggest using a computer or something like that.

_____

8. Suggest writing a postcard or something like that.

_____

D. Make suggestions in response to the following situations using the 〜たらどうですか construction.

[例] おんせんに入りたいんですが、どうしたらいいですか。→
はこねに行ったらどうですか。

1. あたらしいコンピュータを買いたいんですが、どうしたらいいですか。

_____

2. フランス語を勉強したいんですが、どうしたらいいですか。

_____

3. およぎたいんですが、どうしたらいいですか。

_____

4. かさを買いたいんですが、どうしたらいいですか。

_____

5. しずかな所で春休みをすごしたい (want to spend) ですが、どうしたらいいですか。

_____

6. あたまがいたい (head aches) んですが、どうしたらいいですか。

_____

E. Your Japanese acquaintance is planning to come to the United States for two or three weeks. Read your acquaintance's wish list. Then, making suggestions about places to visit and using the ～たら form each time, write a brief itinerary for your acquaintance.

[例] 大きいサボテン (cactus) が見たいです。→
アリゾナのツーソンへ行ったらどうですか。きっとたくさん見られます。

1. きれいな、高い山を見たいです。
2. ちょっとギャンブルもしてみたいですね。
3. 大きい町へも行きたいですが、あぶない (dangerous) 所へは行きたくないですよ。
4. おみやげ (souvenir) をたくさん買ってかえりたいんですが、アメリカらしいもの (something typically American) がいいですね。
5. 私は大西洋 (Atlantic Ocean) を見たことがないので、ぜったいに (by all means) 見たいですね.
6. ふつうのアメリカ人のせいかつ (way of life) が見たいです。小さい町にすんでいる人に会って話がしたいです。
7. アメリカの国りつこうえん (national parks) も二つ、三つ見てみたいです。

SUGGESTED ITINERARY

_____

_____

_____

_____

_____

_____

F. Change the following sentences into statements about a decision by using a form of …ことにする.

[例] 旅行するので、スーツケースを ＿＿＿＿＿＿＿＿＿＿＿＿＿＿＿＿。(買います)

旅行するので、スーツケースを買うことにしました。

1. 寒いので、コートを (着ます)。

寒いので、コートを ＿＿＿＿＿＿＿＿＿＿＿＿＿＿＿＿＿＿。

2. おなかがすいたので、何か (食べます)。

おなかがすいたので、何か ＿＿＿＿＿＿＿＿＿＿＿＿＿＿＿＿。

3. ひまなので、えいがでも (見ます)。

ひまなので、えいがでも ＿＿＿＿＿＿＿＿＿＿＿＿＿＿＿＿＿。

4. 毎朝、30 分ジョギングを (します)。

毎朝、30 分ジョギングを ＿＿＿＿＿＿＿＿＿＿＿＿＿＿＿＿＿。

5. ダイエットをするので、あまい物を (食べません)。

ダイエットをするので、あまい物を ＿＿＿＿＿＿＿＿＿＿＿＿＿＿。

6. お金がないので、ユースホステルに (とまります)。

お金がないので、ユースホステルに ＿＿＿＿＿＿＿＿＿＿＿＿＿＿。

7. バスが来ないので、タクシーに (乗ります)。

バスが来ないので、タクシーに ＿＿＿＿＿＿＿＿＿＿＿＿＿＿＿＿。

8. 明日はしけんがあるので、今日はテレビを (見ません)。

明日はしけんがあるので、今日は ＿＿＿＿＿＿＿＿＿＿＿＿＿＿＿。

G. If you were planning a trip to Japan, you would have a lot of decisions to make. What would you decide to do about each of the following aspects of your trip? Use the …ことにする form.

[例] いっしょに行く人 (何人？だれ？) →

姉と二人で行くことにします。

1. 行く時 (きせつ [season], 何月？)

＿＿＿＿＿＿＿＿＿＿＿＿＿＿＿＿＿＿＿＿＿＿＿＿＿＿＿＿＿＿＿＿＿＿

2. きかん (period of time) (どのくらい日本にいますか。)

＿＿＿＿＿＿＿＿＿＿＿＿＿＿＿＿＿＿＿＿＿＿＿＿＿＿＿＿＿＿＿＿＿＿

3. ひこうき (どのこうくう会社 [airline]? きんえんせき?)

_____

4. にもつ (どんなにもつ? 何こ [pieces]?)

_____

5. ほけん (insurance) (ほけんに入[はい]りますか。)

_____

6. お金[かね] (げんきん [cash]? トラベラーズ・チェック? クレジット・カード?)

_____

H. Today is January 1 and you have made some New Year's resolutions—you intend to be a super person this year! Write what you have decided to do about each of the following aspects of your life, using the ⋯ことにする construction.

今年は：

1. (日本語の勉強)

_____

2. (部屋[へや]のそうじ)

_____

3. (毎日のスケジュール)

_____

4. (アルバイト)

_____

5. (anything else you'd like to do or change)

_____

Vocabulary and Grammar 1B: Transportation and Schedules

A. Fill in the blanks with the correct particles.

1. きっぷ_____ 予約[よやく]しました。

2. じこくひょう_____ しらべなければなりません。

3. ほけん_____ 入[はい]りましょうか。

4. 3時＿＿＿＿、くうこう＿＿＿＿着きました。

5. 5時＿＿＿＿、みなと＿＿＿＿たちます。

6. バス＿＿＿＿ ていりゅうじょはどこですか。

7. 車＿＿＿＿の乗ってください。

8. つぎの駅＿＿＿＿、電車＿＿＿＿おります。

9. 電車＿＿＿＿ おくれています。

10. 車＿＿＿＿ かりるつもりです。

B. Fill in the blanks with the given words. You may need to change the form of the verb.

[例] ごはんを＿＿＿＿＿＿後、テレビを見ます。（食べる）→
ごはんを食べた後、テレビを見ます。

1. テレビを＿＿＿＿＿＿後、勉強します。（見る）

2. テレビを＿＿＿＿＿＿から、勉強します。（見る）

3. テレビを＿＿＿＿＿＿前に、勉強します。（見る）

4. 駅に＿＿＿＿＿＿後、ホテルに電話します。（着く）

5. 駅に＿＿＿＿＿＿から、ホテルに電話します。（着く）

6. 駅に＿＿＿＿＿＿前に、ホテルに電話します。（着く）

7. ひこうきに＿＿＿＿＿＿後、ごはんを食べます。（乗る）

8. ひこうきに＿＿＿＿＿＿から、ごはんを食べます。（乗る）

9. ひこうきに＿＿＿＿＿＿前に、ごはんを食べます。（乗る）

10. 名所 (*famous places*) を見物＿＿＿＿＿＿後、旅館に行きます。（する）

11. 名所を見物＿＿＿＿＿＿から、旅館に行きます。（する）

12. 名所を見物＿＿＿＿＿＿前に、旅館に行きます。（する）

C. Complete the sentences with something that would make sense in the context given.

1. ＿＿＿＿＿＿＿＿＿＿＿＿＿＿＿＿＿＿＿前に、おふろに入りませんか。

2. ＿＿＿＿＿＿＿＿＿＿＿＿＿＿＿＿＿＿＿後、父に電話をします。

3. ＿＿＿＿＿＿＿＿＿＿＿＿＿＿＿＿＿＿＿前に、じこくひょうを見ます。

4. ＿＿＿＿＿＿＿＿＿＿＿＿＿＿＿＿＿＿＿てから、いろいろ見物したいです。

5. _____ 前に、ホテルを予約しました。

6. _____ てから、ガイドをたのみましょう。

7. _____ 後、ふねに乗りました。

D. You are planning a short sightseeing trip to Japan. Would you do the following before you leave for Japan, after you get there, or right before you come home? (Answers may vary, so write what you think *you* would do.)

[例]（ひこうきを予約する）→
　　日本へ行く前にひこうきを予約します。

1. （パスポートをとる）_____

2. （家族におみやげを買う）_____

3. （あたらしいカメラを買う）_____

4. （ホテルを予約する）_____

5. （しんかんせんのきっぷを予約する）_____

6. （にもつをつめる）_____

7. （ドルのトラベラーズチェックを円にかえる [change]）_____

_____

8. （レンタカーをかりる）_____

E. What is your morning routine like? Write what you do before/after the given activity. If you don't do some of these activities, say so.

[例] 新聞を読む →
　　新聞を読む前にコーヒーを飲みます。そして、読んだ後で大学へ行きます。

1. 朝ごはんを食べる _____

_____

2. 服を着がえる _____

_____

3. はをみがく _____

_____

4. シャワーをあびる _____

_____

5. コーヒー／ジュース／こう茶を飲む _____

_____

F. It is March now. The following outlines tell what happened to Ms. Yamamoto, a student from Japan, in the past, and what she plans to do in the future. Write down what happened and when, using 前に／後に and indicating amount of time between events.

last year:	March	came to the United States
	May	enrolled (入る) in an English class
	September	enrolled at the university
this year:	January	changed (かえる) majors
	September	transfer (かわる) to a different university
next year:	March	graduate (そつぎょうする)

[例] 山本さんは1年前にアメリカに来ました。その2ヵ月後に英語のクラスに入りました。

1. _____

2. _____

3. _____

4. _____

Vocabulary and Grammar 1C: Sightseeing and Travel Planning

A. Complete the sentences, filling in the blanks with the appropriate forms of the verb, adjective, or copula. You may need to put some of the verbs or adjectives into the negative.

1. ここをまっすぐ（行く）_____ と、ゆうびんきょくがあります。

2. 部屋が（ひろい）_____ と、五人ねることができません。

3. 私の家（だ）_____ と、よくねられません。

4. ピアノが（上手）_____ と、ピアニストにはなれないでしょう。

5. 風が（強い）_____ と、ふねが出ません。

6. ねだんが（安い）_____ と、だれも買いません。

7. 日本語が（とくい）_____ と、日本を旅行するのにべんりです。

8. やさいを（食べる）_____ と、げんきになります。

B. The following map indicates where some of the students in Professor Yokoi's Japanese class live. Write directions for getting to their homes. Imagine that you are standing in the spot indicated by the "x" on the map.

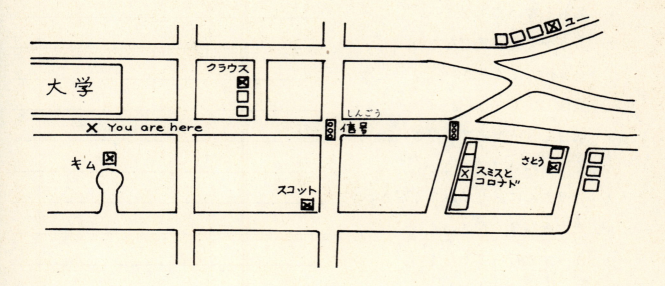

[例] クラウスさん：この道をまっすぐ行って、2つ目のかどを左へ曲がると、左がわにあります。3けん目のたてものです。

1. スミスさんとコロナドさん： _____

   _____

2. ユーさん： _____

   _____

3. キムさん： _____

   _____

4. スコットさん： _____

   _____

5. さとうさん： _____

   _____

C. Change the following requests into commands, as if they were the words of a parent giving directions or advice to a child.

[例] 早く起きてください。→ 早く起きなさい。

1. 名前を書いてください。 _____

2. もう少し食べてください。 _____

3. 全部飲んでください。 _____

4. 勉強してください。 _____

5. 明日もう一度来てください。 _____

6. くつをぬいでください。 _____

7. お母さんに話してみてください。 _____

8. 車に乗ってください。 _____

9. まっすぐ行ってください。 _____

10. 右に曲がってください。 _____

D. Change these commands to the blunt command form.

[例] くすりを飲みなさい。→ くすりを飲め。

1. くつをはきなさい。 _____

2. ホテルを予約しなさい。 _____

3. 私を見なさい。 _____

4. 早く起きなさい。 _____

5. 歩きなさい。 _____

6. よく聞きなさい。 _____

7. ちょっと待ちなさい。 _____

8. お金をはらいなさい。 _____

9. 今すぐに来なさい。 _____

10. 勉強しなさい。 _____

E. How would you advise someone that the following actions are forbidden?

[例] 部屋の中に入る。→ 部屋の中に入ってはいけません。

1. お酒を飲みすぎる。 _____

2. あまい物を食べすぎる。 _____

3. おそくまでねている。 _____

4. となりの人と話す。 _____

5. たばこをすう。 _____

6. テレビを見る。 _____

7. あそびに行く。 _____

8. コンピュータゲームをする。 _____

9. ここで服をぬぐ。 _____

10. しゃしんをとる。 _____

F. Write the blunt negative equivalents for the polite negative requests listed.

[例] 部屋の中に入らないでください。 → 部屋の中に入るな。

1. お酒を飲みすぎないでください。 _____

2. あまい物を食べすぎないでください。 _____

3. おそくまでねていないでください。 _____

4. となりの人と話さないでください。 _____

5. たばこをすわないでください。 _____

6. テレビを見ないでください。 _____

7. あそびに行かないでください。 _____

8. コンピュータゲームをしないでください。 _____

9. ここで服をぬがないでください。 _____

10. しゃしんをとらないでください。 _____

G. Imagine that you are an elementary school teacher. You have a very lively group of children, but they don't always do what you want them to do. Write down what you would like them to do in each of the following situations.

[例] Some children are already eating lunch, even though it's only ten o'clock. You want them to wait until noon. →

今昼ごはんを食べてはいけません。12時まで待ちなさい。

1. They are talking loudly. You want them to quiet down.

_____

2. They are playing (あそぶ). You want them to read their books.

_____

3. One child is asleep. You want him to wake up.

_____

4. They are writing in their books. You want them to write in their notebooks.

_____

5. They are running around (はしりまわる). You want them to sit down (すわる).

_____

6. (something else you have seen and want to change)

_____

H. When you were little, what did your parent(s) or teacher(s) tell you to do and not to do? Write three each following the example.

TO DO

[例] 母は、部屋をかたづけろとよく言いました。私の部屋はいつもとてもきたなかったんです。

1. _____

2. _____

3. _____

NOT TO DO

[例] 私はよくしゅくだいをわすれたので、先生はしゅくだいをわすれるなと毎日言いました。

1. _____

2. _____

3. _____

I. What do you have to do before going to the following countries? (Assume you are an American citizen.)

DESTINATION	VISA NECESSARY?	PASSPORT?	SHOTS? (よぼうせっしゅ)
Japan	no	yes	no
Canada	no	no	no
Australia	yes	yes	no
Kenya	yes	yes	yes
Mexico	no	no	no

[例] 日本へ行く時にはパスポートをとらなければなりません。でも、ビザはいりません。よぼうせっしゅ (vaccinations) もいりません。

1. カナダ _____

_____

2. オーストラリア _____

_____

3. ケニア _____

_____

4. メキシコ _____

_____

J. Does your university dormitory prohibit certain activities? Write down three prohibitions, using 〜てはいけない. Or consult someone about the rules and write down three of them using 〜てはいけないそうです. Or write down three things that are forbidden in the place where you live.

1. _____

2. _____

3. _____

K. Fill in the blanks with the adverbial forms of the adjectives given in parentheses.

[例] _____ ねなさい。(早い) → 早くねなさい。

1. _____ おしえてください。(やさしい)

2. _____ そうじしました。(きれい)

3. _____ 勉強しなさい。(まじめ)

4. _____ 書けましたね。(上手)

5. _____ 歩いてください。(しずか)

6. ＿＿＿＿＿＿＿＿＿＿＿＿ 起きてはいけません。（おそい）

7. ＿＿＿＿＿＿＿＿＿＿＿＿ あそびました。（楽しい）

8. ＿＿＿＿＿＿＿＿＿＿＿＿ 切りました。（みじかい）

9. ＿＿＿＿＿＿＿＿＿＿＿＿ 話しました。（おもしろい）

10. ＿＿＿＿＿＿＿＿＿＿＿＿ うたいました。（楽しい）

L. There are certain manners that you should know when you go to foreign countries. The following are some that Japanese people sometimes do not know when they visit Western countries. Explain them, using 〜てはいけない, 〜なくてはいけない, or 〜なければなりません.

[例] あいて (*the other person*) の目を見ながらあくしゅ (*handshake*) する →
　　　目を見ながらあくしゅしなければなりません。
　　　目を見ないであくしゅしてはいけません。

1. 女の人が部屋に入ってきたら、男の人はたつ (*stand up*)
＿＿＿＿＿＿＿＿＿＿＿＿＿＿＿＿＿＿＿＿＿＿＿＿＿＿＿＿＿＿＿＿＿

2. バスタブの外でからだ (*body*) をあらう (*wash*)
＿＿＿＿＿＿＿＿＿＿＿＿＿＿＿＿＿＿＿＿＿＿＿＿＿＿＿＿＿＿＿＿＿

3. シャワーカーテンをバスタブの中に入れる
＿＿＿＿＿＿＿＿＿＿＿＿＿＿＿＿＿＿＿＿＿＿＿＿＿＿＿＿＿＿＿＿＿

4. フォークにさした (*speared*) 大きい物をかじる (*nibble at*)
(Hint: 小さく切る = *cut into small pieces*) ＿＿＿＿＿＿＿＿＿＿＿＿＿

5. 食事中に手をのばして (*extend*), 遠いところにあるしおをとる
(Hint: …とたのむ = *to ask someone to . . .*) ＿＿＿＿＿＿＿＿＿＿＿＿＿

6. ひじをついて (*leaning on one's elbows*) 食事をする
＿＿＿＿＿＿＿＿＿＿＿＿＿＿＿＿＿＿＿＿＿＿＿＿＿＿＿＿＿＿＿＿＿

M. Complete the following sentences using the construction that expresses obligation. Be sure that the form you write follows logically from the first half of the sentence.

[例] 明日しけんがあるので、→ 明日しけんがあるので、勉強しなければ
　　　なりません。

1. お金がないので、＿＿＿＿＿＿＿＿＿＿＿＿＿＿＿＿＿＿＿＿＿＿＿＿＿

2. 旅行をするので、＿＿＿＿＿＿＿＿＿＿＿＿＿＿＿＿＿＿＿＿＿＿＿＿＿

3. えいがを見に行くので、＿＿＿＿＿＿＿＿＿＿＿＿＿＿＿＿＿＿＿＿＿

4. うちでパーティーをするので、_____

5. アラスカはとても寒いそうなので、_____

6. 車_{くるま}がないので、_____

7. ホテルの予約_{よやく}をしなかったので、_____

8. やさいがきらいなので、_____

9. かんこう名所_{めいしょ}をしらないので、_____

10. 日本語がにがてなので、_____

N. Your friends from Japan have come to visit you and to see the interesting town you live in. Suggest places for them to visit and tell them what they can do there. Also, point out the places they should avoid.

The name of the town _____

1. ばんごはんは、_____ たらいいですよ。

2. しずかな所_{ところ}へ行きたい時は、_____ たらいいですよ。

3. うんどうしたい時は、_____ たらいいですよ。

4. ホテルは、_____ がいいですよ。

   _____ し、_____ し、

   _____ 。

5. きれいな所_{ところ}が見たい時は、_____ たらいいですよ。

6. _____ へ行ってはいけません。

7. _____ てはいけません。

Now make whatever suggestions you like:

8. _____

9. _____

10. _____

O. Complete each of the following sentences with either まで or までに.

1. 五時_____ がっこうに行かなければなりません。

2. 五時_____ がっこうにいなければなりません。

3. 夏_{なつ}が来る_____ 水着_{みずぎ}を買_かいたいです。

4. 明日＿＿＿＿＿＿＿ きっぷを予約しなければなりません。

5. 八時＿＿＿＿＿＿＿ うちで待っています。

6. 午前四時＿＿＿＿＿＿＿ テレビを見ていました。

7. テープが終わる ＿＿＿＿＿＿＿ 聞いていてください。

8. 金曜日＿＿＿＿＿＿＿ りれき書 (résumé) をおくって (send) ください。

9. 四年生は二月＿＿＿＿＿＿＿ そつぎょうろんぶん (senior thesis) を出さなければなり
ません。

10. りんごは赤くなる＿＿＿＿＿＿＿ はすっぱい (sour) です。

P. Choose the appropriate word from among つれていく、つれてくる、もっていく、もってくる、
and put it into the grammatical form indicated by the context. Keep in mind that いく always refers to
motion away from the speaker and くる always refers to motion toward the speaker.

1. デコレーション・ケーキを買って、キムさんのたんじょう日のパーティーに
＿＿＿＿＿＿＿ ました。

2. さとうさん、妹さんに会いたいので、明日私のオフィスへ＿＿＿＿＿＿＿
てください。

3. あのえいがを見に行くのなら、私も＿＿＿＿＿＿＿ てください。

4. 一人で行くのがいやですから、ルームメートを＿＿＿＿＿＿＿ ことに
しました。

5. 山田さん、そのあたらしい電たく (calculator) をこのオフィスへ
＿＿＿＿＿＿＿ てください。

6. 来月インドネシアへしゅっちょうしますが、インドネシア語が話せないので、つ
うやく (interpreter) を ＿＿＿＿＿＿＿ たらいいでしょうね。

7. 土曜日のパーティーか。ぼくはCDプレーヤーを＿＿＿＿＿＿＿ よ。

8. もしもし。ルーム・サービスですか。…シャンパンを一本＿＿＿＿＿＿＿
てください。

9. コンサートのきっぷが二まいあるんだけど、だれを＿＿＿＿＿＿＿ たら
いいかなあ。

10. すずきさんをうちにさそいました (invited) が、かのじょはかってに (without
permission) いぬを＿＿＿＿＿＿＿ ました。

Q. A Japanese acquaintance who has just arrived in the United States from Japan is going to New York City for a few days. Offer five pieces of advice concerning his or her stay there, using such expressions as 〜てはいけない and 〜なくてはいけない.

1. _____

2. _____

3. _____

4. _____

5. _____

Chapter 1 Review

A. What do you call the following in Japanese? Answer using …といいます.

1. とくべつに *(especially, extraordinarily)* はやい電車（てんしゃ）_____

2. 行きとかえりがりょうほう *(both)* あるきっぷ_____

3. タバコをすってもいいせき _____

4. タバコをすってはいけないせき _____

5. 電車（てんしゃ）の中できっぷをしらべる *(check)* 人_____

6. 電車（てんしゃ）に乗（の）る前にはらうお金（かね）_____

7. きっぷをうるきかい *(machine)* _____

8. だれもとまっていない部屋（へや）_____

9. とまると、ばんごはんと朝ごはんがついていること

    _____

10. 電車（てんしゃ）に乗（の）っている人_____

11. 食（た）べ物（もの）や飲（の）み物（もの）を部屋（へや）に持（も）ってきてもらうこと_____

B. Some readers of a Japanese newspaper wrote the following letters to the paper's advice columnist. If you were the advice columnist, what would you say to these people? Write your advice using 〜たらどうですか／いいと思います. Do not hesitate to give creative advice.

1. 私の家内は毎ばん、いびきをかきます *(snores)*。とてもやかましい *(noisy)* のでねむれない *(can't fall asleep)* のですが、家内はじぶん *(she herself)* はぜったいに *(absolutely)* いびきはかかないと言います。どうしたらいいでしょうか。

_____

_____

_____

2. 私の主人は夏には家にかえると、洋服を全部ぬいでパンツ1まいで夕食を食べます。何か着てほしい *(want him to wear)* と何度も言いましたが、ぜんぜん *(not at all)* 聞いてくれません *(won't listen to me)*。どうしたらいいでしょうか。

_____

_____

_____

3. 私の家内は毎日友だちやかのじょの *(her)* 母と電話で話します。1日3時間ぐらいは電話で話しています。電話だい *(phone bill)* も高いし、うるさいのでやめてほしい *(I want her to stop)* のですが、言ってもやめません。どうしたらいいでしょうか。

_____

_____

_____

4. 私の主人は昼ごはんを食べるのがきらいです。私は毎日おべんとうを作るのですが、主人はそれをごみばこにすてて *(throw away)* います。(主人は私がしらないと思っていますが、私はしっています。)私は主人が昼ごはんを食べなければいけないと思うのですが、どうしたらいいでしょうか。

_____

_____

_____

C. You have invited someone special for dinner. Decide what to serve for each of six courses. If you are a good cook, think of a fancy menu that you would not normally cook. If you can't cook, you may have someone help you, use a caterer, or use frozen food (but no fast food, please). Write your selections using …にしようと思います.

[例] ぜんさい (*appetizer*) →

ぜんさいはスモークサーモンにしようと思います。ケイパーとたまねぎとレモンを一緒に出そう (*serve*) と思います。

1. スープ

_____

_____

2. サラダ

_____

_____

3. 肉／魚料理／その他のメインの料理

_____

_____

4. やさい

_____

_____

5. デザート

_____

_____

6. 飲み物

_____

_____

D. Imagine that you are about to leave for an extended trip to Japan. What kind of advice do you think your parent(s) would give you? Write five pieces of advice that you might expect from them. Refer to Activity 31, page 50, in the main text, or call your parent(s) to find out what they would *really* say.

1. _____

2. _____

3. _____

4. _____

5. _____

E. You are at the JR Kyoto Station. You plan to visit several places, but you have only a vague idea of how to get to them. Ask the person at the tourist information counter the questions that follow.

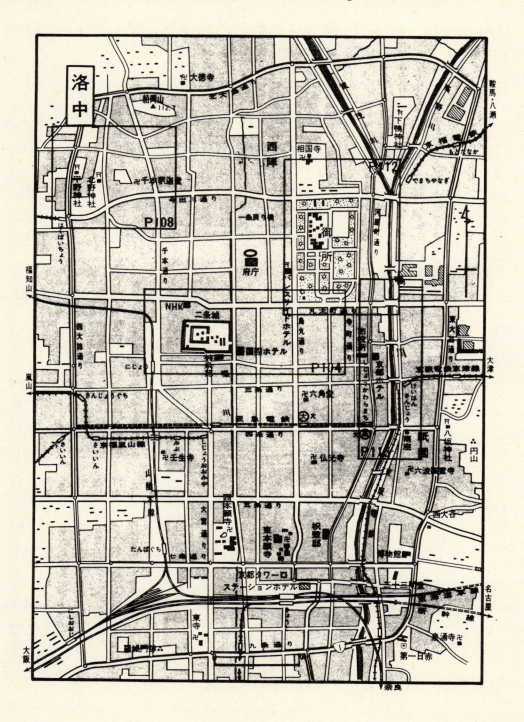

1. You know you can walk to Nishihonganji Temple (西本願寺), but you don't know how to get there. Ask for directions.

   _____

   _____

2. According to the map, the Nijo Castle (二条城) does not seem too far away from the station, so you consider walking there. Ask how long it takes to walk.

   _____

   _____

3. You heard that Kiyomizu Temple (清水寺) is not very far from Yasaka Shrine (八坂神社), but you don't see it on the map. Ask where on the map it is.

   _____

   _____

4. You are to stay at a youth hostel in Utano (宇多野), but you can't find it on the map. Call the hostel and ask how you can get there.

   _____

   _____

5. You would like to go to the Golden Pavilion (金閣寺). You know you can take a bus, but you don't know which one. Find out which bus you should take and where the bus stop is.

   _____

   _____

F. You have received the following answers to the questions in the previous exercise. Which answer is for which question? Write the numbers in the blanks.

1. _____ 25番のです。この駅の南がわから出ますよ。

2. _____ 駅を出て、七条どおり (avenue) を行くと、東本願寺があります。そこから西へ10分ほど歩いたところです。

3. _____ え、あそこまで歩くんですか。ちょっと遠すぎると思いますよ。

4. _____ そうですね。JR ではなぞの駅かさが駅まで行ってそこからタクシーで来るとはやいですよ。

5. _____ そんなに遠くありませんよ。西大谷から歩いてすぐですよ。

G. Give advice to your friends who have the following problems.

[例] 日本を旅行したいんですが、お金がないんです。 →
You: <u>お金をためたら(save up)どうですか。</u>

1. Your friend: 車がこしょうしたんです。

   You: _____

2. Your friend: かん国に行くんですが、ひこうきがこわいんです。

   You: _____

3. Your friend: 引っこしたんですが、部屋がせまいんです。

   You: _____

4. Your friend: ホテルの予約をしたいんですが、高いんです。

   You: _____

5. Your friend: となりの人が毎日うるさいんです。

   You: _____

H. You are a tour conductor showing some Japanese people around New York. They have a lot of questions and problems. Give them advice, using 〜たらどうですか or 〜たらいいです.

1. Tourist: すみません。ひこうきのきっぷがないんですけど…

   You: _____

2. Tourist: 地下てつでウォールストリートへ行こうと思っています。

   You: _____

3. Tourist: すみません。いいレストランをさがしているんですが…

   You: _____

4. Tourist: すみません。ホテルの部屋の電話がこわれているんですけど…

   You: _____

5. Tourist: すみません。地図の見方を教えてください。

   You: _____

6. Tourist: すみません。ホテルの人のえい語がわからないんですけど…

   You: _____

CHAPTER **2**

AT HOME

家で

Listening Comprehension Activities

Vocabulary and Grammar 2A: Houses

A. Listen to the statements and circle the most appropriate room or place for each set of activities.

1. （ドア　　ろうか　　げんかん）
2. （寝室　　トイレ　　居間）
3. （子供部屋　　洗面所　　客間）
4. （浴室　　居間　　庭）
5. （ダイニング・キッチン　　リビング・ルーム　　階段）
6. （屋根　　茶の間　　庭）

B. Listen to Ms, Yamaguchi talk about her experiences looking for a new house. Then mark each of the following statements either true (T) or false (F).

Useful Vocabulary: こんやくしゃ *fiance(e)*

1. _____ The first house had a specious living room and kitchen.

2. _____ They decided not to take the first house because the garden was too big.

3. _____ They liked the second house because it was in a lively neighborhood.

4. _____ The second house had a large yard.

5. _____ They did not take the second house because it was far from a shopping center.

6. _____ The third house was located near a bus stop.

7. _____ The third house had everything except a swimming pool.

8. _____ There were two bathrooms in the third house.

C. Ms. Yamaguchi is talking with Mr. Takada, who has just moved into a new house. Listen to their dialogue and complete each sentence by filling in the blanks.

Useful Vocabulary: とまっていく *spend a night*

1. Takada's previous house was too small for a family of _____.

2. Takada's new house has a _____, two _____, a

   large _____, and a _____.

3. The _____ and _____ are Japanese-style room.

4. Children's rooms are _____ -style rooms.

5. The children can take a shower on the _____.

D. Ms. Yamaguchi is visiting Mr. Takada at his new home. Listen as Takada shows Yamaguchi around the house and indicate which area of the house is best described by the following sentences. (L: Living room, K: Kitchen, Y: Yard)

1. Sunny: _____

2. Large: _____

3. Place for family gatherings: _____

4. Convenient for a housewife: _____

5. Accessible from the living room: _____

6. Quiet place to rest: _____

Vocabulary and Grammar 2B: Furnishing and Appliances

A. Listen to the statements and choose the most appropriate furnishing or appliance for each description.

1. (エアコン　ストーブ　ミシン　テレビ)
2. (そうじき　せんたくき　すいはんき　せんぷうき)
3. (れいぞうこ　時けい　トースター　ラジオ)
4. (ドライヤー　ジューサー　電子レンジ　電気ポット)
5. (かがみ　シェーバー　いす　テーブル)
6. (タンス　つくえ　本だな　ソファー)

B. Takeshi Mimura's sister, Akemi, is visiting the apartment where John Kawamura and Henry Curtis live. Listen as Curtis shows her his room, and choose the best completion for each sentence.

1. Curtis' room is interesting because he _____.
   a. can see the beach from his window
   b. can do a lot of things with various gadgets and equipment
   c. has decorated it with Japanese folk crafts

2. Curtis bought a stereo so that he could _____.
   a. listen to music
   b. record messages to send to his family
   c. listen to Japanese tapes

3. Curtis bought a computer so that he could _____.
   a. practice kanji   b. play games   c. impress people

4. Curtis _____ a good Japanese dictionary for foreigners.
   a. owns   b. asks if Akemi knows of   c. uses

5. Kawamura and Curtis bought _____ for Akemi.
   a. a U.S. travel guide   b. flowers   c. a video game

C. Listen to the statements about giving and receiving, and fill in the blanks with the appropriate words in English.

1. Hayashi _____ Kawamura a necktie.

2. Kawamura gave Hayashi an _____.

3. _____ gave _____ a blouse.

4. Machida _____ money from her mother.

5. Chin _____ Gibson a watch.

6. Chin _____ a CD from Gibson.

7. _____ gave _____ a toaster.

8. Brown _____ me a calendar.

9. I _____ my father a _____.

10. _____ gave _____ a car.

D. Takeshi and Akemi Mimura are discussing what to give their mother for her birthday. Listen to the dialogue, and choose the best completion for each sentence.

1. They find it hard to find a gift for their mother because _____.
   a. she is a difficult person to please
   b. she has everything
   c. they have very little money

2. They won't get their mother a watch because _____.
   a. she got one from their father
   b. she never wanted one
   c. it is too expensive

3. They won't get her a purse because _____ already gave her one.
   a. Akemi   b. Takeshi   c. both

4. Their mother _____ a new camera.
   a. has   b. wants   c. gave her son

5. Takeshi and Akemi think that a trip _____ will be the best gift for their mother.
   a. with their father   b. with lots of money   c. to a hot spring resort

6. _____ will pay the expenses for the trip.
   a. Akemi   b. Takeshi   c. Their father

7. Akemi is excited because _____.
   a. she will take the trip on her birthday
   b. she found what to buy for her mother
   c. she can go on a trip with her mother

E. Listen to what Yoshiko Tanaka, who is traveling the U.S., wrote in a letter to her parents in Tokyo. Then list what the following people have given to, have done for, or will do for her.

Useful Vocabulary: かれの *his*

1. What Smith often does for Yoshiko Tanaka: _____

2. What Smith did for Yoshiko last night: _____

3. What Smith's brother did for Yoshiko: _____

4. What Smith's mother did for Yoshiko: _____

5. What Smith's mother will do for Yoshiko tomorrow: _____

F. Professor Yokoi's students are about to take a chapter test. Listen to the directions she gives them, and choose the correct word in the parentheses.

1. The students (should / should not) write the answers with pen.

2. They (should / should not) write all the answers in Japanese.

3. If they have a question, they (may / may not) ask in English.

4. They (may / may not) use a dictionary.

5. Talking to their classmates and opening the textbook (are / are not) prohibited.

6. During the test, they (can / cannot) eat or drink.

7. When they finish, they (may / may not) leave the class.

G. Yoshiko Tanaka is in a tour group visiting Washington, D.C. Listen as the tour guide explains their schedule for the day, and then complete the following sentences by filling in the blanks.

Useful Vocabulary: じゆう *free,* はくぶつかん *museum,* こえ *voice*

1. The tour guide is going over today's schedule before _____ the bus.

2. They may eat breakfast inside _____.

3. They may take pictures while _____ the town.

4. There will be no time for shopping after lunch because _____

   right after lunch.

5. Inside the museum, they are not allowed to _____ or _____.

6. In the evening after they return to the hotel, they may _____.

7. They should _____ tonight in order to catch the bus at 7:00 tomorrow

   morning.

H. Sometimes it is hard to choose a gift for someone who seems to have everything or someone you don't know well. Listen to the following two conversations, and figure out what each person already has and what would be an appropriate gift.

Useful Vocabulary: たとえば *for example,* ～しなくちゃ *must*

1. What Mr. Yamada already has: _____

   What *you think* will be an appropriate gift for him: _____

2. What Ms. Suzuki already has: _____

   What *you think* will be an appropriate gift for her: _____

Vocabulary and Grammar 2C: Household Chores

A. Listen as Heather Gibson asks three of her friends about household chores, and choose the chores each of them does. There may be more than one answer.

1. Hayashi does (cooking, wiping furniture, ironing, cleaning windows).

2. Kawamura does (cleaning the house, laundry, ironing, mopping the floor).

3. Chin does (cooking, cleaning the house, helping to wash dishes, repairing washing machine).

B. Listen as Henry Curtis asks Takako Matsui about how he can make his room brighter. Then write the advice Matsui gives Curtis about each item.

1. Curtains: _____

2. Color of the walls: _____

3. Picture: _____

4. Table: _____

5. Buying things to improve his room: _____

C. Heather Gibson has just returned to Tokyo from Kyoto. Listen as she gives her classmates advice on visiting the famous city. Then mark each of the following sentences either true (T) or false (F).

Useful Vocabulary: さくらのはな *cherry blossoms,* れきし *history*

According to Gibson:

1. _____ It is best to visit Kyoto in the spring because it is less crowded.

2. _____ Kyoto is a better place than Tokyo to experience traditional Japanese culture.

3. _____ It is easy to get around in Kyoto because it is a small city.

4. _____ People on the street don't like to talk to foreigners in Japanese.

5. _____ It is better to go around Kyoto by taxi because it is economical.

6. _____ Japanese inns are a better place to stay than hotels in Kyoto.

7. _____ It is a good idea to make reservations early if you're going to Kyoto.

D. Professor Yokoi's students are going to have a party this evening at her house. Listen as John Kawamura, who showed up first, asks Professor Yokoi what he can do to help her prepare. Then choose the most appropriate answer.

Useful Vocabulary: じゅんび *preparation*

1. Professor Yokoi _____ the room.
   a. is about to clean   b. is in the midst of cleaning   c. has just cleaned

2. Professor Yokoi's son _____ the table.
   a. is about to clean up   b. is cleaning up   c. has just cleaned up

3. Professor Yokoi's husband _____ the yard.
   a. is going to clean   b. is cleaning   c. has cleaned

4. John Kawamura _____ at home.
   a. is going to eat   b. is now eating   c. has just eaten

E. Listen to what Yoshiko Tanaka wrote to her parents in a postcard from New York. Then complete each of the following sentences.

Useful Vocabulary: もどる *to return*

1. Yoshiko has just returned from _____.

2. She has just _____ Mr. Smith on the phone.

3. She is going to _____ of places Smith has never been to.

4. Yoshiko is about to _____ a restaurant for dinner.

5. She thinks it would be better for her _____

   before going to the restaurant.

6. She _____ about tomorrow's schedule.

F. Yoshiko Tanaka has stopped off in California again at the end of her short vacation in the United States. Her flight for Japan leaves tomorrow. Listen to her conversation with Cody Smith. Then mark each of the following statements either true (T) or false (F).

   Useful Vocabulary: よういする *to get something ready,* しんぱいする, *to worry*

1. _____ Yoshiko will try to rest up before the trip back home.

2. _____ She doesn't have much to take with her because she didn't buy much.

3. _____ Smith will see her off at the airport tomorrow.

4. _____ Smith has reserved a taxi for the airport and talked to the driver.

5. _____ She has done everything she wanted to do before leaving.

6. _____ Smith will call his mother for Yoshiko.

7. _____ She will write to Smith from Japan.

Kanji Practice and Exercises

1	新	新	シン、あたら-しい、あら-た、にい new	新	新
	新しい：あたらしい (new) 新しい車：あたらしいくるま (new car) 新聞：しんぶん (newspaper)				
2	開	開	カイ opening; development あ-ける、あ-く open　　ひら-ける be opened, become developed ひら-く open, develop	開	開
	開ける：あける (open [something]) 本を開けて下さい：ほんをあけてください 　(please open your book)				
3	公	公	コウ public; unbiased, fair; in common; prince, lord ク、おおやけ public	公	公
	公園：こうえん (park) 上野公園：うえのこうえん (Ueno Park) 公開：こうかい (opening to the public)				
4	園	園	エン、その garden	園	園
	公園：こうえん (park) 動物園：どうぶつえん (zoo)				
5	住	住	ジュウ dwelling, residing, living す-む、す-まう live, reside す-まい residence	住	住
	住む：すむ (to live)　　住まい：すまい (dwelling) 住所：じゅうしょ (address) 中野に住んでいる：なかのにすんでいる 　(is living in Nakano)				

6	階 階	カイ stairs; step, grade; floor, story
	一階：いっかい (first floor) 二階：にかい (second floor) 階だん：かいだん (stairs)	

7	広 広	コウ、ひろ-い、ひろ-やか broad, wide, spacious, extensive ひろ-げる extend, enlarge ひろ-がる spread, expand ひろ-める broaden, propagate ひろ-まる spread, be propagated
	広い：ひろい (wide) 広くありません：ひろくありません (not wide) 広い部屋：ひろいへや (spacious room)	

8	直 直	チョク、ジキ straight, immediate, direct, correct なお-す fix, correct, revise; convert into; (as suffix) re; do over なお-る return to normal, be fixed/corrected, recover ただ-ちに immediately す-ぐ immediately; readily, easily; right (near)
	直す：なおす (fix, repair) ドアを直しました：どあをなおしました (repaired the door)	

9	戸 戸	コ door, house(hold) と door
	戸：と (door) 戸を開ける：とをあける (open the door) 神戸：こうべ (Kobe)	

10	古 古	コ、ふる-い old ふる-す wear out ふる-びる become old ふる-ぼける look old; wear out ふる-めかしい old, from long ago いにしえ ancient times
	古い：ふるい (old) 古い家：ふるいいえ (old house) 中古(品)：ちゅうこ(ひん) (secondhand merchandise)	

11	門 門	モン、かど gate
	門：もん (gate) 大きい門：おおきいもん (large gate) 名門大学：めいもんだいがく (prestigious university)	

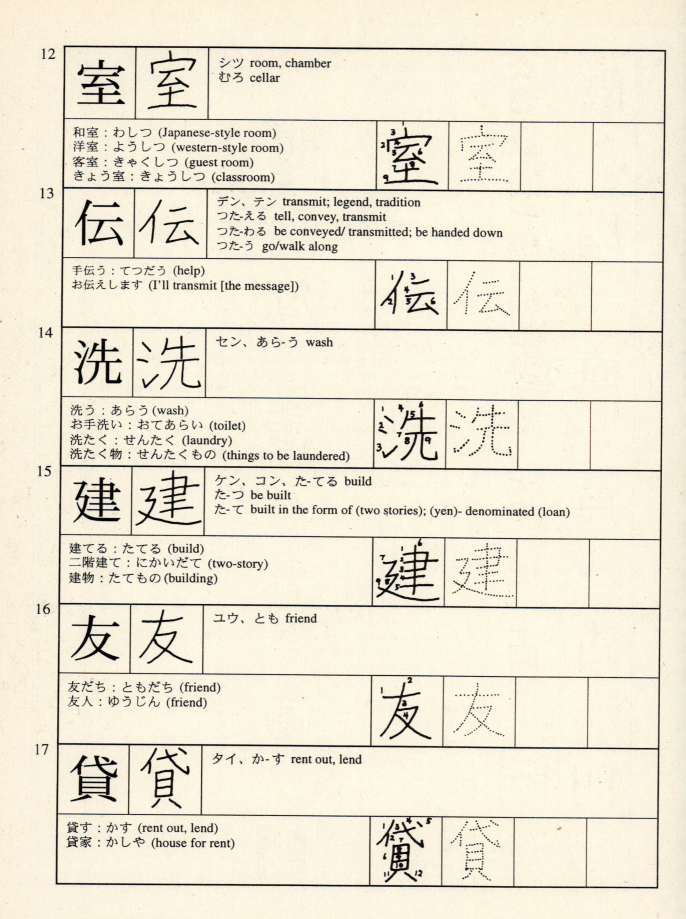

12 室 室	シツ room, chamber むろ cellar	
和室：わしつ (Japanese-style room) 洋室：ようしつ （western-style room) 客室：きゃくしつ (guest room) きょう室：きょうしつ (classroom)		室 室
13 伝 伝	デン、テン transmit; legend, tradition つた-える tell, convey, transmit つた-わる be conveyed/ transmitted; be handed down つた-う go/walk along	
手伝う：てつだう (help) お伝えします (I'll transmit [the message])		伝 伝
14 洗 洗	セン、あら-う wash	
洗う：あらう (wash) お手洗い：おてあらい (toilet) 洗たく：せんたく (laundry) 洗たく物：せんたくもの (things to be laundered)		洗 洗
15 建 建	ケン、コン、た-てる build た-つ be built た-て built in the form of (two stories); (yen)- denominated (loan)	
建てる：たてる (build) 二階建て：にかいだて (two-story) 建物：たてもの (building)		建 建
16 友 友	ユウ、とも friend	
友だち：ともだち (friend) 友人：ゆうじん (friend)		友 友
17 貸 貸	タイ、か-す rent out, lend	
貸す：かす (rent out, lend) 貸家：かしや (house for rent)		貸 貸

18	借 借	シャク、シャ、か-りる borrow, rent かり borrowing, debt, loan			
	借りる：かりる (borrow) 借家人：しゃくやにん (tenant) 借金：しゃっきん (borrowed money)	借 借		
19	置 置	チ、お-く put, place, set, leave behind, leave as is お-き skipping…, at intervals of…, every (other/third day), (five meters) apart			
	置く：おく (put) つくえの上に本を置いておきました：つくえのう えにほんをおいておきました (I put the book on top of the desk for now.)	置 置		
20	静 静	セイ、ジョウ、しず、しず-か quiet, peaceful, still しず-める calm, soothe, quell しず-まる grow quiet/calm, subside, die down			
	静か：しずか (quiet) 静かな公園：しずかなこうえん (quiet park)	静 静		
21	庭 庭	テイ、にわ garden, yard			
	庭：にわ (garden) 家庭：かてい (household)	庭 庭		
22	便 便	ベン convenience, facilities, excrement, feces ビン mail; transport, flight; opportunity たよ-り news, things			
	便利：べんり (convenient) 便乗する：びんじょうする (get a lift [in a friend's car])	便 便		
23	利 利	リ advantage; interest (on a loan) き-く take effect, work き-かす make effective, use, exercise			
	便利：べんり (convenient) 利子：りし (interest [on a loan])	利 利		

24	不	不	フ、ブ not, un-				
	不便：ふべん (inconvenient) 不動さん屋：ふどうさんや (real estate agent) 不明：ふめい (unclear)						

Kanji Exercises

A. Match each kanji or kanji compound with its closest English equivalent.

1. 公園 _____
2. 不 _____
3. 開 _____
4. 階 _____
5. 建 _____
6. 古 _____
7. 戸 _____
8. 便 _____

9. 広 _____
10. 室 _____
11. 借 _____
12. 貸 _____
13. 住 _____
14. 新 _____
15. 静 _____
16. 洗 _____

17. 置 _____
18. 直 _____
19. 庭 _____
20. 手伝う _____
21. 公 _____
22. 門 _____
23. 友 _____
24. 利 _____

a. door b. to open c. public d. yard e. to live f. floor/story g. wide h. to fix
i. new j. old k. gate l. room m. to help n. to wash o. to listen p. friend
q. to rent out/lend r. to borrow s. left t. quiet u. park v. to build w. not/un-
x. convenience y. advantage z. to put/place

B. Write the hurigana for each kanji or kanji compound.

1. 静か
   _____

2. 庭
   _____

3. 門
   _____

4. 住む
   _____

5. 住所
   _____

6. 開ける
   _____

7. 新しい
   _____

8. 古い
   _____

9. 広い
   _____

10. 新聞

_____

11. 便利

_____

12. 不便

_____

13. 洗う

_____

14. お手洗い

_____

15. 洗たく

_____

16. 手伝う

_____

17. 公園

_____

18. 洋室

_____

19. 建てる

_____

20. 二階建て

_____

21. 建物

_____

22. 直す

_____

23. 置く

_____

24. 貸す

_____

25. 借りる

_____

26. 戸

_____

27. 友だち

_____

C. Write the appropriate kanji for the hiragana under the lines.

1. _____ だちに _____ を _____ してもらった。
   とも   くるま   か

2. _____ い _____ はそのつくえの _____ に _____ いて _____ さい。
   ふる しんぶん   うえ お   くだ

3. _____ から _____ をたくさん _____ りた。
   としょかん   ほん   か

4. _____ い _____ のある、_____ しい _____ ての _____ です。
   ひろ にわ   あたら にかいだ   いえ

5. _____ はさらを _____ いながら、_____ で _____ しています。
   はは   あら   でんわ はな

6. _____ の _____ がこわれたから _____ して _____ さい。
   もん と   なお くだ

7. _____ も _____ もある _____ に _____ みたい。
   わしつ ようしつ いえ す

8. _____ を _____ けて _____ さい。
   ほん あ くだ

9. _____ で _____ ごはんを _____ べましょう。
   こうえん ひる た

10. この＿＿＿＿＿＿は＿＿＿かだし、＿＿＿＿＿＿だし、＿＿＿みやすい＿＿＿＿
　　　　きんじょ　　しず　　　　　　　べんり　　　　す　　　　　ところ
　　だと＿＿＿います。
　　　　　おも

11. ＿＿＿＿＿＿＿は＿＿＿のしごとを＿＿＿＿＿＿っていました。
　　　きのう　　　ちち　　　　　　てつだ

12. ＿＿＿がないと＿＿＿＿＿＿な＿＿＿ですから＿＿＿いのでも＿＿＿ったら
　　　くるま　　　　　ふべん　　ところ　　　　ふる　　　　か
　　どうですか。

13. ＿＿＿＿＿＿＿は＿＿＿たくをしたり、＿＿＿い＿＿＿をしたりするつもりです。
　　　あした　　　せん　　　　　　か　　もの

Kanji in Everyday Life

1. You're in the National Diet Library, and you see a sign pointing to the 新館. What is it?

   _____

2. Who owns the company known as 広田建設? What kind of company is it?

   _____

3. A land-use map labels a certain part of a town as 住宅地. What is the land used for?

   _____

4. The word 国際 means *international*. What is 国際友情?

   _____

5. In a bookstore you find a dictionary labeled 古語辞典. What do you think this dictionary specializes in?

   _____

6. While reading a sociological study of a rural village, you see that its population is listed as 四十五戸. Does this figure tell you the exact number of people living there or something else?

   _____

7. In a music store you find a CD of フランスの室内音楽, featuring a string quartet. What do you think 室内音楽 is?

   _____

8. Your Japanese pen pal writes that he or she is earning extra money as a 家庭教師. You happen to know that 教師 is another word for *teacher*, so can you figure out what your pen pal's new アルバイト is?

_____

Writing Activities

Vocabulary and Grammar 2A: Houses

A. Match the following activities with the part of a house where you do them. It may be possible to do some of these activities in more than one part of the house.

1. _____ ごはんを作る
2. _____ テレビを見る
3. _____ ねる
4. _____ 友だちとあそぶ
5. _____ おふろに入る
6. _____ 手を洗う
7. _____ ざっしを読む
8. _____ お客さんと話す
9. _____ 花をそだてる
10. _____ 勉強する

a. げんかん
b. ダイニングルーム
c. いま
d. 客間
e. 勉強部屋
f. しん室
g. よく室
h. せんめん所
i. トイレ
j. 庭
k. 台所

B. What kind of house do you want to live in? Look at the choices listed and write your preferences. Do you want these rooms? If so, how many? What kind? Be specific where you can.

[例] 庭 → 庭がいる／庭はいらない
部屋 → ひろい部屋がたくさんある方がいい。

1. 一戸建てじゅうたく (*single-family dwelling*) ／ マンション／アパート (*choose one*)

_____

2. 客間 _____

3. 勉強部屋 _____

4. 子ども部屋 _____

5. しん室 _____

6. よく室 _____

7. 洗めん所 _____

8. トイレ _____

9. 和室 _____

10. 洋室 _____

11. 天じょうが高い／天じょうがひくい _____

12. ベランダ _____

C. Describe your family's house and your own room either by filling in the blanks or circling one of the two alternatives given in parentheses.

私の家は(大きくて/小さくて)、(新しい／古い)です。＿＿＿＿＿階建てです。しん室が、

＿＿＿＿＿つあります。げんかんを入って、右に＿＿＿＿＿＿＿＿＿＿、左に

＿＿＿＿＿＿＿＿＿＿＿があります。

私の部屋は＿＿＿＿＿＿階にあります。(広い／せまい)です。部屋のかべの色は

＿＿＿＿＿＿＿＿＿＿＿です。てんじょうの色は＿＿＿＿＿＿＿＿です。部屋のまどから、

＿＿＿＿＿＿＿＿＿＿＿が見えます。

部屋の中に＿＿＿＿＿＿＿＿＿や、＿＿＿＿＿＿＿＿＿＿や、＿＿＿＿＿＿＿＿＿＿や、

＿＿＿＿＿＿＿＿＿＿があります。

家のとなりには、＿＿＿＿＿＿＿＿＿＿が住んでいます。家のむかいには、

＿＿＿＿＿＿＿＿＿＿＿＿＿＿＿。家をでて、右に行くと、

＿＿＿＿＿＿＿＿＿＿＿があります。左に行くと、＿＿＿＿＿＿＿＿＿＿があります。

家のそばに、＿＿＿＿＿＿＿＿＿や、＿＿＿＿＿＿＿＿＿や、＿＿＿＿＿＿＿＿＿

があります。でも、＿＿＿＿＿＿＿＿＿や、＿＿＿＿＿＿＿＿＿＿はありません。家

からがっこうまで＿＿＿＿＿＿＿＿＿＿ぐらいかかります。

D. The following are diagrams of (A) a house and (B) a condominium. Study them carefully.

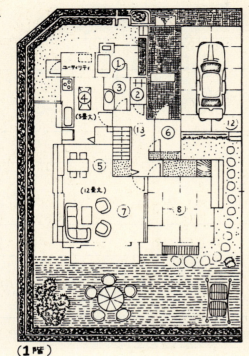

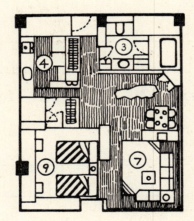

What are the numbered rooms called in Japanese? Write them down.

1. _____   6. _____   10. _____

2. _____   7. _____   11. _____

3. _____   8. _____   12. _____

4. _____   9. _____   13. _____

5. _____

E. Referring to diagrams A and B in Exercise D, answer the following questions.

1. Ａは家ですか、マンションですか。Ｂは？

_____

_____

2. Ａには部屋^{へや}がいくつありますか。Ｂには？

_____

_____

3. Ａには和室^{わしつ}がありますか。Ｂには？

_____

_____

4. Ａにはえんとつがあるでしょうか。Ｂは？

_____

_____

5. Ａは何階建^{かいだ}てでしょうか。

_____

_____

6. もしあなたの家族がＡの家を買^かったら、あなたはどの部屋^{へや}をあなたのしん室^{しつ}に
   したいですか。

_____

_____

7. Ａは東京^{きょう}から電車^{でんしゃ}で一時間半のところにあって、Ｂは東京^{きょう}のまん中にあります。
   ＡとＢのねだんは同^{おな}じです。
   あなただったら、どちらを買^かいますか。どうして。

_____

_____

F. A Japanese acquaintance would like to know what a typical American home is like. Draw a diagram of a house that *you* think is typical and describe it in Japanese. Write at least five sentences. (You will draw furniture on the diagram later, so make sure it is large enough.)

_____

_____

_____

_____

_____

G. Combine each of the following pairs of phrases into a single sentence using the 〜たり〜たり form.

[例] テレビを見る、新聞を読む → テレビを見たり、新聞を読んだりします。

1. ステレオを聞く、友だちと話す

_____

2. 食事をする、えいがを見る

_____

3. 勉強する、ねる

_____

4. 行く、来る

_____

5. 出る、入る

_____

6. うたをうたう、おどる

_____

7. かんじを書く、ひらがなを書く

_____

8. お酒を飲む、たばこをすう

_____

H. What do you do in the following places? Describe the activities typical of each place using the 〜たり 〜たり construction.

[例] 客間で → 客間でお客さんと話したりお茶を飲んだりします。

1. 台所で _____

2. ダイニングルームで _____

3. いまで、_____

4. 勉強部屋で _____

5. しん室で、_____

6. よく室で、_____

7. 洗めん所で、_____

8. 庭で _____

9. げんかんで _____

10. 車こで、_____

11. ベランダで、_____

12. 書さいで、_____

I. What would you do on the following days? Use 〜たり〜たり in your answers.

[例] 天気のいい日 →

天気のいい日には、さんぽしたり、外でキャッチボールをしたりします。

1. 雨の日

_____

2. きまつしけん (final exams) が終わった日

_____

3. ひまで、何もすることがない日

　　_____

4. お金^{かね}がぜんぜんない日

　　_____

5. きゅうりょう (salary) をもらった日

　　_____

J. A Japanese student wants to find out more about American student life. Answer his/her questions using ～たり～たり.

1. アメリカの学生はたいていどこで勉強するんですか。_____

　　_____

2. アメリカの日本語の学生はどうやって日本語を勉強するんですか。_____

　　_____

3. アメリカの学生はデートではどんなことをするんですか。

　　_____

4. アメリカの学生はみんなビールを飲みますか。_____

　　_____

5. アメリカの学生はみんなアルバイトをしますか。_____

　　_____

6. アメリカの学生は休みの日にはどんなことをするんですか。_____

　　_____

7. アメリカの学生はみんなパーティーが好きですか。_____

　　_____

8. アメリカの大学のキャンパスはみんなきれいですか。_____

　　_____

Vocabulary and Grammar 2B: Furnishings and Appliances

A. In what rooms do you find the following furniture and electrical appliances? Some of the rooms will be used more than once.

1. _____ 本だな
2. _____ たんす
3. _____ 花びん
4. _____ はいざら
5. _____ かがみ
6. _____ るすばん電話
7. _____ 電子レンジ

8. _____ れいぞうこ
9. _____ せんたくき
10. _____ クーラー
11. _____ そうじき
12. _____ すいはんき
13. _____ せんぷうき
14. _____ ストーブ
15. 電気 (light)

16. _____ とけい
17. _____ ベッド
18. _____ ソファ
19. _____ シェーバー
20. _____ コンピュータ

a. げんかん
b. ろうか
c. いま
d. 台所
e. ダイニングルーム
f. 勉強部屋
g. 子ども部屋
h. せんめんじょ

i. よく室
j. トイレ
k. 客間
l. しゃこ
m. 庭
n. しん室
o. どこでも (anywhere)

B. Take out the diagram that you made in Exercise **F** in section **2A** (**Houses**), and draw the following furnishings with labels in the appropriate rooms.

本だな　　　　スタンド　　　ソファー
たんす　　　　テーブル　　　いす
とけい　　　　テレビ　　　　ステレオ
電話　　　　　ベッド　　　　コンピュータ
電子レンジ　　オーブン　　　ガスレンジ
れいぞうこ　　つくえ　　　　げたばこ
せんたくき　　こたつ　　　　ざぶとん

C. Answer the questions, telling what item or part of the house is used for the following purposes.

[例] しゃしんをとるために使うものは何ですか。 →
カメラです。

1. 服や下着をしまっておく (put away) ためのものは何ですか。 _____

2. 時間をしりたい時に使うものは何ですか。 _____

3. だれもいない時にかかってきた電話のメッセージを入れるためのものは何
ですか。_____

4. くつをしまっておくためのものは何ですか。_____

5. はやく料理を作ったり、つめたいものをあたためたり (warm up) するために使う
ものは何ですか。_____

D. Complete sentences 1–4 by telling what the purpose of the item mentioned is. Complete sentences 5–8 by stating which household item you would use for the purpose mentioned.

[例] _____ ために、せんたくきを買いました。→
服を洗うために、せんたくきを買いました。

1. _____ ために、ワープロを買いました。

2. _____ ために、ミシンを買いました。

3. _____ ために、そうじきを使います。

4. _____ ために目ざましとけいを使います。

5. 部屋をすずしくするために_____。

6. ごはんをたく(cook) ために_____。

7. 部屋をあたたかくするために_____。

8. 洋服をしまっておく(put away) ために _____。

E. State the reasons for the results given in sentences 1–5 by using ⋯ために. Then state the results of the situations given in sentences 6–8.

[例] _____ ために、せんたくきが買えませんでした。→
お金がなかったために、せんたくきが買えませんでした。

1. _____ ために、何も見えませんでした。

2. _____ ために、あまり聞こえませんでした。

3. _____ ために、先生に会えませんでした。

4. _____ ために、アパートをさがさなければなりません
でした。

5. _____ ために、車を借りなければなりませんでした。

6. コンピュータが古かったために、＿＿＿＿＿＿＿＿＿＿＿＿＿＿＿＿＿＿＿＿＿。

7. 目ざましどけいがなかったために、＿＿＿＿＿＿＿＿＿＿＿＿＿＿＿＿＿。

8. 部屋がせまいために、＿＿＿＿＿＿＿＿＿＿＿＿＿＿＿＿＿。

F. What do you need to do in order to become proficient in Japanese? Continue the sequence of sentences and see what you come up with.

- 日本語が上手になるためには、日本へ行くのがいいです。
- 日本へ行くためには、お金をつくらなければなりません。
- お金をつくるためには、＿＿＿＿＿＿＿＿＿＿＿＿＿＿＿＿＿
- ＿＿＿＿＿＿＿＿＿＿＿＿＿＿、＿＿＿＿＿＿＿＿＿＿＿＿＿＿
- ＿＿＿＿＿＿＿＿＿＿＿＿＿＿、＿＿＿＿＿＿＿＿＿＿＿＿＿＿
- ＿＿＿＿＿＿＿＿＿＿＿＿＿＿、＿＿＿＿＿＿＿＿＿＿＿＿＿＿
- ＿＿＿＿＿＿＿＿＿＿＿＿＿＿、＿＿＿＿＿＿＿＿＿＿＿＿＿＿

So, what do you need to do in order to be proficient in Japanese? Write in your last sentence from above. Does it make sense?

日本語が上手になるためには、＿＿＿＿＿＿＿＿＿＿＿＿＿＿＿＿＿

G. Using the sentence elements given, write out each situation first in terms of who gave what to whom and then in terms of who received what from whom. Be sure to make any necessary adjustments for politeness.

[例] カワムラさん → ブラウンさん （日本語のじしょ）
    a. カワムラさんはブラウンさんに日本語のじしょをあげました。
    b. ブラウンさんはカワムラさんに日本語のじしょをもらいました。

カワムラさん → 私 （白いシャツ）
    a. カワムラさんは私に白いシャツをくれました。
    b. 私はカワムラさんに白いシャツをもらいました。

私 → カワムラさん （ぼうしとマフラー）
私はカワムラさんにぼうしとマフラーをあげました。

よこい先生 → 私 （ペン）
    a. よこい先生は私にペンをくださいました。
    b. 私はよこい先生にペンをいただきました。

1. 山本さん → 町田さん （赤くてきれいなブラウス）

    a. ＿＿＿＿＿＿＿＿＿＿＿＿＿＿＿＿＿＿＿＿＿＿＿＿＿＿＿＿＿＿

    b. ＿＿＿＿＿＿＿＿＿＿＿＿＿＿＿＿＿＿＿＿＿＿＿＿＿＿＿＿＿＿

2. 山口さん → 私 (便利なじしょ)

   a. _____

   b. _____

3. 大野さん → ひら山さん (とけい)

   a. _____

   b. _____

4. 山口さん → ギブソンさん (新しい黒いかさ)

   a. _____

   b. _____

5. カワムラさん → 私の妹 (古い車)

   a. _____

   b. _____

6. 私 → 山本さん (お酒とビール)

   _____

7. 大野さん → (私の)母 (アメリカのジャム)

   a. _____

   b. _____

8. 私 → 山口先生 (日本のお茶)

   _____

9. よこい先生 → 私 (おもしろい本)

   a. _____

   b. _____

10. さのさんのお母さん → いぬ (ドッグ・フード)

    a. _____

    b. _____

H. Here are some situations in which someone performed an action as a favor for someone else. Write up each situation twice, the first time stating it in terms of who did the favor, and the second time stating it in terms of who received the favor.

[例] 町田さん → ブラウンさん（日本語をおしえる）　→
   a. 町田さんはブラウンさんに日本語をおしえてあげました。
   b. ブラウンさんは町田さんに日本語をおしえてもらいました。

1. ブラウンさん → カワムラさん（おいしいレストランをおしえる）

   a. _____

   b. _____

2. 山本さん → 私の弟（静かなきっさてんにつれて行く）

   a. _____

   b. _____

3. はやしさん → 私（和食を料理する）

   a. _____

   b. _____

4. 町田さん → チンさん（ノートを見せる）

   a. _____

   b. _____

5. 先生 → カーティスさん（会う）

   a. _____

   b. _____

6. 先生 → 私（しゃしんを見せる）

   a. _____

   b. _____

I. The following is John Kawamura's gift-giving record for last year's おせいぼ. Taking Kawamura's point of view, study the list, and then complete the sentences using verbs of giving and receiving.

NAME	GAVE	RECEIVED
Prof. Yokoi	candy	
Linda Brown	T-shirt	ham
Hitomi Machida	cookies	apples
Henry Curtis	T-shirt	juice
Prof. Oono	nuts from the U.S.	dictionary
Sayuri Yamamoto		coffee set
the Yamaguchis	a set of towels	

[例] キャンディーはよこい先生にさしあげました。

1. ハムは _____

2. クッキーは _____

3. 町田さんからは _____

4. りんごは町田さんが _____

5. 山本さんは _____

6. 山口さんに _____

7. 大野先生は _____

8. じしょは大野先生に _____

9. カーティスさんに _____

10. アメリカのナッツは _____

J. List your three favorite gifts out of those you received last year for holidays, your birthday, or any other gift-giving occasions. Indicate who gave you what.

[例] 姉が新しいじてん車をくれました。

1. _____

2. _____

3. _____

K. Now restate the situation in terms of whom you received each gift from.

[例] 新しいじてん車は姉からもらいました。

1. _____
2. _____
3. _____

L. What did people do for you on your last birthday or on some other occasion when you received presents? Answer using 〜てくれる.

[例] 父が新しいステレオを買ってくれました。

1. _____
2. _____
3. _____

M. You are in bed with a bad case of the flu. List three things you would like someone to do for you in such a situation.

[例] 母にチキンスープを作ってもらいたいです。

1. _____
2. _____
3. _____

N. Your significant other's birthday is coming up. What kinds of things would you like to do for him or her on that day? Use the 〜てあげる construction.

[例] シャンパンを買ってあげようと思います。

1. _____
2. _____
3. _____

O. Would you like to do each of the following for someone (if so, for whom?), or would you rather have someone do it for you? If neither, state so.

[例] (to lend money)

こまっている友だちにお金を貸してあげたいです。 →

or 母にお金を貸してもらいたいです。

or お金をだれにも貸してあげたくないし、貸してもらいたくもないんです。

1. (to help with Japanese homework) _____

2. (to lend a car) _____

3. (to clean the room) _____

4. (to do massage) _____

5. (to invite to a party) _____

P. Use 〜てもいいですか to ask permission in the following situations. Try to adjust the request to the proper level of politeness.

[例] Ask your instructor for permission to turn in the homework next week.

来週しゅくだいを出^だしてもいいですか。

Ask your best friend in Japan if it's all right to borrow that magazine.

そのざっしを貸^かりてもいい？

1. Ask a waiter in a restaurant for permission to smoke.

_____

2. Ask your Japanese host mother for permission to eat a banana that is on the table.

_____

3. Ask your Japanese host father for permission to use his car this Saturday night.

_____

4. Ask your instructor for permission to enter his/her office (けんきゅう室^{しつ}).

_____

5. Ask a fellow train passenger for permission to sit down here.

_____

6. Ask Ms. Machida for permission to take a look at her room.

_____

7. Ask Mr. Mimura for permission to borrow his new CD until next Sunday.

_____

8. Ask Ms. Yamaguchi for permission to go to her home at 6:00 P.M., Friday.

_____

9. Ask your instructor for permission to ask a question now.

_____

10. Ask your boss for permission to go home early today.

_____

Q. You have a new Japanese instructor. Ask this instructor if you can do or do not have to do certain things, using ～てもいいですか.

　　　[例] (ask questions in English)
　　　　このクラスでは、えい語でしつもんしてもいいですか。

1. (work with classmates on home assignments)

　　　_____

2. (write answers without using [使わないで] kanji)

　　　_____

3. (not do your homework when you are busy)

　　　_____

4. (leave early when you have to work)

　　　_____

5. (sit alone in the back of the classroom [きょうしつの後ろのほう])

　　　_____

6. Make up your own questions to ask the instructor.

　　　_____

　　　_____

　　　_____

R. You have just moved into a new apartment in Tokyo. Japanese apartments are almost never furnished, so you need furniture and appliances. Your former host mother has all the items that you need, but you do not yet know which ones she is still using herself. Choose five items that you want from the list below. Then make up dialogues between yourself and your host mother. You are a bit of a spoiled brat (your host family was secretly relieved to see you move out), so you make outrageous demands, but your host mother tells you that you may or must not take the item, that she cannot give it away, heavens no (とんでもない！), that you must be joking (じょうだんでしょう), and so on. Be creative, and make the dialogue as long as you wish.

stereo	sofa	dining table	microwave oven
TV	toaster	coffee maker	washing machine
bed	telephone	blender	vacuum cleaner
clock	radio	refrigerator	chest of drawers

[例]　　　YOU: お母さん、その新しいステレオ、もらってもいい？
　　HOST MOTHER: いいえ、それはあげられないけど、古いのを使ってもいいわ。
　　　　　YOU: お母さんが古いのを使ったらどう？
　　HOST MOTHER: じょうだんでしょう！

1. _____

_____

_____

_____

2. _____

_____

_____

_____

3. _____

_____

_____

_____

4. _____

_____

_____

_____

5. _____

_____

_____

_____

S. Refuse the following requests politely with 〜ないでください.

[例] ここでたばこをすってもいいですか。 →
　　　もうしわけありませんが、ここではすわないでください。*

1. 中に入ってもいいですか。

　　わるいですが、今服を着がえているから、＿＿＿＿＿＿＿＿＿＿＿＿＿＿＿

2. 電気をつけてもいいですか。

　　わるいですが、＿＿＿＿＿＿＿＿＿＿＿＿＿＿＿＿＿

3. ドアを開けてもいいですか。

　　もうしわけありませんが、少し寒いですから、＿＿＿＿＿＿＿＿＿＿＿＿＿

4. このブラウスをせんたくきで洗ってもいいですか。

　　いいえ、＿＿＿＿＿＿＿＿＿＿＿＿＿＿＿＿＿

5. 今から、そうじきをかけてもいいですか。

　　わるいですが、今勉強しているので、＿＿＿＿＿＿＿＿＿＿＿＿＿＿＿

6. ここに車を止めてもいいですか。

　　もうしわけありませんが、＿＿＿＿＿＿＿＿＿＿＿＿＿＿＿

T. You are guiding a group of elderly Japanese tourists around the largest park complex in your area. There are a number of signs, and because most of these people went to school before English instruction was widespread in Japan, they ask you what the signs mean. Explain the meaning of each of these signs in Japanese.

1. 　　　　　　　2.

3. 　　　4. 　　　5.

---

* もうしわけありません (*lit., there is no excuse*) is a polite apology used when you think that the person you are talking to will be disappointed at your refusal. On a more informal level, you could say わるいですが (*it's bad of me [to say this] but . . .*).

Useful Vocabulary: しばふ *lawn*, えさ *animal food*, ごみ *trash*

[例] ここでローラースケートをしないでください。

1. _____

2. _____

3. _____

4. _____

5. _____

U. You have completed extensive training in Japanese and lived in Japan for a while, and now you are teaching a beginners' class. Your students ask you for permission to do certain things, and you either grant permission or deny it. Use any of the appropriate forms you know.

1. じしょを見て書いてもいいですか。

   _____

2. ひらがなだけで書いてしゅくだいを出してもいいですか。

   _____

3. クラスメートと話をするとき、えい語を使ってもいいですか。

   _____

4. メモを見てスピーチをしてもいいですか。

   _____

5. きょうかしょを見てこたえてもいいですか。

   _____

6. たん語 (*vocabulary item*) をわすれたとき、えい語のたん語を使ってもいいですか。

   _____

7. クラスメートのしゅくだいをうつして (*copy*)、出してもいいですか。

   _____

8. カタカナをおぼえなくてもいいですか。

   _____

9. 天気のいい日にじゅぎょう (*class session*) を休んでもいいですか。

   _____

10. 日本人の友だちをじゅぎょうにつれてきてもいいですか。

_____

Vocabulary and Grammar 2C: Household Chores

A. Fill in the blanks with the name of an item that best completes each sentence.

1. _____ をほす。

2. _____ をみがく。

3. _____ をふく。

4. _____ をはく (*sweep*)。

5. _____ を直<ruby>直<rt>なお</rt></ruby>す。

6. _____ を洗<ruby>洗<rt>あら</rt></ruby>う。

7. _____ を手伝<ruby>手伝<rt>てつだ</rt></ruby>う。

B. Make suggestions in response to the following statements. Use the …ほうがいい construction.

[例] 来週、東京<ruby>東京<rt>きょう</rt></ruby>へ行くんですが、東京は今、寒いですか。
　　ええ、コートを_____ →
　　ええ、コートをもって行ったほうがいいですよ。

1. 明日の朝、四時に起きなければならないんです。

　　こんばんは早<ruby>早<rt>はや</rt></ruby>く_____

2. 私のアパートはとてもうるさいんです。

　　新しいアパートを_____

3. 来週エジプトへ行くんですが、アラビア語がわからないんです。

　　ツアーガイドを_____

4. 昨日お酒を飲んで、今日はあたま (*head*) がいたいんです。

　　あまりお酒を_____

5. 今ダイエットをしているんです。

　　じゃ、あまりあまいものを_____

6. たばこが大好きで、一日50本ぐらいすいます。

　　たばこはそんなに_____

7. 部屋が暗いんです。

   新しいスタンドを _____

8. このシャツはせんたくきで洗ってもいいですか。

   いいえ、これはシルクだから、せんたくきで _____

9. 車が動かないんです。

   早く _____

10. むしば (cavities) がたくさんあるんです。

    はいしゃ (dentist) へ _____

    そして、毎日はを _____

C. Traveling on crowded holiday weekends can be stressful. Your Japanese acquaintance visiting your area is planning a short vacation trip on one of those weekends. Using 〜たほうがいい, offer him/her some advice about choosing destination, making reservations, departure/arrival time, planning meals, and means of transportation.

[例] ひこうきの予約は３ヶ月ぐらい前からしておいたほうがいいですよ。

1. _____
2. _____
3. _____

D. Rewrite the following sentences using …しか…ない.

[例] ビールを１本だけ飲みました。→ ビールは１本しか飲みませんでした。

1. トーストを１まいだけ食べました。

   _____

2. 手紙が１つだけ来ました。

   _____

3. 明日だけ行きます。

   _____

4. ディズニーランドにだけあります。

   _____

5. 私(わたし)だけしっています。

　　_____

6. ぎゅうにゅうだけ飲みました。

　　_____

7. パーティーに15人だけ来ました。

　　_____

E. Put each of the following sentences into the two ところ constructions.

[例] 車(くるま)を直(なお)す →
　　車を直すところです。(*I am about to repair the car*)
　　車を直しているところです。(*I am in the midst of repairing the car*)

1. テーブルの上をふく

　a. _____

　b. _____

2. せんたくものをほす

　a. _____

　b. _____

3. アイロンをかける

　a. _____

　b. _____

4. くつをみがく

　a. _____

　b. _____

5. にわいじりをする

　a. _____

　b. _____

6. 料理を手伝う

   a. _____

   b. _____

7. おさらを洗う

   a. _____

   b. _____

F. John Kawamura took the photographs below. Using a ところです construction, write what each person is doing in the picture.

1.

2.

3.

4.
5.

[例] このしゃしんはブラウンさんが台所で料理をしているところです。

1. _____

2. _____

3. _____

4. _____

5. _____

G. The telephone rings. It's someone who your roommate does not want to speak to, so you have to come up with an excuse. Try the following excuses, using …ところだ.

[例] (is taking a shower)
すみません、今シャワーをあびているところなんです。

1. (has just gone out)

   _____

2. (has just gone to the university)

   _____

3. (is about to take a bath)

   _____

4. (is taking a nap)

   _____

5. Think of your own excuses.

   _____

   _____

   _____

H. Rephrase the following expressions using 〜中(ちゅう). If you don't remember the exact phrasing, reread the language note on p. 107 of your main text.

[例] 今食事をしているところです。→
今食事中です。

1. 今かいぎ (meeting) をしています。_____

2. 今しごとをしているところです。_____

3. 今電話で話しているところです。_____

4. 今使っているところです。_____

5. 今勉強しているところです。_____

6. 今はいません。ちょっと出かけました。_____

7. 今じゅぎょう (class session) に出ています。_____

I. Your Japanese friend just called and wants to get together with you right now. You need more time because of the following. Explain your situation, and tell your friend how much more time you need.

[例] (ironing)

今スカートにアイロンをかけているところだから、30分ぐらい待ってください。

1. (getting dressed)

   _____

2. (doing homework)

   _____

3. (about to eat a meal)

   _____

4. (cleaning the house)

   _____

5. (just about to take a bath)

   _____

6. Think of your own reasons.

   _____

   _____

   _____

J. You are planning a birthday party for your roommate. What would you do in preparation? Answer using ～ておく.

[例] ビールを買って、れいぞうこに入れておきます。

1. _____

2. _____

3. _____

K. You are in Japan. You hear on the radio that a big typhoon is due to hit your area in a couple of days. What should you do to be prepared? Write three things, using 〜ておく. (A few hints: It may rain quite a bit, so you cannot have a leaky roof. You may lose electricity. It may become very windy, so you can't leave anything loose outside in the yard or on the porch. Nearby stores may be closed.)

Useful Vocabulary: ろうそく *candle*

[例] 天気よほうを聞きたいから、ラジオのかん電ち (*dry battery*) を買っておきましょう。

1. _____

2. _____

3. _____

L. What would you do in advance to prepare for a trip to Japan? Write three things using 〜ておく.

[例] 日本へ行く前に日本語を勉強しておくつもりです。

1. _____

2. _____

3. _____

M. The following picture shows the mess in John's room. He is going to give a party tonight, so offer him some advice on how to straighten up the room.

[例] (トースター) トースターは台所へもって行っておいた方がいいです。

1. (さらやコップ) _____

2. (本やノート) _____

3. (せんたくもの) _____

4. (テーブルの上) _____

5. (ゆか) _____

N. You are going on vacation for one week and have decided to hire a house sitter while you're gone. Using 〜ておく, ask the house sitter to do various things, such as taking care of your pets and garden and doing other necessary household chores.

[例] 庭の野さいをとって、れいぞうこに入れておいてください。

1. _____

2. _____

3. _____

Chapter 2 Review

A. A Japanese person new to the United States has some questions about American customs. Answer in Japanese.

1. アメリカでは、靴をぬがないで家の中に入ってもいいんですか。

   _____

2. アメリカでは、レストランでタバコをすってもいいんですか。

   _____

3. アメリカでは、ほかの人の家に行ったとき、コートをぬいでから家の中に入ってもいいですか。

   _____

4. アメリカでは、お手洗いを使っていないときに、ドアをしめておいてもいいですか。

   _____

5. アメリカではおうだんほどう (pedestrian crossing) ではないところで道をわたってもいいんですか。

   _____

B. List six things you would like to or plan to give your friends, family members, or acquaintances during the coming year.

[例] 妹のたん生日にカバンをあげるつもりです。／…あげたいと思っています。／…あげようと思っています。

1. _____
2. _____
3. _____
4. _____
5. _____
6. _____

C. John Kawamura and his classmates and acquaintances frequently help one another with household chores and other work. How would the participants describe each of the following situations? First describe the situation from the point of view of the person who did the favor, and then from the point of view of the person who received the favor.

[例] カワムラさん → ブラウンさん（洗たくをする）
カワムラ：せんたくをしてあげました。
ブラウン：カワムラさんがせんたくをしてくれました。

1. ブラウンさん → 町田さん（車を洗う）

ブラウン：_____

町田：_____

2. 山本さん → ギブソンさん（部屋をかたづける）

山本：_____

ギブソン：_____

3. カワムラ → 先生（まどをみがく）

カワムラ：_____

先生：_____

4. ギブソンさん → カーティスさん（花に水をやる）

ギブソン：_____

カーティス：_____

5. 先生 → 高田さん（すいせんじょう [letter of recommendation] を書く）

先生： _____

高田： _____

D. How would you prepare if you had the following situations coming up? Answer using 〜ておく.

[例] 明日日本語のしけんがあります。 →
　　　かんじを勉強しておきます。
　　　きょうかしょを読んでおきます。

1. 今日の午後、家にお客さんが来ます。

_____

_____

2. 明日うちでバースデーパーティーがあります。

_____

_____

3. しゅっちょうで、来週日本へ行かなければいけません。

_____

_____

4. 今夜デートをします。

_____

_____

5. 今日は、お客さんが来るので、日本料理を作るつもりです。

_____

_____

E. You are helping your Japanese friend find an apartment. You have seen a number of apartments, and you have limited your choices to the following six. Read about the kind of apartment that your friend wants, and then help him/her decide which one is the best by answering the questions on the following page in Japanese. (● = yes   ○ = no)

	1	2	3	4	5	6
しん室がある	●	○	●	●	●	●
よく室にシャワーがある	●	●	●	○	●	○
かぐがある	○	●	●	●	●	○
せんたくきがある	●	○	●	○	●	●
エアコンがある	●	●	●	●	○	○
カーペットがある	○	●	●	●	●	○
大きいクローゼットがある	●	●	○	●	○	●
庭がある	○	○	○	●	○	●
しんちくのアパートだ	○	●	○	○	●	●
家主がとてもしんせつだ	○	○	●	●	○	○
スーパーが近い	●	●	○	●	●	○
大学に近い	○	●	●	○	●	●
バスのていりゅうじょに近い	●	●	●	●	●	○
やちんがやすい	●	○	●	●	○	○

「私はワンルームマンションは好きじゃありません。たいていベッド・メーキングはしませんから、ベッドは人に見えない所におきたいです。いそがしくてゆっくりおふろに入る時間はありませんから、毎日シャワーをあびるだけだと思います。かぐやもちもの (possessions) はほとんどありませんから、ベッドやソファーのあるアパートがいいですね。せんたくも家でできる方がいいです。私は夏の暑いのと冬の寒いのは大きらいですが、外で花をうえたり (plant) やさいをつくったりするのは好きです。新しくなくてもいいけど、家主さんがいつも手入れを (care) よくしてくれる所がいいです。やちんはもちろんやすいほうがいいですが、少しぐらい高くても、買い物やつう学 (commuting to school) に便利なほうがいいですね。」

1. Is there a perfect apartment? If yes, which is it? If not, which comes closest to what your friend wants?

    _____

    _____

2. What are some of the problems with each apartment that you mentioned in question 1?

    _____

    _____

3. Which one would *you* recommend? Why?

    _____

    _____

4. Which of the six apartments would you rent? Why?

    _____

    _____

F. The following is a copy of a page from a gift catalog for the Nissho food store. Read the passage on お歳暮 (おせいぼ), which was written by a Japanese student, and then answer the questions that follow while looking at the catalog page.

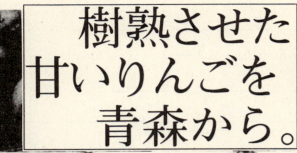

樹熟させた甘いりんごを青森から。

産 **D7-2** 〈青森県〉
サンふじ (5kg) (14〜18個入)
5,000円

産 **D7-3** 〈青森県〉
王林 (5kg) (14〜18個入)
5,200円

産 **D7-7** 〈青森県〉
サンふじ・王林 (5kg) (14〜18個入)
5,100円

産 **D7-5** 〈青森県〉
陸奥 (5kg) (14〜18個入)
6,500円

産 **D7-6** 〈青森県〉
ふじ (5kg) (14〜18個入)
5,000円

12月1日(金)以降のお届けとなります。

12月1日(金)以降のお届けとなります。

産 **D7-8** 〈青森県〉
Mr.完熟アップルコンボ
Mr.完熟りんごツイン(サンふじ＋王林)(5袋)
Mr.完熟アップルジュース(195mℓ・10缶)
Mr.完熟アップルスナック(80g×2袋)
4,800円

12月1日以降のお届けとなります。

トロピカルフルーツを全国へ

ご注文は12月20日(水)まで。

産 **TF-2** 〈トロピカルフルーツ〉
グレープフルーツ
[ホワイト] (12個)
2,900円

産 **TF-4** 〈トロピカルフルーツ〉
グレープフルーツ [ホワイト] (6個)
パパイヤ (2個)
パイン (1個)
アボガド (3個)
3,900円

産 **TF-9** 〈トロピカルフルーツ〉
グレープフルーツ [ホワイト] (6個)
オレンジ (16個)
3,400円

産 **TF-12** 〈トロピカルフルーツ〉
オレンジ (32個)
3,800円

産 **TF-13** 〈トロピカルフルーツ〉
オレンジ (48個)
5,000円

Useful Vocabulary: おくる *send, give as a gift,* すっぱい *sour,* おっしゃる *the honorific form of* 言う

今年はおせいぼにくだものをあげることにしました。友だちの山下さんと、大家さんのさとうさんと、まつおか先生とホイットン先生におくりたいと思います。山下さんのおせいぼは3000円ぐらいでいいと思います。さとうさんは5000円ぐらい、先生はどちらも4000円ぐらいでいいでしょう。さとうさんはりんごやりんごジュースが大好きだし、まつおか先生はすっぱいものはあまりお好きではないから、グレープフルーツはさしあげない方がいいかもしれません。ホイットン先生はアボカドが大好きですが、日本では高くてなかなか食べられないとおっしゃっていたそうだから、アボカドの入ったセットをさしあげたいです。

1. Make suggestions in Japanese about what to give each person. Use constructions with 〜たら to frame your suggestions.

   山下さん _____

   さとうさん _____

   まつおか先生 _____

   ホイットン先生 _____

2. For a couple of people you could have chosen some other items. What are your reasons for choosing the items you did? Write the reasons in Japanese.

   _____

   _____

   _____

3. もしあなたがこの学生の大家だったら、どんなおせいぼをもらいたいと思いますか。

   _____

G. Answer the following questions about your home life.

1. あなたはたいていいつ家のそうじをしますか。そうじをするときには、どんなことをしますか。(use 〜たり…〜たり)

   _____

   _____

2. あなたのしん室にはどんなかぐがありますか。今買いたい、または、買ってもらいたいのはどんなかぐですか。

_____

_____

_____

3. あなたの家の台所にない電気せい品で、ほしいものはありますか。それは何のために使うものですか。

_____

4. 友だちがきゅうに (suddenly) 来ましたが、あなたは料理をしているところです。どうしますか。

_____

5. あなたは3ヶ月間、日本へ行くことにしました。その間アパートをほかの人に貸すことにしました。あなたがいない間に、その人にしてもらいたくないことは何ですか。

_____

_____

6. あなたの近所の店であなたが好きな店は何の店ですか。どうしてその店が好きですか。

_____

_____

7. 今住んでいるところに来る前はどんなところに住んでいましたか。

_____

8. 大学から帰った後で、まずさいしょに自分の部屋ですることは何ですか。

_____

9. あなたのとなりの家／部屋／アパートの人はどんな人ですか。あなたがいないときに、はいたつ (delivery) の人が来たら、にもつをあずかって (hold for safekeeping) くれますか。

_____

_____

AUTOMOBILES AND TRANSPORTATION

くるま　こうつう
車と交通

Listening Comprehension Activities

Vocabulary and Grammar 3A: Cars and Driving

A. Listen to the following descriptions and identify which part of the car is being described.

Useful Vocabulary: ふむ *to step on*

1. _____
2. _____
3. _____
4. _____
5. _____

a. ワイパー
b. ブレーキ
c. ミラー
d. アクセル
e. ハンドル
f. ウィンカー
g. タイヤ

B. What or whom do you consult when you don't know how to do something? Listen to four people wondering what to do, and choose the best source of help for each question. Do not use the same answer twice.

1. _____
2. _____
3. _____
4. _____

a. せつめい書
b. じ書
c. 料理の本
d. きょうしゅうじょ　(driving school)
e. テレビ

C. Masao Hayashi is telling Mei Lin Chin what to do when getting ready to drive. Listen to their conversation, and number Hayashi's instructions in the order in which he gives them, from 1 to 7.

_____ Turn on engine

_____ Release hand break

_____ Fasten seatbelt

_____ Back up

_____ Shift into reverse gear

_____ Step on accelerator

_____ Adjust mirror

D. Masao Hayashi is giving Mei Lin Chin a ride home. Listen to their conversation and then fill in the blanks to complete the summary.

In the car, Hayashi told Chin to push the _____ button to _____ the window, and to push the _____ button to turn on the _____. Chin asked him to _____ the car in front of the _____, and thanked Hayashi for the _____.

E. John Kawamura invites Hitomi Machida to his apartment. Listen to their conversation as they enter the apartment. Then write what condition the following things were in when they entered.

Useful Vocabulary: どろぼう *burglar, thief,* 気をつける *to be careful*

1. door: _____

2. lights: _____

3. radio: _____

4. window: _____

5. things on the desk: _____

Vocabulary and Grammar 3B: Car Maintenance and Repairs

A. Masao Hayashi is asking John Kawamura about the date he had yesterday. Listen to their conversation, and figure out what Kawamura tried to do.

1. Kawamura tried to _____, but the CD player didn't work.

2. He planned to go to the _____, but it started to rain.

3. He tried to _____, but there was no space in the parking lot at the movie theater.

4. He tried to _____, but was rejected.

B. It is Sunday, and Masao Hayashi and Mei Lin Chin are going on a picnic by a lake in Hayashi's car. Listen to their conversation, and then choose the answers that complete the following sentences.

1. Hayashi is in charge of _____.
   a. car maintenance   b. food   c. map

2. The condition of Hayashi's car is _____.
   a. not so good   b. so-so   c. very good

3. There was a problem with the car _____, but it has been fixed.
   a. radio   b. air conditioning   c. seats

4. There should be no problem finding the way to the lake, because _____.
   a. there is a car navigation system
   b. Chin bought a map
   c. Hayashi has a good sense of direction

5. Chin brought _____.
   a. sandwiches and coffee   b. camera   c. both a and b

C. Mei Lin Chin is at a car dealer's looking for a used car. Listen to her conversation with the salesperson and answer the questions.

1. Things that are quite new are: _____

2. Things that are broken are: _____

3. Things that are quite old are: _____

4. Things that have been checked/changed are: _____

5. Thing that is missing is: _____

D. Masao Hayashi and Henry Curtis have been looking forward to watching the baseball game on TV on Sunday afternoon at Hayashi's house. Listen to their conversation and choose the most appropriate answer.

Useful Vocabulary: えだまめ *(boiled) soybeans,* しかたがない *can't be helped*

1. Hayashi thinks that the TV should be working because _____.
   a. it was expensive   b. it is brand new   c. it has just been repaired

2. Hayashi suggests going to a shokudoo (dining place) because _____.
   a. their food is good   b. the TV is always on there   c. it is the closest restaurant

3. Curtis doesn't want to go to the shokudoo because he _____.
   a. has just eaten lunch   b. doesn't like Japanese food   c. is on a diet

4. Curtis does not want to drink beer because he _____.
   a. doesn't drink alcohol   b. just had some coffee   c. doesn't have any money

5. Curtis doesn't want to go to Machida's house because _____.
   a. her TV is old   b. he doesn't like her   c. he just went to her house yesterday

6. Hayashi finally suggests that they go to an electric appliance shop to _____.
   a. have the TV repaired   b. buy a new TV   c. watch the game

E. Masao Hayashi, who knows that Mei Lin Chin is looking for a car, picked up on campus an ad for a used car for sale. So he called Mei Lin Chin, but she wasn't home. So he left a message on her answering machine about the car. Listen to his message and fill in the information he gave her.

1. Make: _____

2. Model: _____

3. Year: _____

4. Mileage: _____

5. Color: _____

6. Number of passengers: _____

7. Automatic?: _____

8. Trunk: _____

9. Tires: _____

10. Engine: _____

11. Price: _____

F. Masao Hayashi and Hitomi Machida happened to meet on the street one day. Listen to their conversation, and choose the most appropriate answer to each question.

1. Hayashi bought a new _____ car.
   a. foreign made   b. sports   c. two-door

2. Hayashi sold his former car because _____.
   a. it was not economical   b. it had engine trouble   c. the garage owner wanted to buy it

3. Hayashi was told that it would cost ¥60,000 _____.
   a. to replace the radiator   b. to buy auto insurance   c. to fix the engine

4. Hayashi wanted to buy a brand-new car because he _____.
   a. wanted airbags   b. had plenty of money   c. wanted to take Machida-san for a drive

5. Hayashi had a car accident _____.
   a. at a traffic signal   b. at a corner   c. in a parking lot

6. The accident occurred because Hayashi was _____.
   a. driving drunk   b. speeding   c. sleeping

7. Hayashi had lots of part-time jobs during the summer in order to _____.
   a. pay for the accident   b. buy a new car   c. purchase a house

Vocabulary and Grammar 3C: Transportation and Traffic in the City

A. What kind of transportation should the following people use? Choose the best one for each.

1. _____

2. _____

3. _____

4. _____

   a. ひこうき
   b. タクシー
   c. バス
   d. じてんしゃ
   e. ちかてつ

B. Hitomi Machida saw John Kawamura on campus, and noticed that he looked pale. Listen to their conversation, and fill in the blanks to complete the summary.

Kawamura came to school without _____ and without combing _____

this morning. He is very tired because he studied without _____ at all last night. He had

to write a report without using a _____ because it was not working properly.

Machida hopes that Kawamura will get home safely without _____ while driving.

Kanji Practice and Exercises

1	自 自	ジ、シ self みずか-ら oneself, personally, (on) one's own おの-ずから of itself, spontaneously, naturally				
	自動車：じどうしゃ (automobile) 自分で：じぶんで (on one's own) 全自動：ぜんじどう (completely automatic)					
2	路 路	ロ、～じ、みち road, path, way, street				
	道路：どうろ (road) 路上：ろじょう (on the street)					
3	交 交	コウ intersect; coming and going; associate with ま-じる／ざる (intr.) mix ま-える、ま-ぜる (tr.) mix まじ-わる associate with か-わす exchange (greetings) ～か-う go past each other				
	交通：こうつう (traffic, transportation) 交通安全：こうつうあんぜん (traffic safety) 外交：がいこう (diplomacy)					
4	通 通	ツウ、ツ go through, pass; in common; (as suffix) thorough knowledge of, an expert; (counter for letters/copies) とお-る go through, pass とお-す let through かよ-う commute とお-り street; way, manner -どお-り street; as per, as, in accordance with, according to				
	交通：こうつう (traffic, transportation) 通る：とおる (to pass through) 一方通行：いっぽうつうこう (one-way traffic) 通行人：つうこうにん (passerby)					

5	転車云	テン turn; change　ころ-ぶ tumble, fall down; roll over ころ-がる／げる roll, tumble, fall, lie down/about ころ-がす／ばす roll (a ball), knock down, trip (somebody)		
	運転：うんてん (driving) 自転車：じてんしゃ (bicycle)	車云 転		
6	駐馬主	チュウ be resident/stationed in; stop		
	駐車する：ちゅうしゃする (to park) 駐車場：ちゅうしゃじょう (parking lot)	馬主 駐		
7	教教	キョウ teaching; religion おし-える teach　おし-え a teaching, precept おそ-わる be taught		
	教える：おしえる (to teach, to explain) 教室：きょうしつ (classroom) 教か書：きょうかしょ (textbook) 教会：きょうかい (church)	教 教		
8	窓窓	ソウ, まど window		
	窓：まど (window) 窓を開ける：まどをあける (to open the window) 窓口：まどぐち (window for buying tickets, etc.) 同窓会：どうそうかい (class reunion)	窓 窓		
9	閉閉	ヘイ, し-める, と-じる／ざす close, shut し-まる be(come) closed	tr Trtran	
	本を閉じる：ほんをとじる (to close a book) 窓を閉める：まどをしめる (to close a window) 窓が閉まる：まどがしまる (a window closes) 閉館：へいかん (closing a building)	閉 閉		
10	消消	ショウ, け-す extinguish, turn off (a light), erase, cancel out き-える go/die out, disappear		
	電気を消す：でんきをけす (to turn off the electricity)　電気が消える：でんきがきえる (the electricity goes off)　消しゴム：けしごむ (pencil eraser)　消ぼう車：しょうぼうしゃ (fire truck)	消 消		

11 変変　ヘン change; strange; flat (in musical keys); mishap; disturbance
か-わる (intr.) change; be different
か-える (tr.) change

色を変える：いろをかえる (to change the color)
きせつが変わった：きせつがかわった (the season changed) 大変なしごと：たいへんなしごと (tough job)

12 故故　コ old, former, deceased, (as prefix) the late . . . ; intentional; matter
ゆえ reason, cause; circumstances
ふる-い old

事故：じこ (accident)
交通事故：こうつうじこ (traffic accident)
故しょうする：こしょうする (to have a mechanical breakdown)

13 差差　サ difference
さ-す hold (an umbrella); wear (a sword); extend (a hand); offer; thrust; insert
さ-し〜 (emphatic verb prefix) さ-しで between two persons

交差点：こうさてん (intersection)
時差：じさ (difference in time)
時差ぼけ：じさぼけ (jet lag)

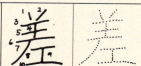

14 点点　テン point
とも-る (intr.) burn, be lighted とも-す、つ-ける (tr.) burn, light, turn on (a lamp)
つ-く catch (fire), be lit, (lights) come on

交差点：こうさてん (intersection)
点けんする：てんけんする (to spot-check)
百点：ひゃくてん (100 points)

15 信信　シン fidelity, sincerity, trust, credit, reliability
シン-じる／ずる believe, believe in
まこと sincerity, fidelity

信号：しんごう (traffic light)
通信：つうしん (correspondence)
信じる：しんじる (to believe)

16 号号　ゴウ number; name; signal, sign; cry out

信号：しんごう (traffic light)
番号：ばんごう (number in a series)
電話番号：でんわばんごう (telephone number)
3号車：さんごうしゃ (car no. 3 on a train)

17	走 走	ソウ, はし-る run はし-り first (produce) of the season			
	走る：はしる (to run) 走って行く：はしっていく (to go away running)	走	走		
18	帰 帰	キ, かえ-る return かえ-す let (someone) return, send (someone) back			
	家に帰る：いえにかえる (to return home) 昨日、旅行から帰って来ました：きのう, りょこうからかえってきました (Yesterday I came home from a trip)	帰	帰		
19	横 横	オウ horizontal よこ side; horizontal direction			
	…の横：…のよこ (at the side of…) 道路を横切る：どうろをよこぎる (to cross the road) 横だん歩道：おうだんほどう (pedestrian crossing)	横	横		
20	働 働	ドウ, はたら-く work はたら-き work, function			
	働く：はたらく (to work) その店で働いている：そのみせではたらいている (is working at that shop)	働	働		
21	工 工	コウ, ク artisan; manufacturing, constuction たくみ craftsman, workman			
	工事：こうじ (construction, process) 工事中：こうじちゅう (under construction) 工学：こうがく (engineering) 人工：じんこう (artificial)	工	工		
22	速 速	ソク, はや-い fast はや-める quicken, accelerate すみ-やか speedy, prompt			
	速い：はやい (fast) 速度：そくど (rate of speed) 高速道路：こうそくどうろ (freeway) 時速：じそく (speed per hour)	速	速		

23	違 違	イ, ちが-う be different; be mistaken; cross/pass (someone) ちが-える alter たが-う (intr.) differ from; violate たが-える (tr.) violate, break (a promise)

| | 違う：ちがう (to be different)
いいえ、違います：いいえ、ちがいます (No,
　that's wrong)
違反：いはん (violation) | 違 | 違 | | |

24	反 反	ハン,ホン against, opposite, anti-　タン (unit of measurement) そ-る／らす (intr./tr.) warp, bend back

| | ルールに違反する：ルールにいはんする (to
　violate a rule)
反日：はんにち (anti-Japanese) | 反 | 反 | | |

Kanji Exercises

A. Match each kanji or kanji compound with its closest English equivalent.

1. 違 _____
2. 横 _____
3. 帰 _____
4. 教 _____
5. 事故 _____
6. 交 _____
7. 工 _____
8. 番号 _____

9. 差 _____
10. 自 _____
11. 消 _____
12. 信号 _____
13. 窓 _____
14. 走 _____
15. 速 _____
16. 通 _____

17. 駐車 _____
18. 転 _____
19. 点 _____
20. 働 _____
21. 反 _____
22. 閉 _____
23. 変 _____
24. 路 _____

a. accident b. intention c. construction d. difference e. extinguish f. fast g. intersect
h. number i. open j. pour k. pass l. point m. return n. road o. roll p. run q. self
r. shut s. side t. strange u. teach v. traffic lights w. be mistaken x. walk y. window
z. work aa. parking bb. against

B. Write the hurigana for each kanji or compound. Pay special attention to the changes in pronunciation that may occur when kanji are compounded.

1. 自動車

_____

2. 自転車

_____

3. 駐車場

_____

4. 交通

_____

5. 一方通行

_____

6. 通る

_____

7. 教える

_____

8. 教室

_____

9. 窓

_____

10. 閉じる

_____

11. 閉める

_____

12. 閉まる

_____

13. 消す

_____

14. 消える

_____

15. 消ぼう車

_____

16. 変える

_____

17. 変わる

_____

18. 大変

_____

19. 横

_____

20. 横切る

_____

21. 横だん歩道

_____

22. 事故

_____

23. 働く

_____

24. 工事中

_____

25. 速い

_____

26. 速度

_____

27. 高速道路

_____

28. 違う

_____

29. 違反

_____

30. 交差点

_____

31. 信号

_____

32. 走る

_____

33. 帰る

_____

C. Fill in the blank with the kanji for the word or phrase that is spelled out in hiragana under the line.

1. この ＿＿＿ たくきは＿＿＿＿＿＿＿＿ ですから、とても ＿＿＿＿＿ です。
   せん　　　　　　　　ぜんじどう　　　　　　　　　　　べんり

2. ＿＿＿＿＿ の ＿＿＿ は ＿＿＿ 、 ＿＿＿ 、 ＿＿＿ です。
   しんごう　　　いろ　　あか　　あお　　きいろ

3. ＿＿＿＿＿ のし ＿＿＿ を ＿＿＿ えてくれませんか。
   ちゅうしゃ　　　かた　　　おし

4. ＿＿＿＿＿ で ＿＿＿ を ＿＿＿＿＿ するのは ＿＿＿＿＿ です。
   にほん　　　くるま　　うんてん　　　　　たいへん

5. ＿＿＿ いですね。＿＿＿ を ＿＿＿ めましょう。
   さむ　　　　　　まど　　　し

6. このボタンをおすと、＿＿＿＿＿ が ＿＿＿ えます。
   でんき　　　　き

7. ＿＿＿＿＿＿＿＿ の ＿＿＿＿＿ はどこですか。
   こうそくどうろ　　　いりぐち

8. ＿＿＿＿＿＿ を ＿＿＿＿＿ ろうとしたら、＿＿＿＿＿＿＿＿
   こうさてん　　　　よこぎ　　　　　　　　　こうつうじこ

   にあってしまいました。

9. ＿＿＿＿＿＿ のサインが ＿＿＿ ていますよ。
   こうじちゅう　　　　　で

10. スピード＿＿＿＿＿ をしてはいけません。
    いはん

11. ＿＿＿＿＿ は ＿＿＿＿＿＿＿ 、 ＿＿＿ いていました。
    きのう　　　いちにちじゅう　　はたら

12. ＿＿＿＿＿ が ＿＿＿ わりましたので、おしらせします。
    じゅうしょ　　か

D. Circle the kanji whose meaning is closest to the English definition.

1.	teach	教	散	孝	7.	open	間	閉	開
2.	return	帰	寝	掃	8.	room	室	屋	空
3.	trip	族	旅	遊	9.	convenience	使	便	住
4.	walk	歩	走	赤	10.	old	広	公	古
5.	friend	反	友	左	11.	fix	真	直	置
6.	shrine	寺	社	神	12.	lend	借	貸	貸

13.	self	首	百	自		19.	wait	待	持	特
14.	exchange	交	文	父		20.	bend	由	甲	曲
15.	advantage	利	私	和		21.	capital	都	部	者
16.	ground	池	他	地		22.	quick	速	連	返
17.	not/un-	木	不	ネ		23.	stop	上	止	正
18.	ride	乗	垂	東		24.	guest	店	各	客

E. Write the appropriate kanji for the hiragana written below the lines.

1. ＿＿＿ は ＿＿＿＿＿＿ へ ＿＿ まつり (festival) を ＿＿ に ＿＿
    ふゆ　　　　　ほっかいどう　　　ゆき　　　　　　　　　　み　　　　い

    こうと ＿＿＿ っています。
    　　　　　おも

2. ＿＿＿ は ＿＿＿＿ ＿＿ く ＿＿ きて、30 ＿＿ ぐらい ＿＿＿＿
    ちち　　　　まいあさ　　はや　　　お　　　　　　　ぶん　　　　　こうえん

    を ＿＿＿ きます。
    　　　ある

3. ＿＿＿＿ に ＿＿ の ＿＿＿＿ のし ＿＿ を ＿＿ えてもらった。
    かない　　　　くるま　　　うんてん　　　　かた　　　おし

4. ＿＿＿ だちが ＿＿＿＿＿＿ のしゅくだいを ＿＿＿＿＿ ってくれました。
    とも　　　　　　にほんご　　　　　　　　　　　てつだ

5. A: すみません。この ＿＿＿＿＿＿ を ＿＿ していただけますか。
    　　　　　　　　　　　　　　ちず　　　　　　か

    B: いいですよ。でも、＿＿＿＿＿ までに ＿＿ して ＿＿ さい。
    　　　　　　　　　　　　あした　　　　　　かえ　　　　　くだ

6. ＿＿＿ は ＿＿ かな ＿＿ で ＿＿＿＿＿＿ するのが ＿＿ きです。
    わたし　　　しず　　　ところ　　　べんきょう　　　　　　　す

7. すみませんが、＿＿＿＿＿＿ を ＿＿ って ＿＿ て ＿＿ さい。
    　　　　　　　　　しんぶん　　　　も　　　　き　　　　くだ

8. ＿＿＿＿ ではホテルより ＿＿＿＿＿ にとまった ＿＿ がいい。
    きょうと　　　　　　　　りょかん　　　　　　　ほう

9. あっ、＿＿ ですよ。＿＿ って ＿＿ りましょう。
    　　　あめ　　　　　　はし　　　　かえ

10. ＿＿＿＿＿＿＿＿＿ はどこに ＿＿ ってみたいですか。
    かいがいりょこう　　　　　　　い

11. ＿＿＿の＿＿＿でタクシーを＿＿＿つことにした。
<small>えき　　まえ　　　　　　ま</small>

12. ＿＿＿＿＿に＿＿＿って＿＿＿きましょう。
<small>でんしゃ　　　の　　　い</small>

13. ＿＿＿が＿＿＿＿＿んでいる＿＿＿は＿＿＿くて＿＿＿しいです。
<small>わたし　　いま　す　　　　いえ　　ひろ　　　あたら</small>

14. その＿＿＿は＿＿＿くて＿＿＿けにくいから＿＿＿した＿＿＿がいいと
<small>もん　　ふる　　　あ　　　　　　なお　　　ほう</small>

＿＿＿います。
<small>おも</small>

15. このじ＿＿＿は＿＿＿＿＿＿でいつもそばに＿＿＿いている。
<small>しょ　　べんり　　　　　　　お</small>

16. あのレストランは＿＿＿＿＿して＿＿＿った＿＿＿がいいでしょう。
<small>よやく　　　　い　　　ほう</small>

17. ＿＿＿が＿＿＿まっているし、＿＿＿＿＿も＿＿＿えているし、
<small>まど　　し　　　　　　　でんき　　　き</small>

＿＿＿＿＿さんは、＿＿＿かけているようですね。
<small>たかだ　　　　で</small>

18. ＿＿＿＿＿な＿＿＿＿＿やお＿＿＿を＿＿＿たいです。
<small>ゆうめい　　じんじゃ　　てら　　み</small>

19. この＿＿＿は＿＿＿＿＿＿＿てで＿＿＿＿＿が＿＿＿つもある。
<small>いえ　　　にかいだ　　　わしつ　　ふた</small>

20. あの＿＿＿は＿＿＿＿＿＿＿＿の＿＿＿＿＿が＿＿＿に
<small>くるま　　　こうさてん　　　しんごう　　あか</small>

＿＿＿わっても、＿＿＿まらないで＿＿＿って＿＿＿ってしまった。
<small>か　　　　と　　　　はし　　　い</small>

21. ＿＿＿＿＿さんは、＿＿＿＿＿＿に＿＿＿っていて、
<small>まちだ　　　　じてんしゃ　　の</small>

＿＿＿＿＿＿＿にあいました。
<small>こうつうじこ</small>

22. ＿＿＿＿＿＿＿をしてはいけません。
<small>ちゅうしゃいはん</small>

23. ＿＿＿＿＿から＿＿＿をたくさん＿＿＿りて＿＿＿たけど、＿＿＿む
<small>としょかん　　　ほん　　　　か　　　き　　　　よ</small>

＿＿＿にならない。
<small>き</small>

24. _____ でお ____ を _____ みながら _____ しましょう。
     きゃくま   ちゃ   の   はな

25. _____ の _____ を _____ って、_____
     こうじちゅう   どうろ   よこぎ   こうえん

へもどりました。

Kanji in Everyday Life

1. What kind of work do the 教員 of a school do?

   _____

2. The kanji 暴 appears in words having to do with *violence*. If you saw a newspaper headline mentioning 暴走族, would you know what that referred to? (Hint: They ride motorcycles.)

   _____

3. You can pay extra to have a letter delivered 速達. Why would you do that?

   _____

4. If you read the following statement 「田口さんは自信があります。」 what would you know about Mr./ Ms. Taguchi?

   _____

5. If you read that a celebrity who had lived abroad for a long time would soon 帰国, what would you know about that person?

   _____

6. The label of an item for sale in the store says that it is made of 人工 materials. What kind of materials are those?

   _____

Writing Activities

Vocabulary and Grammar 3A: Cars and Driving

A. The following sentences describe the procedure for starting a car with a manual transmission. Number the steps in the proper order. If there are vocabulary items you are not familiar with, try to guess them from the context. There may be individual variations in the answers.

1. _____ かぎをかぎあなに入れて、右に回す。

2. _____ 車のドアを開けて、運転せきにすわる。

3. _____ 左あしでクラッチをふみこむ。

4. _____ シートベルトをしめる。

5. _____ ギアを1に入れる。

6. _____ バックミラーやサイドミラーで、後ろや横に、ほかの車や人がいるかどうか見る。

7. _____ アクセルをふむ。

B. Change the following verbal phrases into expressions meaning *how to . . .*

[例] 車を運転する → 車の運転のしかた

1. ていきけん (commuter pass) を買う _____

2. 車を止める _____

3. カーラジオを聞く _____

4. スピードをコントロールする _____

5. スピードメーターを読む _____

6. シートを動かす _____

7. シートベルトをしめる _____

8. ガソリンを入れる _____

9. トランクを開ける _____

10. ヘッドライトをつける _____

C. What, in your opinion, are the five most difficult things in learning to drive a car? Give advice to a Japanese student who is just starting driving lessons. (You can either advise caution or offer to teach the difficult point.) If you can't think of any difficult things, here are some hints: parking, shifting gears in manual cars (ギアチェンジをする), controlling speed, turning onto a busy street, changing lanes (しゃせんをへんこうする), driving on highways, driving on narrow streets, and so forth.

[例] 駐車のし方はむずかしいですから、よくれんしゅうした方がいいですよ。

1. _____

2. _____

3. _____

4. _____

5. _____

D. Complete the following brief dialogues using either ⋯かしら (if you are female) or ⋯かなあ (if you are male).

[例]　A: あれは何ですか。
　　　B: さあ、何かしら。
　　　　　or
　　　　　さあ、何かなあ。
　　　A: このとけいを<ruby>直<rt>なお</rt></ruby>してください。
　　　B: さあ、<ruby>直<rt>なお</rt></ruby>せるかなあ。
　　　　　or
　　　　　さあ、<ruby>直<rt>なお</rt></ruby>せるかしら。

1.　A: あのしけんはできましたか。

　　B: さあ、_____

2.　A: ギブソンさんは、どの<ruby>車<rt>くるま</rt></ruby>が好きでしょうか。

　　B: さあ、どれが _____

3.　A: ブラウンさんのたんじょう日は今日ですね。

　　B: さあ、今日 _____

4.　A: カワムラさんも<ruby>運転<rt>うんてん</rt></ruby>できますか。

　　B: さあ、カワムラさんは、_____

5.　A: すみません。このかんじの読み方、しっていますか。

　　B: さあ、_____

6.　A: スミスさんに手がみを書いてください。

　　B: さあ、えい語で _____

7.　A: 明日、また来てね。

　　B: さあ、_____

E. Fill in the blanks with the appropriate transitive or intransitive verbs. Be sure to put the verbs in the grammatical form indicated by the endings given.

1.　open　　　　まずドアを _____ てください。

2.　close　　　　トランクの _____ <ruby>方<rt>かた</rt></ruby>を<ruby>教<rt>おし</rt></ruby>えてください。

3.　stop　　　　前の<ruby>車<rt>くるま</rt></ruby>が _____ ました。

4.　drop, fall　　<ruby>車<rt>くるま</rt></ruby>のスピードが _____ ました。

5.　enter　　　　<ruby>車<rt>くるま</rt></ruby>にガソリンが _____ ていません。

6. move　　　　　ハンドルを右に＿＿＿＿＿＿　てください。

7. begin　　　　　きょ年運転を＿＿＿＿＿＿　ました。

8. broken　　　　タコメーターが＿＿＿＿＿＿　ています。

9. fix　　　　　　エンジンを＿＿＿＿＿＿　なければいけません。

10. turn on　　　ヘッドライトが＿＿＿＿＿＿　ていません。

11. close　　　　電車のドアが＿＿＿＿＿＿　ますから、ご注意ください。

F. Fill in the blanks with the appropriate particles. Do not use は.

1. アクセルをふむとスピード＿＿＿＿　出ます。

2. 学こうへ行くときは、バス＿＿＿＿　乗ります。

3. ドライビング・スクール＿＿＿＿　午後五時に終わります。

4. ルームライト＿＿＿＿　消えていませんね。

5. ワイパー＿＿＿＿　動きません。

6. バッテリー＿＿＿＿　上がりました。

7. エンジン＿＿＿＿　直りました。

8. 友だちが車のドア＿＿＿＿　こわしました。

9. つぎの駅＿＿＿＿、東京行＿＿＿＿　電車＿＿＿＿　乗りかえます。

10. オレンジカード (*prepaid debit card*) ＿＿＿＿　使って、JR のきっぷ＿＿＿＿　買いました。

G. Fill in the blanks and complete the conversations using transitive verbs.

[例]　A: ガソリンが入っていますか。
　　　B: はい、もう入れてありますよ。

1. A: ラジエーターに水が入っていますか。

　　B: はい、もう ＿＿＿＿＿＿＿＿＿＿＿＿＿＿＿＿＿＿＿

2. A: 車は止まりましたね。

　　B: はい、もう ＿＿＿＿＿＿＿＿＿＿＿＿＿＿＿＿＿＿＿

3. A: タイヤのパンクは直っていますか。

　　B: はい、もう ＿＿＿＿＿＿＿＿＿＿＿＿＿＿＿＿＿＿＿

4. A: ボンネットは開いていますか。

　　B: はい、もう ＿＿＿＿＿＿＿＿＿＿＿＿＿＿＿＿＿＿＿

5. A: ヘッドライトはついていますか。

   B: はい、もう _____

6. A: スーツケースはもうならんでいますか。

   B: はい、もう _____

7. A: うま (horse) はもう、トラックに乗っていますか。

   B: はい、もう _____

8. A: 駅の窓口は閉まっていますか。

   B: はい、もう _____

H. There is a haunted house in your neighborhood. No one is supposed to be living in it, but all sorts of strange things happen there. Fill in the blanks with appropriate intransitive verbs, and complete the passage that describes what happens in this haunted house.

この家は、だれも住んでいないと思うんですが、人が近くに行くと、ドアが

_____[1]。家の中に入ると、ドアが_____[2]。スイッチを入れなくても、

電気が_____[3]。そして、人が家を出ると、電気が_____[4]。中に入った

人が何かこわしても、つぎの日には_____[5] います。長い間ドアの外にたって

いると、時々二階の窓から大きいいし (stones) が_____[6] くるから、あぶないで

す。この家は三階建てですが、エレベーターがあります。そのエレベーターは、人が

乗っていなくても、かってに (of its own free will)_____[7] たり_____[8] たり

します。かべにきれいなえ (pictures) が_____[9] いますが、そのえは時々

_____[10] (disappear)。

What other things do you think could happen in a haunted house? Write at least two of them.

11. _____

12. _____

I. Actually, there is no such thing as a haunted house. The house described in the previous exercise is really a hideout for a criminal gang. They create all those weird effects so that people won't come near the house. The following describes what they do to make the house appear to be haunted. Fill in the blanks with appropriate transitive verbs.

この家のドアと電気のかかりはバッド・バートです。人が近くに来ると二階のリモー

トコントロールを使ってドアを_____[1] て、中に入るとドアを_____[2]。

そして、人が家に入ると、二階のスイッチで電気を_____³。人が家から出ると電気を_____⁴。中に入った人が何かこわしたら、つぎの日までにフランキーが_____⁵。人がげんかんに長い間たっていると、フランキーは時々二階からいしを_____⁶。この家は三階建てですけれど、エレベーターがあります。そのエレベーターはブルーザーが三階から_____⁷たり_____⁸たりします。ブルーザーはいま (living room) のかべのきれいなえを_____⁹ (move)。

The two haunted-house phenomena that you mentioned in the previous exercise are actually carried out by a fourth accomplice, Brutus (ブルータス). Write down what he does.

10. _____

11. _____

J. You are having a big party at 8:00 P.M. tonight, and you have worked all day to get ready for it. It is now 7:30, and you think you're done with the preparations. Now look at the illustration, check to see if everything is in order, and write down a sentence confirming this fact using 〜てあります. If you think some other preparations need to be done, write them down, too, using 〜てありません. (Use もう and まだ when appropriate.)

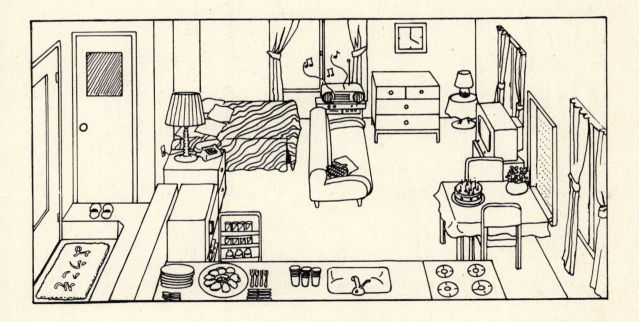

Write about:

1. the beverages _____

2. the flowers _____

3. the table _____

4. the potato chips _____

5. the cake _____

6. the radio _____

7. the plates, cups, and forks _____

8. the room _____

9. (something else you have observed) _____

    _____

10. (something else you have observed) _____

    _____

K. A burglar broke into your room and caused a lot of damage while you were away for a few days. Look at the picture, and report to the police about the following, using 〜ています。

[例] ステレオがこわれています。

1. the door _____

2. the window _____

3. the refrigerator door _____

4. the lights _____

5. the drawers (たんすの引き出し) _____

6. the clock (stopped) _____

7. the money _____

8. the telephone line (電話せん) _____

9. the TV _____

Vocabulary and Grammar 3B: Car Maintenance and Repairs

A. Please complete the following sentences by writing what happened for 1 through 5 and what you may have tried to to do for 6 through 10.

1. 毎日５時間日本語を勉強しようとしましたが、_____

    _____。

2. ６時のひこうきに乗ろうとしたんですが、_____

    _____。

3. ブレーキをかけようとしたんですが、_____

    _____。

4. フランス料理を作ろうとしたんですけれど、_____

    _____。

5. 窓を開けようとしたら、_____。

6. _____、高くて買えませんでした。

7. _____、とても寒かったので、

    かかりませんでした。

8. _____、むずかしくてできません

    でした。

9. ＿＿＿＿＿＿＿＿＿＿＿＿＿＿＿＿＿＿＿＿＿＿＿、時間がありませんでした。

10. ＿＿＿＿＿＿＿＿＿＿＿＿＿＿＿＿＿＿＿＿＿＿＿、雨がふってきました。

B. Children and teenagers sometimes try to do things that their parents have forbidden. Did you ever try to get away with something like that when you were younger? Were you successful, or did you get caught? If you can't think of any such incidents in your own life, write the experiences of some of your friends.

[例] 友だちのジョンは、中学生の時、家出（いえで ＝ *run away*）しようとしました。でも窓から出ようとした時にお父さんに見つかりました。

1. ＿＿＿＿＿＿＿＿＿＿＿＿＿＿＿＿＿＿＿＿＿＿＿＿＿＿＿＿＿＿＿＿

2. ＿＿＿＿＿＿＿＿＿＿＿＿＿＿＿＿＿＿＿＿＿＿＿＿＿＿＿＿＿＿＿＿

3. ＿＿＿＿＿＿＿＿＿＿＿＿＿＿＿＿＿＿＿＿＿＿＿＿＿＿＿＿＿＿＿＿

C. Have you ever tried to do something but failed to accomplish it, no matter how hard you tried? Write about three such incidents. If you can't remember any such incidents in your own life, ask some of your classmates to tell you about their experiences, and then write about those incidents.

[例] 小さい時の話ですが、「スーパーマン」のえいがを見てから、そらをとぼう（*fly*）としましたが、どうしても（*no matter what*）とべませんでした。

1. ＿＿＿＿＿＿＿＿＿＿＿＿＿＿＿＿＿＿＿＿＿＿＿＿＿＿＿＿＿＿＿＿

2. ＿＿＿＿＿＿＿＿＿＿＿＿＿＿＿＿＿＿＿＿＿＿＿＿＿＿＿＿＿＿＿＿

3. ＿＿＿＿＿＿＿＿＿＿＿＿＿＿＿＿＿＿＿＿＿＿＿＿＿＿＿＿＿＿＿＿

D. Your acquaintance is asking you the reason for your action or situation. Answer with an explanation containing …ばかりなんです.

[例] どうしてもっと食べないんですか。 →
今ごはんを食べたばかりなんです。

1. どうしてつかれているんですか。
   うんどうしたばかりなんです。

2. どうしてお金（かね）がないんですか。
   車を買ったばかりなんです。

3. どうしてあのえいがに行かないんですか。
   あのえいがを見（み）たばかりなんです。

4. どうして部屋（へや）がこんなにきれいなんですか。
   さっきそうじしたばかりなんです。

5. どうしてまだパジャマを着ているんですか。

おきたばかりなんです。

E. The members of Professor Yokoi's class have gone to the mountains for a weekend retreat. They are staying at a ペンション (*a Western-style establishment similar to a bed and breakfast, except that it also serves dinner*). It's almost time for dinner, and everyone has just gathered in the living room. Look at the drawing, figure out what everyone was doing before the group gathered, and fill in the speech balloons with each person's explanation of what he or she was doing, using …ところ or …ばかり.

F. An acquaintance has made the following requests and offers. Turn down each request or offer, explaining that you have just done something that makes it impossible or inconvenient to fulfill the request or accept the offer.

[例] X: 日本語を教えてくださいませんか。
　　Y: すみません、私も日本語の勉強を始めたばかりですから…

1. X: このケーキ、私が作ったんですよ。食べませんか。

　 Y: すみません、ケーキを食べたばかりんですから

2. X: 明日いっしょにディズニーランドへ行きませんか。

　 Y: すみませんが、私きのうD.L.に行ったばかりんです

3. X: 今からジョギングに行くんですけど、いっしょにいかがですか。 *Would you like to go*

   Y: <u>すみません、けさ ジョギングに 行った ばかりんです</u>

4. X: このコンピュータの使い方を教えてください。

   Y: <u>すみません、コンピュータの つかい方 をならった ばかりんで</u>

5. X: ビール、飲みませんか。 *の*

   Y: <u>すみませんが (さき) あさけをたくさん 飲んたばか</u> *just* て

G. Suppose you are going to buy a small, used 1990 car for $3,000. Would the following problems prevent you from buying it? Check the five problems that you are concerned about most.

_____ トランスミッションがこわれている。

_____ サイドミラーがとれている (*has come off*)。

_____ クラッチがすりへっている (*is worn down*)。

_____ シートベルトがとれている。

_____ タコメーターが動かない。

_____ エアコンが使えない。

_____ ブレーキがよくきかない。

_____ フェンダーがとれている。

_____ ウィンカーがはたらかない。

_____ ボンネットが閉まらない。

H. Your rich aunt is giving you money to buy a car. It should not cost any more than $25,000. (You may get a cheaper car and save the rest of the money for tuition or whatever, but your aunt wants you to buy a new car.) Describe the car that you want, using at least six sentences. (Refer to Activity 27.)

1. _____

2. _____

3. _____

4. _____

5. _____

6. _____

Vocabulary and Grammar 3C: Transportation and Traffic in the City

A. Which motorized or nonmotorized means of transportation would you use or summon in the following situations? Write the name of the means of transportation.

1. くうこうからホテルまで行きたいとき: _____

2. 引っこし (*moving*) するとき: _____

3. 道のよくないところをドライブしたいとき: _____

4. となりの家からけむり (*smoke*) が出るのを見たとき: _____

5. となりの家にどろぼう (*thief*) が入るのを見たとき: _____

6. けっこんしき (*wedding ceremony*) の後で: _____

7. 運動したいとき: _____

8. 車を使わないでがっこうや会社に通いたい (*want to commute*) とき: _____

B. Combine the two clauses using the conjunctive form, following the example.

[例] (ふたを開ける)(お金を入れる) → ふたを開け、お金を入れました。

1. (ドアを閉める)(かぎをかける)

   _____

2. (ドアが開く)(町田さんが出てくる)

   _____

3. (ガソリンスタンドへ行く)(車を洗う)

   _____

4. (ロードマップをもらう)(ガソリンスタンドを出る)

   _____

5. (私はスパゲッティーを食べる)(林さんはシチューを食べる)

   _____

6. (母は本を読む)(父はステレオで音楽を聞く)

   _____

7. (車を止める)(道を聞く) _____

8. （おふろに入る）（ゆっくりする）

   _____

9. （山本さんはケーキを作る）（私はすしを作る）

   _____

10. （高田さんに手がみを書く）（電話番号を教える）_____

C. There was a Japanese test today. All of the students in class did an excellent job. We interviewed them and found out that each one had given up an everyday activity for the last two days to devote more time to studying. Guess how each person studied, referring to that person's activity.

   Student 1 (likes to sleep)

   Student 2 (never misses a meal or snacks)

   Student 3 (likes to watch TV)

   Student 4 (always studies for every other class, too)

   Student 5 (exercises regularly)

   Student 6 (talks on the phone with his girlfriend a lot)

   [例] Student 1: 私はぜんぜんねないで勉強しました。

   Student 2: _____

   Student 3: _____

   Student 4: _____

   Student 5: _____

   Student 6: _____

   You (think of your own): _____

D. The following sentences each paraphrase one of the signs shown here. Fill in the blanks with the proper forms of the verbs to reflect the meanings of the signs.

1.   2.   3.

[例]  4.   5.

[例] (A) ここを _____（通る）→

ここを通ってはいけません。

1. ここでは一度_____。（止まる）

2. 右に_____。（曲がる）

3. 時速50キロいじょう (above) で_____（走る）

4. ユーターンを_____。（する）

5. おうだん歩道があるので_____。（注意する）

E. Sometimes it seems that you get into a troublesome situation only when you're unprepared for it. The following are some of these situations. Fill in the blanks to provide the condition under which they occur, using 〜ないで〜と.

[例] 運転めんきょをもたないで車を運転すると、けいかんにひっかかります (be stopped at a roadblock)。

1. _____と、ぬきうちテスト (pop quiz) があります。

2. _____と、雨がふります。

3. _____と、友だちは出かけています。

4. パーティーでたくさん食べ物があるだろうと思って_____

と、飲み物しかありません。

5. 明日はテストがあるはずなので_____

と、先生が病気でクラスがなかったりします。

Chapter 3 Review

A. There are many kinds of public transportation systems around the world. Which do you think are the five most important features for a public transportation system to have? Number them in order of importance.

1. _____ うんちん (*fare*) がやすい

2. _____ きっぷを買わないで、乗りかえられる

3. _____ 24 時間乗れる

4. _____ かいすう (*frequency of runs*) が多い

5. _____ 電車やバスの中がきれいだ

6. _____ 学生わりびきがある

7. _____ 一ヵ月のていきけん (*commuter's pass*) が買える

8. _____ ラッシュアワーの時、かいそく (*limited stop*) のバスや電車がある

9. _____ けいさつ (*police*) がいつも乗っているから、あんぜん (*safe*) だ

10. _____ いつでも、どこへでも行けるから、車がいらない

B. The map on page 140, which depicts the JR Osaka Station area, is part of a bank advertisement. You are a traveler from the United States who has just arrived at Osaka Station. The following paragraphs tell what happens as you explore the area, and each one ends with a question or an instruction. The answers to most of the questions can be inferred from the information given on the map, although you may have to use your imagination for others.

1. アメリカの旅行会社にヒルトンホテルの部屋を予約しておいてもらいました。駅でホテルへの道を日本人に聞いたら、しんせつに (*kindly*) 教えてくれました。日本人は何と言ったでしょうか。

   _____

   _____

2. ヒルトンホテルに着いたら、部屋がありませんでした。アメリカの旅行会社が予約するのをわすれていたのです。ホテルの人に何と言いますか。

   _____

3. ヒルトンホテルの人がとなりの大阪マルビルにもホテルがあると教えてくれました。電話して、部屋を予約してください。(みじかいダイアログを書いてください。)

_____

_____

_____

_____

_____

4. ホテルの部屋ににもつを置いて、出かけることにしました。まず、ゆうびんきょくへ行って、切手を買って、それから、阪急百貨店 (Hankyu Department Store) で買い物をしました。少し歩くと、けいさつ (police) と学校があったので、その間の道をまっすぐ歩いて、お初天神という小さい神社を見て、ホテルに帰りました。歩いた所を地図に書いてください。(Trace your path on the map.)

5. この近所に梅田コマげき場というげき場 (live theater) があると聞きました。行き方をだれかに聞くダイアログを書いてください。

_____

_____

_____

_____

6. げき場もおもしろかったです。明日は阪急梅田駅から電車に乗って、友だちの家へ行きます。朝の9時ごろホテルを出ようと思っています。にもつがあるから、タクシーで行こうと思います。フロントデスクに電話して、タクシーをたのんでください。(ダイアログを書いてください。)

_____

_____

_____

_____

ご来店をお待ちしております

C. The Unicorn is a jetfoil (an advanced hydrofoil) that travels between the ports of Aomori (青森) and Hakodate (函館), providing a link between the islands of Honshu and Hokkaido. The following is some information on the Unicorn's schedule, fares, and dock locations at Hakodate and Aomori ports. Study these charts carefully and answer the questions.

UNICORN 営業の御案内

運航ダイヤ

～8月のダイヤ

函館発	青森着	便	青森発	函館着
5:30	07:10	1	07:40	09:20
9:50	11:30	5	12:10	13:50
4:30	16:10	9	16:50	18:30

※9月～3月のダイヤ

便	函館発	青森着	便	青森発	函館着
4	08:10	09:50	3	10:20	12:00
8	12:30	14:10	7	14:40	16:20

運賃・料金

	運　賃	特別急行料	合　　計
人	2,800	3,500	6,300
己	1,400	1,750	3,150

乗り場案内 (フェリー乗り場とは異なります)

函館……函館駅より車で10分・徒歩30分

青森……青森駅より車で10分・徒歩20分

東日本フェリー株式会社

─ お問い合せ ─

トフォイル函館 ☎(0138)27-2222 函館市末広町14番17号地先
トフォイル青森 ☎(0177)74-3333 青森市安方2丁目14番23号
予約センター ☎(011)518-2718 札幌市中央区南4条西11丁目
京 営業部 ☎(03)5561-0211 東京都港区赤坂2丁目17番22号
阪 支店 ☎(06)445-6100 大阪市西区京町堀2丁目2番1号

1. スケジュールが2つありますね。どう違いますか。もし今日北海道へ行くんだったら、どちらのスケジュールを使いますか。

   _____

2. 今青森にいます。明日の朝できるだけ早く (as early as possible) 函館へ行きたいんですが、何便 (which boat) に乗ったらいいでしょうか。

   _____

3. 青森から函館まではどのぐらいかかりますか。

   _____

4. 運賃料金ひょう(fare table) を見てください。あなたがユニコーンに乗ると、いくらかかりますか。

   _____

5. このひょう (chart) には書いてありませんが、おうふくきっぷを買うと10% やすくなります。友だちと2人でおうふくきっぷを買うと、いくらになりますか。

   _____

6. 乗り場案内を見てください。今あなたは函館駅にいます。ユニコーンの乗り場まで歩いたら何分かかりますか。タクシーでは？

   _____

7. 函館駅から乗り場までの行き方を書いてください。

   _____

8. 青森駅から青森港 (port) の乗り場まではどうやって行ったらいいですか。

   _____

   _____

9. あなたはユニコーンに乗ってみたいですか。どうして。

   _____

   _____

THE BODY AND HEALTH

からだ けんこう
体と健康

Listening Comprehension Activities

Vocabulary and Grammar 4A: Body Parts

A. Listen to the following definitions and choose the name of each body part being described.

1. _____
2. _____
3. _____
4. _____
5. _____
6. _____
7. _____

a. くち
b. め
c. はな
d. は
e. みみ
f. あたま
g. ゆび
h. あし
i. かお

B. Listen to John Kawamura describe his first love, and fill in the blanks.

When I was in high school, I fell in love with a girl who was _____ like snow.

Her hair was _____ and smelled good like _____.

Also, she played the piano with _____ fingers. She used to sing for me with a

voice like _____. And, she had a figure like a _____.

Besides all these, she was _____ enough to help me study just like

_____. Someday, I want to see her again.

C. Listen to the descriptions of four people and mark each description either true (T) or false (F) based on the picture.

Sayuri Yamamoto   Yooichi Takada   Kunio Sano   Yoshiko Sano   Yayoi Murayama

1. _____   3. _____   5. _____

2. _____   4. _____

D. Masao Hayashi and Henry Curtis are talking about their mothers. Listen to the conversation and complete the following summary by filling in the blanks.

    Useful Vocabulary: うそをつく *to tell a lie*

The person whom Curtis is the most afraid of is _____. She is so

_____ that she can tell whenever her children _____. She has

extraordinarily sharp _____, _____ and even

_____. Her children are a bit afraid of her, but they also love her because she is

_____ and _____. These days, she scolds her children

_____ than she used to. On the other hand, Hayashi's mother scolds her son

_____ than before.

Vocabulary and Grammar 4B: Feeling and Emotions

A. Listen to the statements and choose the most appropriate emotional response for each occasion.

1. （うれしい　かなしい　こわい）
2. （あんしんする　こわがる　がっかりする）
3. （はずかしい　さびしい　たのしい）
4. （たのしい　こまる　くるしい）
5. （しんぱいする　おこる　あんしんする）

B. John Kawamura has been keeping a diary in Japanese in order to improve his writing skills. Listen to two entries from February 20 and 21, and mark the statements either true (T) or false (F).

Useful Vocabulary: 食よく *appetite*

2月20日。土曜日。

1. _____ 林さんは、今日の朝、かなしそうだった。
2. _____ 林さんのねこは、病気で死んだそうだ。
3. _____ そのねこは、とてもしずかなねこだったようだ。
4. _____ そのねこは、きれいな目をしていたらしい。
5. _____ 林さんは、私と話しながら泣いていた。

2月21日。日曜日。

1. _____ カワムラさんは今日ひまだったようだ。
2. _____ ブラウンさんはデートに行くようだった。
3. _____ 林さんは今朝はやく起きたようだ。
4. _____ 横井先生は本屋ですわって本を読んでいた。
5. _____ 夕方も雨がふっていた。
6. _____ 林さんはたくさん食べてから、カワムラさんの家に来た。
7. _____ 林さんはまだかなしそうで、食よくもなさそうだった。

C. Hitomi Machida and John Kawamura are talking about one of their classmates, Masao Hayashi. Listen to their conversation and choose the words that describe how Hayashi has been recently.

Useful Vocabulary: きっと *for sure*

Hayashi seems:

a. grouchy
b. happy
c. addicted to cigarettes
d. more irritable
e. healthier
f. active in sports
g. less energetic
h. not to be drinking

Vocabulary and Grammar 4C: Health and Illness

A. Listen to the three short dialogues between a doctor and a patient, and circle the symptoms of each patient on the doctor's chart.

PATIENT #1	PATIENT #2	PATIENT #3

• Ache or soreness
   head, stomach, throat
• Cough   yes/no
• Fever   yes/no
	• Ache or soreness
	   head, stomach, throat
	• Nausea yes/no
	• Diarrhea yes/no
	• Fever yes/no
		• Injured part
		   legs, arms, face, head
		• Pain yes/no
		• Medicine taken yes/no

B. Listen to the conversation between a doctor and Takeshi Mimura, and mark the statements either true (T) or false (F).

Useful Vocabulary: しかたありません *can't be helped*

1. _____ Mimura's throat is normal.

2. _____ It was raining all day yesterday.

3. _____ Mimura met Julia Roberts at the bus stop yesterday.

4. _____ Mimura did not use his own umbrella because he lent it to a pretty woman.

5. _____ Mimura has a high fever but has no headache.

6. _____ He doesn't have diarrhea but feels no appetite.

7. _____ It seems that Mimura has caught a cold.

C. Listen as Mrs. Suzuki talks about her dream last night, and write the initials of the persons whom she made to do the following activities.

(husband = H, children =C, dog = D, robot = R)

1. Fix breakfast: _____

2. Bring the newspaper: _____

3. Wash dishes: _____

4. Drive a car: _____

5. Do office work: _____

6. Do house chores: _____ _____

D. Yoshiko Tanaka's mother is reading a magazine article in which the author criticizes Japanese parents for over-scheduling their children. Listen as she discusses the article with her daughter, Yoshiko, who has just returned from a trip to the United States. Then fill in the blanks in the following paragraph.

Useful Vocabulary: じゅく *cram academy (where students go after school to do extra studying),* ならいごと *lessons*

As she reads the magazine article, Mrs. Tanaka notes that Japanese parents make their children

_____ and _____. Yoshiko tells her that American

parents let their children _____. Mrs. Tanaka wonders

_____ if they aren't very busy with study or lessons, but Yoshiko tells her that

American parents make their children _____, take out trash, and

_____. Many parents also have their children _____,

and _____. Mrs. Tanaka wonders which system is better.

E. Listen to the conversation between a doctor and Mr. Suzuki, who hit his head yesterday and lost his memory temporarily. Then mark the statements either true (T) or false (F).

Useful Vocabulary: おちる *to fall,* 自分 *self*

1. _____ 自分の名前をおぼえていた。

2. _____ 頭をうつ前にどこにいたかおぼえている。

3. _____ 階だんからおちた後のことをおぼえていない。

4. _____ 自分がどこで働いているかおぼえていない。

5. _____ おくさんの顔をおぼえていた。

F. Henry Curtis and Takeshi Mimura have noticed a new building being built near the campus of their university. Listen to their dialogue and complete the following newspaper advertisement by filling in the blanks.

New Sports Center Opens _____! Come over and see our great

facilities for _____, weight training, and _____. There are many

classes offered at the center, such as _____ and _____. We also have

classes for elderly people such as _____ and gateball. Free T-shirt with our logo if

_____ on the opening day. We guarantee your good health and 100%

satisfaction!!

G. John Kawamura meets Heather Gibson on campus before their Japanese class. Listen to their conversation and choose the correct answer for each sentence.

1. _____ saw Henry Curtis in front of the library a while ago.
   a. John Kawamura   b. Heather Gibson   c. both Kawamura and Gibson

2. Kawamura believes Curtis is sick in bed with _____.
   a. a headache   b. a cold   c. both a and b

3. Curtis _____ the cafeteria.
   a. went into   b. didn't go into   c. got sick in

4. Curtis _____ now.
   a. feels the same as last night   b. feels worse   c. feels better

5. Takako Matsui _____ Curtis this morning.
   a. called   b. went to see   c. prepared breakfast for

6. Matsui will _____ Curtis this morning.
   a. call   b. go to see   c. not see

7. Curtis feels well enough to _____.
   a. visit Matsui   b. cook for Matsui   c. take the exam

H. Listen to a conversation between Yoshiko Tanaka and Akira Yamada, and mark the statements either true (T) or false (F).

1. _____ Yoshiko looked happy when she met Akira.

2. _____ Yoshiko's father seems not to care about Yoshiko.

3. _____ It seems that Yoshiko's father has been enthusiastic about educating his daughter.

4. _____ Yoshiko has been healthy since she was a child.

5. _____ Yoshiko's father made her take a swimming lesson.

6. _____ Akira was not allowed to play with his friends when he was a child.

7. _____ Akira can play the piano.

8. _____ Akira's father was hospitalized because of a traffic accident.

9. _____ Akira's father doesn't allow his son to drive a car.

10. _____ Akira thinks that his father doesn't care about him.

Kanji Practice and Exercises

1	体 体	タイ body; object, thing; style, form テイ appearance; condition, state からだ body			
	体：からだ (body) 人間の体：にんげんのからだ (human body)				
2	頭 頭	トウ、ズ、ト、あたま、こうべ、かぶり head かしら head, leader, top			
	頭：あたま (head) 頭上：ずじょう (on/over your head)				
3	顔 顔	ガン、かお face			
	顔：かお (face) 顔色が悪い：かおいろがわるい (look pale)				
4	鼻 鼻	ビ、はな nose			
	鼻：はな (nose) 鼻が高い：はながたかい (to be proud)				
5	耳 耳	ジ、みみ ear			
	耳：みみ (ear) 右耳：みぎみみ (right ear) 左耳：ひだりみみ (left ear)				

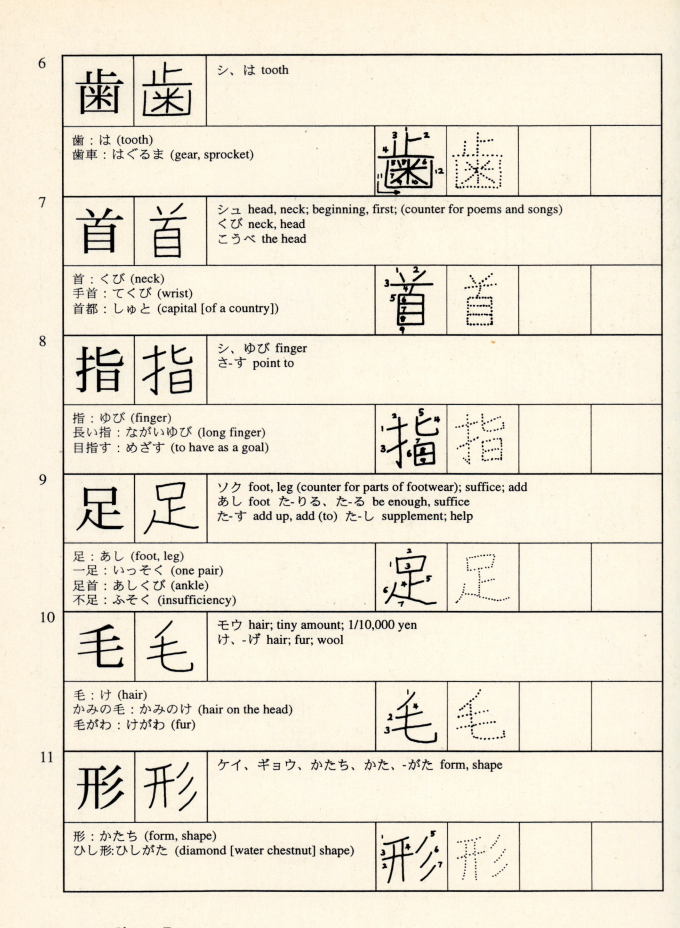

6	歯 歯	シ、は tooth
	歯：は (tooth) 歯車：はぐるま (gear, sprocket)	
7	首 首	シュ head, neck; beginning, first; (counter for poems and songs) くび neck, head こうべ the head
	首：くび (neck) 手首：てくび (wrist) 首都：しゅと (capital [of a country])	
8	指 指	シ、ゆび finger さ-す point to
	指：ゆび (finger) 長い指：ながいゆび (long finger) 目指す：めざす (to have as a goal)	
9	足 足	ソク foot, leg (counter for parts of footwear); suffice; add あし foot た-りる、た-る be enough, suffice た-す add up, add (to) た-し supplement; help
	足：あし (foot, leg) 一足：いっそく (one pair) 足首：あしくび (ankle) 不足：ふそく (insufficiency)	
10	毛 毛	モウ hair; tiny amount; 1/10,000 yen け、-げ hair; fur; wool
	毛：け (hair) かみの毛：かみのけ (hair on the head) 毛がわ：けがわ (fur)	
11	形 形	ケイ、ギョウ、かたち、かた、-がた form, shape
	形：かたち (form, shape) ひし形：ひしがた (diamond [water chestnut] shape)	

12	丸 丸	ガン、まる circle; entire, complete, full (month); (suffix for names of ships) まる-い、まる-っこい round まる-で quite, utterly, completely; just like, as it were まる-める make round, form into a ball			
	丸：まる (circle) 丸い形：まるいかたち (round shape)		丸	丸	

13	角 角	カク angle; corner; (animal's) horn; compare, compete かど corner, angle すみ corner, nook つの horn, antlers			
	三角：さんかく (triangle) 四角：しかく (square or rectangle) 四角い形：しかくいかたち (square or rectangle shape) 五つ目の角：いつつめのかど (fifth corner)		角	角	

14	持 持	ジ、も-つ have, possess; hold, maintain; wear, last も-ち wear, durability; charge, expenses; (ladies') wear も-てる be popular with; can hold/carry; propertied, the haves も-たす let (someone) have, give; have (someone) hold/carry/hear, preserve, make last			
	持つ：もつ (to have) 気持ち：きもち (feeling/emotion) （お）金持ち：（お）かねもち (rich person)		持	持	

15	立 立	リツ、リュウ、た-つ stand, rise た-てる set, raise リットル liter			
	立つ：たつ (to stand [up]) 立場：たちば (standpoint) 国立：こくりつ (national)		立	立	

16	心 心	シン、こころ heart, mind; core			
	心：こころ (heart, mind) 安心する：あんしんする (to be relieved) 中心：ちゅうしん (center)		心	心	

17	配 配	ハイ、-バイ distribute, allot; arrange, place; be together; exile くば-る distribute, pass out, allocate			
	心配する：しんぱいする (to worry) 心配事：しんぱいごと (worries, cares, troubles)				

18	苦 苦	ク、くる-しむ／しがる suffer くる-しめる torment くる-しい painful にが-い bitter にが-る scowl				
	苦しい：くるしい (oppressively painful) 苦い：にがい (bitter) 苦手なスポーツ：にがてなすぽーつ (a sport that one is bad at and dislikes)	苦	苦			
19	死 死	シ、し-ぬ、し-する die				
	死ぬ：しぬ (to die) 病死：びょうし (death from illness)	死	死			
20	元 元	ゲン origin; **yuan** (Chinese monetary unit); Mongol (dynasty) ガン origin もと origin, basis; (as prefix) former, ex-				
	お元気ですか：おげんきですか (How are you?) 元日：がんじつ (first day of the year) 元年：がんねん (first year of an era)	元	元			
21	病 病	ビョウ、ヘイ、や-む、や-める get sick, be ill, suffer from やまい illness, disease; bad habit; weakness for				
	病気：びょうき (illness) 病人：びょうにん (sick person)	病	病			
22	院 院	イン institution, palace, temple, hospital, school, house (of a legislature); ex- emperor				
	病院：びょういん (hospital) 入院：にゅういん (entering the hospital) 大学院：だいがくいん (graduate school)	院	院			
23	痛 痛	ツウ pain いた-い painful いた-み pain, ache いた-む be painful, hurt; be damaged, spoil いた-める hurt, pain, afflict				
	痛い：いたい (painful) 頭痛：ずつう (headache) 頭が痛い：あたまがいたい (head aches)	痛	痛			

24	熱 熱	ネツ heat; fever; mania, enthusiasm あつ-い hot (not used for weather; that's 暑い)			
	熱：ねつ (fever) 熱いお茶：あついおちゃ (hot tea) 熱心：ねっしん (zeal, enthusiasm)		熱	熱	
25	薬 薬	ヤク、ヤッ-、くすり、-ぐすり medicine; chemical			
	薬：くすり (medicine) かぜ薬：かぜぐすり (cold medicine) 薬屋：くすりや (drugstore)		薬	薬	
26	局 局	キョク bureau, office; (radio/TV) station; situation つぼね court lady			
	薬局：やっきょく (pharmacy) ゆう便局：ゆうびんきょく (post office)		局	局	

Kanji Exercises

A. Match each kanji or kanji compound with its closest English equivalent. (Each letter is used once.)

1. 入院 _____
2. 角 _____
3. 顔 _____
4. 局 _____
5. 苦 _____
6. 形 _____
7. 元 _____
8. 指 _____
9. 死 _____

10. 立 _____
11. 歯 _____
12. 持 _____
13. 耳 _____
14. 首 _____
15. 心 _____
16. 足 _____
17. 体 _____
18. 痛 _____

19. 頭 _____
20. 熱 _____
21. 配 _____
22. 鼻 _____
23. 病 _____
24. 毛 _____
25. 丸 _____
26. 薬 _____

a. angle b. body c. bureau d. die e. distribute f. ear g. face h. fever i. finger j. foot
k. hair l. have m. head n. heart o. hospitalization p. illness q. medicine r. neck s. nose
t. origin u. pain v. round w. shape x. stand y. suffer z. tooth

B. Write the hurigana for each kanji or kanji compound.

1. 人間の体

   _____

2. 休み

   _____

3. 頭が痛い

   _____

4. 頭痛

   _____

5. 顔

   _____

6. 鼻

   _____

7. 耳

   _____

8. 聞く

   _____

9. 歯

   _____

10. 道

    _____

11. 首

    _____

12. 指

    _____

13. 足

_____

14. 一足

_____

15. 手

_____

16. 毛

_____

17. 変な形

_____

18. 丸

_____

19. 九

_____

20. 死ぬ

_____

21. 三つ目の角

_____

22. 三角

_____

23. 元気

_____

24. 待つ

_____

25. 持つ

_____

26. 立つ

_____

27. 苦手

_____

28. 苦い

_____

29. 苦しい

_____

30. 心

_____

31. 心配

_____

32. 病院

_____

33. 薬

_____

34. 薬局

_____

35. 薬屋

_____

36. 熱

_____

37. 熱い

_____

husband

C. Write the appropriate kanji for the hiragana under the blanks.

1. ご＿＿＿（しゅじん）は＿＿＿（きょう）はあまり＿＿＿（げんき）がないようですね。

2. ＿＿（わたし）の＿＿（い）ったようにケーキを＿＿（つく）りましたか。

3. ＿＿（ねつ）があったので、＿＿（くすり）を＿＿（の）んでねた。

4. ＿＿（かお）のまん＿＿（なか）にあるのは＿＿（はな）です。

5. ＿＿＿（ひだりて）で＿＿＿（みぎみみ）をさわって＿＿（くだ）さい。

6. きりん (giraffe) は＿＿（くび）も＿＿（あし）も＿＿（なが）い。

7. ＿＿（は）が＿＿（いた）くて、＿＿＿（きのう）は＿＿＿（たいへん）だった。

8. ＿＿（あね）は＿＿（えき）の＿＿（ちか）くの＿＿＿（びょういん）で＿＿＿（はたら）いている。

9. ゆう＿＿＿＿＿（びんきょく）に＿＿＿（い）って、＿＿＿＿＿（きって）を＿＿＿（か）ってきて＿＿＿＿＿（くだ）さいませんか。

10. たくさん＿＿＿（た）べたので、＿＿＿（くる）しくて＿＿＿（し）にそうだった。

11. ＿＿＿＿＿＿＿（まいにち）かみの＿＿＿＿（け）を＿＿＿＿（あら）いますか。

12. あの＿＿＿＿＿＿＿（たてもの）は＿＿＿＿（へん）な＿＿＿＿＿（かたち）をしています。

13. お＿＿＿（からだ）に＿＿＿＿（き）をつけて＿＿＿＿（くだ）さい。

14. ＿＿＿＿＿＿＿＿＿（しんぱいごと）がたくさんあって、＿＿＿＿（あたま）が＿＿＿＿（いた）い。

15. だれかが＿＿＿（にわ）の＿＿＿（き）の＿＿＿（まえ）に＿＿＿＿（た）って＿＿＿＿（おお）きな＿＿＿＿（まる）い＿＿＿＿（め）で＿＿＿＿（わたし）たちを＿＿＿＿（み）ていました。それは、＿＿＿＿＿＿＿＿（しかく）い＿＿＿＿（かお）をした

うちゅう_____ で、_____ の _____ におもそうな
　　　　じん　　　　　　　　　　　さんぼんゆび　　　　　　て

_____ のじ _____ を _____ っていました。
　　にほんご　　　　　　　　しょ　　　　　も

Kanji in Everyday Life

1. You are reading about a famous doctor who is described as being a 耳鼻咽喉専門医. What is this doctor's specialty?

   _____

2. What do you think the students at a 歯科大学 study?

   _____

3. The verb 感じる means *to feel an emotion or sensation*. What do you think the verbal noun 痛感する means in reference to emotions?

   _____

4. You are trying to get money out of the automatic teller machine, but when you insert your card and press all the right buttons, you get a message on the screen that contains the word 不足. What is the problem?

   _____

5. What part of your body is your 指先?

   _____

6. You read in the newspaper that the police found a 死体 in your neighborhood. How does that make you feel?

   _____

7. What is the shape of the stomach medicine known as 正露丸?

   _____

8. The word 糸 means *yarn* or *thread*. What do you think 毛糸 is?

   _____

Writing Activities

Vocabulary and Grammar 4A: Body Parts

A. The following words are all the names of body parts. Rewrite the list in order, from top (*head*) to bottom (*foot*).

<ruby>足<rt>あし</rt></ruby>　目　口　むね　かみ　<ruby>鼻<rt>はな</rt></ruby>　<ruby>首<rt>くび</rt></ruby>

_____

_____

_____

_____

_____

_____

_____

B. What if human beings' body parts were made or placed differently from how they really are? Use your imagination and complete the following sentences.

[例] もし目が<ruby>頭<rt>あたま</rt></ruby>の上にあったら、
* 前がよく見えないから、<ruby>交通事故<rt>こうつうじこ</rt></ruby>がふえるかもしれません。
* みな、いつもおじぎ (*bowing*) をしながら歩くかもしれません。
* 雨の日にはだれも外に出ないかもしれません。etc.

1. もし目が3つあったら、_____

_____

2. もし<ruby>鼻<rt>はな</rt></ruby>が2つ、<ruby>頭<rt>あたま</rt></ruby>の<ruby>横<rt>よこ</rt></ruby>(<ruby>耳<rt>みみ</rt></ruby>のあるところ)　にあったら、_____

_____

3. もしおや<ruby>指<rt>ゆび</rt></ruby> (*thumb*) がなかったら、_____

_____

4. もしおへそがなかったら、_____

_____

5. もしさる (*monkey*) のように、<ruby>体中<rt>からだじゅう</rt></ruby>に<ruby>毛<rt>け</rt></ruby>があったら、_____

_____

C. Write な or に in the blanks. If no particle is required, write X.

1. ねこのよう＿＿な＿＿顔

2. ねこのよう＿＿に＿＿歩く

3. レモンのよう＿＿X＿＿黄色い

4. レモンのよう＿＿X＿＿すっぱい (sour)

5. 月みたい＿＿に＿＿丸い

6. 月のよう＿＿な＿＿顔

7. ドーナツのよう＿＿な＿＿くも (cloud)

8. いぬみたい＿＿X＿＿です。

9. 日本人のよう＿＿X＿＿です。

10. さとうみたい＿＿X＿＿あまい

D. Write を or が in the blanks, depending on which one is correct in the context.

1. さるのような顔＿＿＿＿している。

2. スーパーマンみたいなすがた＿＿＿＿している。

3. みかんのような味＿＿＿＿する。

4. ピザみたいなにおい＿＿＿＿する。

5. きれいな色＿＿＿＿している。

6. 変な音＿＿＿＿する。

7. 丸い形＿＿＿＿している。

8. 水みたいな味＿＿＿＿する。

9. モデルのようなスタイル＿＿＿＿している。

10. いいかんじ＿＿＿＿する。

E. You have just concocted a tasty new dish. Describe its smell, appearance, and taste, comparing each of them to something people can relate to.

[例] この料理はカレーのようなにおいがします。

1. smell: _____

2. appearance: _____

3. taste: _____

F. A strange-looking person has just moved into your neighborhood. Describe how unusual his or her appearance is, including, but not limited to, face, hair style and color, and clothes. (You may draw a picture, too, if you like.)

[例] 耳はぞう (*elephant*) のように大きいです。

1. _____

2. _____

3. _____

G. The following are all sentences in the は…が pattern. Fill in the blanks with nouns that would make sense. Be imaginative.

[例] 私は_____がこわい。→ 私は<u>ゴジラ</u> (*Godzilla*) がこわい。

1. 私のがっこうは_____が有名だ。

2. 父は_____が上手だ。

3. てんぷらは_____がむずかしい。

4. 田中さんは_____が長い。

5. カーティスさんは_____が高い。

6. 山口さんは_____がきれいだ。

7. 私のしゅっしん地は_____がいい。

8. このレストランは_____がおいしい。

9. 田中さんは_____が痛い。

10. 私は_____がしたい。

11. 私の部屋は_____が見える。

12. 私の部屋は_____が聞こえる。

13. 日本語は_____がむずかしい。

H. Interview a classmate and ask about the following. Write your partner's answers in the spaces indicated.

Name of the classmate you interviewed: _____

[例] favorite music
スミスさんはクラシックが好きです。

1. favorite academic subjects _____

2. athletic skills _____

3. foods that he or she cannot eat _____

4. what he or she wants to do right now _____

5. what sounds, if any, can be heard in his or her room at night _____

6. what can be seen out of the bedroom window _____

I. Complete the following sentences using a は…が… construction.

1. 私は _____

2. 私の日本語の先生は _____

3. 母は _____

4. 私のとなりの人は _____

5. 私の大学は _____

J. An elderly Japanese couple has asked you for advice on places to visit in the United States and Canada. These people are interested in some states and provinces, but they have no idea what they are like. Please tell them something special about each of the following states, using the は…が construction.

[例] (アイオワ) アイオワはとうもろこし (corn) がおいしいです。
(フロリダ) フロリダは冬が暖かくていいですよ。

1. ハワイ _____

2. オレゴン _____

3. カリフォルニア _____

4. テキサス _____

5. バーモント _____

6. ユーコン _____

7. ケベック _____

8. ルイジアナ _____

9. Your own state or region (if not included above) _____

K. What is your idea of a good-looking man or good-looking woman? Describe your ideal type, using at least three sentences.

[例] うでと指が長くて、つめがきれいです。

1. _____

2. _____

3. _____

Vocabulary and Grammar 4B: Feeling and Emotions

A. Choose the descriptions of the facial expressions that pertain to the following conditions. In some cases, more than one choice may be appropriate.

Useful Vocabulary: せいせき *grades,* おばけ *ghost,* おとす *to drop,* うそをつく *to tell a lie*

1. _____ せいせきがよかったです。
2. _____ おばけを見ました。
3. _____ 車がこわれました。
4. _____ お金をおとしました。
5. _____ 家族がみんな旅行に行きました。
6. _____ 明日までにしゅくだいを出さなければ

   なりません。
7. _____ 友だちがうそをつきました。

a. うれしそうな顔をしています。
b. こわそうな
c. かなしそうな
d. さびしそうな
e. イライラしているような
f. 気げんの悪そうな
g. びっくりしたような

B. What would you do in the following situations? Give specific examples, e.g., かなしいとき：私はかなしいときには楽しいえいがを見ます。

1. うれしいとき：_____

   _____

2. かなしいとき：_____

   _____

3. はずかしいとき：_____

   _____

4. こわいとき：_____

   _____

5. さびしいとき：_____

   _____

C. Can you think of a person, either someone you know or a famous person, who fits each of the following descriptions? Give an example of that person's behavior.

[例] はずかしそうな人 →
　　　私のルームメートです。パーティーに行ったとき、だれとも話をしません。

1.　よくストレスをかんじる人

_____

_____

2.　おこりやすい (*easily angered*) 人

_____

_____

3.　よくなく人

_____

_____

4.　よくわらう人

_____

_____

5.　何でも心配するような人

_____

_____

6.　かなしそうな人

_____

_____

7.　プレッシャーに強い人

_____

_____

8.　どこでも、いつでもリラックスできる人

_____

_____

D. Fill in the blanks to complete the sentences using 〜そうです (*it looks…*). You might have to conjugate some words.

1. いつも（元気）＿＿＿＿＿＿＿＿＿＿＿。

2. しけんは（むずかしい）＿＿＿＿＿＿＿＿＿＿＿。

3. このケーキは（おいしくない）＿＿＿＿＿＿＿＿＿＿＿。

4. 今日は（寒い）＿＿＿＿＿＿＿＿＿＿＿。

5. 雨が（ふる）＿＿＿＿＿＿＿＿＿＿＿。

6. このきょうりゅう (*dinosaur*) は（こわい）＿＿＿＿＿＿＿＿＿＿＿。

7. たくさん（食べられる）＿＿＿＿＿＿＿＿＿＿＿。

8. 日本語が（できる）＿＿＿＿＿＿＿＿＿＿＿。

9. 頭が（いい）＿＿＿＿＿＿＿＿＿＿＿。

10. ピアノが（上手）＿＿＿＿＿＿＿＿＿＿＿。

11. 心配することは（ない）＿＿＿＿＿＿＿＿＿＿＿。

E. Change the words in parentheses to either their …よう（な）, 〜そう（な）, or らしい form, depending on which one makes the most sense in the context.

朝起きて、カーテンを開けると、そらがくもっていて、雨が(1. ふる)

＿＿＿＿＿＿＿＿＿ だった。それに、外はとても (2. 寒い)＿＿＿＿＿＿＿＿＿ だった。下から (3. おいしい)＿＿＿＿＿＿＿＿＿ なにおいがしてきた。さとみさんがハムエッグを (4. 作っている)＿＿＿＿＿＿＿＿＿ だった。ダイニングキッチンに行くと、さとみさんは (5. うれしい)＿＿＿＿＿＿＿＿＿ だった。何かとくべつなことがあるのかと聞くと、「ええ」とだけ言った。ボーイフレンドとデートが (6. ある)

＿＿＿＿＿＿＿＿＿。さいきん、かれとのなかがうまくいって (7. いる)

＿＿＿＿＿＿＿＿＿。まもなく、だいすけさんが起きてきた。とても (8. ねむたい

[*sleepy*]) ＿＿＿＿＿＿＿＿＿ な顔をしていた。昨日の夜もおそくまでしごとを (9. していた) ＿＿＿＿＿＿＿＿＿。だいすけさんのしごとはとても (10. きつい [*demanding*])

＿＿＿＿＿＿＿＿＿。だいすけさんは朝起きるとすぐ、コーヒーを飲む。とても (11.

こい [*strong*]) ＿＿＿＿＿＿＿＿＿ なコーヒー。目をさますためにはコーヒーが一番だといつも言っている。さとみさんが作ったハムエッグとトーストを (12. おいしい)

_____ に食べている。だいすけさんはいつもしょくよく (appetite) が (13. ある) _____。山口さんのご主人が朝のさんぽから帰ってきた。ご主人はとてもさんぽが (14. 好き) _____ だ。どんなお天気でも、さんぽに出かける。ご主人のしごとはたいへんだが、いつも (15. 元気) _____ だ。やはり、さんぽをかかさない (not leave out) からだろう。おくさんはいっしょじゃない。さとみさんによると、まだねているということだ。気分が (16. よくない) _____。昨日、くしゃみ (sneeze) をしていたが、かぜがはやっていて (going around)、クラスでもかぜをひいている人が (17. 多い) _____。今年のかぜは (18. ひどい) _____。薬を飲んでも、なかなか (19. なおらない) _____。

F. You are talking with a friend about events or situations that you know only by hearsay. React to your friend's statements with a comment ending in …らしいです。

[例] Your friend: 町田さんはお兄さんがいるそうですね。
You: ええ、とてもハンサムらしいです。

1. Your friend: 昨日パーティーがあったそうですね。

   You: ええ、とても _____

2. Your friend: 明日は雨がふるそうですね。

   You: ええ、風も _____

3. Your friend: カワムラさんは車を買ったそうですね。

   You: ええ、とても _____

4. Your friend: 先週ブラウンさんはおきなわに行ったそうですね。

   You: ええ、_____

5. Your friend: 昨日、ギブソンさんはしゅっせき (show up) しませんでしたね。

   You: ええ、_____

G. Answer these questions in the negative.

[例] 外は風が強いですか。→
いいえ、強くなさそうです。

今日は雨がふりますか。→
いいえ、ふりそうじゃないです。
or
いいえ、ふらなさそうです。

1. このしけんはむずかしいですか。

_____

2. 今日は早く帰れますか。

_____

3. このかんじが読めますか。

_____

4. 新しい先生はきびしいですか。

_____

5. 友だちは元気ですか。

_____

6. お父さんはアメリカが好きですか。

_____

H. There has been a murder. An American businessman was killed in his apartment in Aoyama. You are a detective called to the murder scene to investigate the case. Study the picture and answer the questions by making guesses from evidence in the picture. (Use ⋯よう／みたい.) Give the reasons for your answers.

Useful Vocabulary: きんこ *safe* (*n.*)

[例] この部屋に人が何人いたんでしょうか。
2人のようですよ、グラスが2つありますから。

1. どこから出ていったんでしょうか。

_____

2. さっき (*just previously*) この部屋にいたのは男でしょうか、女でしょうか。

_____

3. ひがいしゃ (*victim*) は、出かけるところだったんでしょうか。帰ってきたところ
だったんでしょうか。

_____

4. きょうき (*weapon*) は何だったんでしょうか。

_____

5. ぬすまれた (*stolen*) ものはあるんでしょうか。

_____

I. Rewrite the following sentences using 〜そう, よう, or らしい, depending on the background information described under each subheading. Pay attention to the tenses of the verbs and adjectives, too.

1. 今日はとても寒いです。

    a. You have just looked outside. It's snowing and windy, and you can see icicles.

    _____

    b. You look out the window and see that your neighbor is going out all bundled up.

    _____

    c. You have not been outside today, but you have heard on the radio that the temperature has dropped to –10 degrees.

    _____

2. 雨がふります。

    a. You didn't see or hear it rain, but when you got up, you saw puddles on the sidewalk.

    _____

    b. It's been cloudy, and now it's getting really dark, even though it's the middle of a summer afternoon.

    _____

    c. One part of the country had been suffering from drought. You heard on today's news, however, that the drought is over.

    _____

    d. Your friend is planning to go hiking in the mountains tomorrow. You have heard on the radio, however, that it will rain in that region tomorrow, so you warn your friend.

    _____

3. あのアパートは静かじゃありません。
    (You are thinking about moving to a certain apartment, so you visited it yesterday. When you were there, you didn't hear much noise, but . . .)

    a. You were told that one of the buildings nearby houses students who play music in an alternative band and practice every evening.

    _____

    b. One neighbor whom you talked to was constantly yawning and telling you that it's hard to get a good night's sleep in that building because the radiators are always clanging.

    _____

    c. The apartment is located in an area close to the main road.

    _____

    d. Someone who lived there before told you it was noisy there.

    _____

Vocabulary and Grammar 4C: Health and Illness

A. Match the following words with the appropriate verbs or adjective, and fill in whatever else is necessary to produce a complete sentence.

[例] <u>h.</u>　頭 →　<u>頭が痛いです。</u>

1. _____ 食よく	_____	a.	ひく
2. _____ 学校	_____	b.	行く
3. _____ かぜ	_____	c.	見てもらう
4. _____ 病気	_____	d.	のむ
5. _____ けが	_____	e.	なる
6. _____ はき気	_____	f.	する
7. _____ 入院	_____	g.	休む
8. _____ 薬	_____	h.	痛い
9. _____ 薬屋	_____	i.	ない
10. _____ いしゃ	_____		
11. _____ 歯	_____		

B. Use the causative form to ask for permission to do the following things.

[例]　テレビが見たいです。
　　　テレビを見させてください。

1. 本が買いたいです。 _____

2. 9時にねたいです。 _____

3. あそびたいです。 _____

4. 明日は休みたいです。 _____

5. しけんを明日うけたいです。 _____

6. ビールが飲みたいです。 _____

7. アイスクリームが食べたいです。 _____

8. 近いうちに (in the near future)、また来たいです。 _____

9. けっこんしたいです。 _____

10. しごとをやめたいです。 _____

11. 車を運転したいです。 _____

C. Some high school students are complaining about the chores their parents make them do and the obligations they have in their family. Below are the orders that the parents continually give their sons and daughters. Rewrite each one as a young person's complaint about what the parents force him or her to do.

[例] Parents: みんなの洋服を洗たくしなさい。

High school student: りょうしんは私にみんなの洋服を洗たくさせるんです。

1. Parents: 朝ごはんを作りなさい。

   High school student: りょうしんは私に _____

2. Parents: 部屋をそうじしなさい。

   High school student: りょうしんは私に _____

3. Parents: 手がみを出してきなさい。

   High school student: りょうしんは私に _____

4. Parents: 休まないでしごとをつづけなさい。

   High school student: りょうしんは私に _____

5. Parents: コーラじゃなくて、ぎゅうにゅうを飲みなさい。

   High school student: りょうしんは私に _____

6. Parents: テレビを見る前に、しゅくだいをしなさい。

   High school student: りょうしんは私に _____

7. Parents: にもつを持ちなさい。

   High school student: りょうしんは私に _____

8. Parents: 10時までに家に帰りなさい。

   High school student: りょうしんは私に _____

9. Parents: ソファを動かしなさい。

   High school student: りょうしんは私に _____

10. Parents: 窓を開けなさい。

    High school student: りょうしんは私に _____

D. Suppose you got hold of Aladdin's lamp. What three things would you make the genie do? Be as creative as you can, but do not attempt structures and vocabulary that you have no knowledge of. Stay within your current ability.

[例] 私を日本へつれて行かせます。

1. _____
2. _____
3. _____

E. Do you know the story of Cinderella and her mean stepmother and stepsisters, who made her do all the household chores? List three things that you think they made her do.

[例] お姉さんはシンデレラにアイロンをかけさせました。

1. _____
2. _____
3. _____

F. Many parents are strict, but even the strictest parents often let children do certain things they want to do. Write three things that your parents let you do when you were little.

[例] 私のりょうしんは、時々ワインを一口 (one sip) だけ飲ませてくれました。

1. _____
2. _____
3. _____

G. Pets need proper health care, too. Suppose you have a very old dog (or cat, bird, or anything else you like), and you have to leave it with a housesitter for three days while you are out of town on business. What three things would you like the sitter to make/let your pet do?

[例] あまりたくさん食べさせないでください。

1. _____
2. _____
3. _____

H. When speaking Japanese to her non-Japanese friends, Midori Momoi occasionally uses words that they don't understand. Assume in each of the following exchanges that the person she is talking to does not understand the underlined word. Have that person ask what the word means.

Useful Vocabulary: こくばん消し *chalkboard eraser,* パルコ *the name of an upscale department store,* きゅうか *vacation,* きゅうこう *cancellation of classes,* かごしま *a city at the southern end of Kyushu,* がくちょう (学長) *school principal or university president*

[例]　Momoi: 横山さんはいますか。

　　Lois Johnson: 横山さんというのはだれですか。

1.　Momoi: こくばん消しをください。

　　Cody Smith: こくばん消し＿＿＿＿＿＿＿＿＿＿＿＿＿＿＿＿＿ ですか。

2.　Momoi: 日本に行ったとき、パルコに行きましたか。

　　Lois Johnson: パルコ＿＿＿＿＿＿＿＿＿＿＿＿＿＿＿＿＿＿ ですか。

3.　Momoi: きゅうかには何をするんですか。

　　Jin Mi Kim: きゅうか＿＿＿＿＿＿＿＿＿＿＿＿＿＿＿＿＿ ですか。

4.　Momoi: 明日はきゅうこうですね。

　　Peggy Yu: きゅうこう＿＿＿＿＿＿＿＿＿＿＿＿＿＿＿＿ ですか。

5.　Momoi: 私はかごしまのしゅっしんです。

　　Antonio Coronado: かごしま＿＿＿＿＿＿＿＿＿＿＿＿＿＿ ですか。

6.　Momoi: 学長はいますか。

　　Hans Kraus: がくちょう＿＿＿＿＿＿＿＿＿＿＿＿＿＿＿ ですか。

I. You have just started corresponding with a Japanese student, but this student's first letter includes several expressions and words that you do not know and cannot guess. Read the letter and write down three questions about the unfamiliar words and phrases using "…というのは interrogative ですか" so you can ask your Japanese teacher about them in Japanese later.

　私のふるさとは岡山です。岡山は瀬戸内海に面していて、景色もとてもきれいだし、魚もおいしいです。気候も温暖で、いろいろなくだものがとれるので有名です。

1.　＿＿＿＿＿＿＿＿＿＿＿＿＿＿＿＿＿＿＿＿＿＿＿＿＿＿＿＿＿＿＿＿

2.　＿＿＿＿＿＿＿＿＿＿＿＿＿＿＿＿＿＿＿＿＿＿＿＿＿＿＿＿＿＿＿＿

3.　＿＿＿＿＿＿＿＿＿＿＿＿＿＿＿＿＿＿＿＿＿＿＿＿＿＿＿＿＿＿＿＿

J. Make up dialogues, following the example given.

[例] 北海道/ どこ
   — 北海道はどこですか。
   — どこにあるかしりません。

1. ハリスさんの日本語の先生／どなた

   _____

   _____

2. マダガスカル／どんな所

   _____

   _____

3. 町田さんのボーイフレンド／だれ

   _____

   _____

4. まっ茶＊／何

   _____

   _____

5. カワムラさんがしゅくだいをしなかったのは／なぜ

   _____

   _____

6. きまつしけん(*final exam*) ／ いつ

   _____

   _____

7. いいCDプレーヤー／いくらぐらい

   _____

   _____

8. 安いスーパー／どこ

   _____

   _____

_____

＊ まっ茶 is the type of green tea used in the tea ceremony.

K. Someone has asked you the following questions. Unfortunately, you don't know the answers to any of them. Respond appropriately.

[例] Q: この人はかんごふですか。
A: さあ、かんごふかどうかわかりません。

Q: ジョンソンさんはいつそつぎょう (graduate) しますか。
A: いつそつぎょうするかわかりません。

1. Q: 明日は雨がふるでしょうか。

   A: さあ、＿＿＿＿＿＿＿＿＿＿＿＿＿＿＿＿＿ わかりません。

2. Q: 先生は何が一番好きですか。

   A: さあ、＿＿＿＿＿＿＿＿＿＿＿＿＿＿＿＿＿ わかりません。

3. Q: この人の名前は田中でしたか。

   A: さあ、＿＿＿＿＿＿＿＿＿＿＿＿＿＿＿＿＿ おぼえていません。

4. Q: 明日はしけんがありますか。

   A: さあ、＿＿＿＿＿＿＿＿＿＿＿＿＿＿＿＿＿ しりません。

5. Q: いつしけんがあるんですか。

   A: さあ、＿＿＿＿＿＿＿＿＿＿＿＿＿＿＿＿＿ わすれました。

6. Q: キムさんのおじいさんは入院しましたか。

   A: さあ、＿＿＿＿＿＿＿＿＿＿＿＿＿＿＿＿＿ わかりません。

L. How would you ask a classmate whether he or she knew or could tell you the answers to the following questions? Write the questions you would ask, using the embedded question construction.

[例] your instructor's age
先生は何さいかしっていますか。or …教えてください。

1. where your instructor was born

   ＿＿＿＿＿＿＿＿＿＿＿＿＿＿＿＿＿＿＿＿＿＿＿＿＿＿＿＿＿＿＿＿＿＿

2. what your instructor's office phone number is

   ＿＿＿＿＿＿＿＿＿＿＿＿＿＿＿＿＿＿＿＿＿＿＿＿＿＿＿＿＿＿＿＿＿＿

3. where some famous person of your choice lives

   ＿＿＿＿＿＿＿＿＿＿＿＿＿＿＿＿＿＿＿＿＿＿＿＿＿＿＿＿＿＿＿＿＿＿

4. what this famous person's phone number is

   ＿＿＿＿＿＿＿＿＿＿＿＿＿＿＿＿＿＿＿＿＿＿＿＿＿＿＿＿＿＿＿＿＿＿

5. what kind of car the famous person drives

   _____

6. what one of your classmates (you choose) ate for lunch yesterday

   _____

7. what time one of your classmates got up this morning

   _____

8. who the best friend (しんゆう) of one of your classmates is

   _____

M. A classmate of yours is sick and staying home today. Go see or call your classmate and ask three questions concerning the symptoms of the illness and what he or she has been doing about it. Then report here what questions you asked, following the example.

[例] 熱があるかどうか聞きました。or 熱が何度か聞きました。

(The actual question you asked was either 熱がありますか。or 熱は何度ですか。)

1. _____

2. _____

3. _____

N. Make a conclusion from the following information using はず.

[例] あの人は日本にりゅうがく (study abroad) していました。
だから、あの人は日本語を話すはずです。

1. カワムラさんはアメリカで生まれました。

   だから、_____

2. 明日しけんです。

   だから、_____

3. これは先生が書きました。

   だから、_____

4. この車はイタリアで作られました。

   だから、_____

5. ギブソンさんは昨日アメリカへ帰りました。

   だから、_____

6. このレストランはあのレストランより高いです。

   だから、_____

7. ブラウンさんは毎日スポーツをしています。

   だから、_____

8. 今日は日曜日です。

   だから、_____

O. Following the example, complete these sentences by using はずです or はずがありません.

   [例] むら山さんは大学でフランス文学をせんこうしましたから →
   むら山さんは大学でフランス文学をせんこうしましたから、<u>フランス語が
   読めるはずです</u>。

1. このとけいはスイスせいだから、_____

2. 今日は土曜日だから、_____

3. カワムラさんはよく図書館へ行くから、_____

4. かのじょはアメリカの大学をそつぎょうしたから、_____

5. かれは去年にけっこんしたから、_____

6. みむらさんはかぎをなくした (lost the key) から、_____

7. はやしさんは今、あまりお金がないから、_____

8. さのさんはもうしごとをしていないから、_____

P. It is 3:00 P.M. on Saturday, and Cody Smith is bored. It is raining heavily outside, he has read all the books he owns, his stereo is being repaired, and there's nothing interesting on TV. He's thinking of calling some classmates and asking if they want to do something. He is now thinking about what everyone said yesterday, so he can decide whom to call. Write in Japanese what everyone *can be expected to be doing now*.

   [例] Peggy Yu: She teaches Chinese every Saturday afternoon.
   ユーさんは今中国語を教えているはずです。

1. Maria Nakajima: She was very sick in bed with the flu yesterday.

   _____

2. Midori Momoi: Cody saw her yesterday afternoon going to the train station with a suitcase.

   _____

3. Hans Kraus: He said he was going to take a big test on Monday.

   _____

4. Antonio Coronado: His parents are scheduled to arrive at the airport from Mexico around 5:00 P.M.

_____

5. Jin Mi Kim: She was planning to go on a hike.

_____

Whom do you think Cody is going to call? _____

Q. An acquaintance has made the following statements, but you are pretty sure that the statement is wrong. Respond using はずがないんですが.

[例] A: 昨日がっこうで山口さんに会いました。

B: え、それはおかしいですね。山口さんは病気だからがっこうに来るはずがないんですが。

1. A: この車はやすかったです。

B: え、それはおかしいですね。その車は _____

_____

2. A: カワムラさんはお父さんといっしょに買い物に行きましたよ。

B: え、それはおかしいですね。カワムラさんのお父さんは _____

_____

3. A: ユーさんはもうがっこうへ行きましたよ。

B: え、それはおかしいですね。今日は _____

_____

4. A: 今日ははやしさんのたんじょう日ですね。

B: え、それはおかしいですね。はやしさんのたんじょう日は _____

_____

5. A: みむらさんはお金がないそうです。

B: え、それはおかしいですね。みむらさんは _____

_____

6. A: ジョンソンさんは今アルバイトをしています。

B: え、それはおかしいですね。ジョンソンさんは _____

_____

R. When you know a person well, you have a pretty good idea of what he or she is likely or unlikely to do. Think of your best friend and write whether that friend could be expected to do the following things. Give a reason for your assumption.

[例] skip class today
今日はしけんがあるから、クラスを休むはずがありません。
or
今日はしけんがあるんですが、Ｘさんはしけんがきらいですから、休むはずです。
or
来るはずがありません。

1. get married next month _____
_____

2. quit school _____
_____

3. go to Japan next year _____
_____

4. break up with boy/girl friend _____
_____

5. go to the homecoming dance _____
_____

6. not eat any dessert for the next three months _____
_____

S. What could you do in Japanese if you studied it hard for four years? Write three sentences using はず. The following are some examples of things you may or may not be able to do: translate (ほんやくする) Japanese books, write letters to friends, write research papers (ろんぶん), interpret (通やくする) for the Japanese prime minister (そうりだいじん), show a friend's mother around town (あんないする), fully understand Japanese movies without subtitles (じまく), read newspapers, and so on.

[例] 日本語のろんぶんはまだ書けないはずです。
友だちと日本語で話せるはずです。

1. _____

2. _____

3. _____

Chapter 4 Review

A. Do you know people with the following personality traits? Describe them by using comparisons. If you can, give an example of a time when the person exhibited that personality trait.

[例] けち (*stingy*)
私のおじはスクルージのようにけちです。
けっこんきねんび (*wedding anniversary*) におばをファーストフードレストランにつれていって、ハンバーガーを食べさせました。

1. いじわる (*mean*) _____

   _____

2. つめたい (*coldhearted*) _____

   _____

3. 明るい (*cheerful*) _____

   _____

4. やさしい (*nice, kind*) _____

   _____

5. じゅんしん (*pure, naive, innocent*) _____

   _____

B. Tomorrow morning you are going to meet a Japanese person for the first time at the airport. You are talking with this person on the phone now. Since the two of you have never met before, you need to describe yourself in terms of your hair, eyes, and any other physical features so that he or she can recognize you. Write at least three sentences describing yourself.

1. _____

2. _____

3. _____

C. When do you think you may have had the following expressions on your face? Give one example from your real life.

[例] うれしそうな顔
しけんでまん点 (*perfect score*) をとったときに、うれしそうなかおをしていたと思います。

1. かなしそうな顔: _____

   _____

2. イライラしているような顔^{かお}: _____

_____

3. おどろいているような顔^{かお}: _____

_____

4. おこっているような顔^{かお}: _____

_____

5. うれしそうな顔^{かお}: _____

_____

D. The Japanese term for apple-polishing or brown-nosing is ごますり (*sesame grinding*), from the phrase ごまをする. What do you think a "sesame grinding" student might say to the teacher? Limit your answers to the offers to help the teacher that such a student would make, and write four things using the causative 〜 てください(ませんか)/いただけますか。

[例] 先生のお書きになった本を読ませていただけますか。

1. _____

2. _____

3. _____

4. _____

E. Under what circumstances do you feel the following emotions or have the following reactions?

[例] ストレスをかんじる →
しけんがたくさんあるとき、ストレスをかんじます。

1. おこりやすく (*easily angered*) なる

_____

2. なく

_____

3. わらう

_____

4. 心配^{しんぱい}する

_____

5. さびしくなる

   _____

6. がっかりする (*be disappointed*)

   _____

7. はずかしくなる

   _____

8. こわくなる

   _____

F. Choose any two members of your family and make five contrastive statements about them, using the は…が construction.

[例] 姉はせが高いですが、妹はせがひくいです。

1. _____
2. _____
3. _____
4. _____
5. _____

G. Fill in the blanks with a form of either よう (or みたい), 〜そう, or らしい.

[例] 今朝の新聞によると、ひどい交通事故があった<u>らしいです。</u>

1. はっきり見えませんが、あの人は島田さんじゃない_____。

2. そのコンピュータはすごく便利_____ です。

3. あら、あの子どもが木からおち_____。

4. ちょうぼ (*ledger*) を見ると、だれかがお金を使いこんでいる (*embezzle*)

   _____。

5. 外は寒_____。

6. はんにん (*criminal*) はこの窓から出ていった_____。

7. よく使う_____ 物はつくえの上に出してあります。

H. Studying at a foreign university can be very stressful. A Japanese classmate of yours, who has been in the United States for less than a year, tells you that he has not been feeling well recently. Give him some advice for maintaining good health, both physically and psychologically. Write at least three suggestions.

[例] 夜おそくまで勉強しないで、早くねた方がいいですよ。毎日7時間はねてください。

1. _____

2. _____

3. _____

I. Do you know the symptoms of the following illnesses or conditions? Describe as many as you can, but write at least one symptom for each.

[例] 水ぼうそう(chicken pox) → ひふがかゆいです。

1. インフルエンザ (the flu) _____

2. 盲腸炎 (appendicitis) _____

3. 胃潰瘍 (stomach ulcers) _____

4. 結膜炎 (conjunctivitis or "pink eye") _____

5. 心臓麻痺 (heart attack) _____

J. Under which of these conditions would you go to a doctor? Go to the emergency room at a hospital? Just stay home and take care of yourself? Write D (for doctor), E (for emergency room), or H (for home care) for each condition below.

Useful Vocabulary: こぼす *to spill,* 下がる *to decrease, to go down,* おちる *to fall from a height*

1. ____ 昨日からげりをしています。熱はありません。

2. ____ 2日ぐらい前から、食べるとはくので、何も食べられません。

3. ____ 100度のお湯を1リットル、足にこぼしました。

4. ____ 頭がとても痛いです。熱も高いです。アスピリンを飲んでいますが、ぜんぜん熱が下がりません。

5. ____ せきがでて、鼻がつまっています(stuffed)。

6. ____ 昨日、高いところからおちました。けがはないようでしたが、今日は、足首がとても痛いです。

7. ____ 今、交通事故にあいました。けがはないようですが、首が痛いです。

CHAPTER **5**

LIFE AND CAREERS

人生<ruby>じんせい</ruby>とキャリア

Listening Comprehension Activities

Vocabulary and Grammar 5A: From Cradle to Grave

A. Listen to Masao Hayashi recounting his life past and present, and his future plans. Then write down in Japanese what happened—and what he hopes will happen—in his life for each age listed.

2 さい：

7 さい：

13 さい：

16 さい：

19 さい：

23 さい：

26 さい：

35 さい：

B. Mei Lin Chin came to Hitomi Machida's house and found her in tears in front of the TV. Listen to their conversation and find the answers that best complete the following sentences.

1. When the heroine was a baby, _____

2. When she was in kindergarten, _____

3. When she was in high school, _____

4. After graduating from high school, _____

5. At the work place, _____

6. After quitting her job, _____

   a. her parents got married
   b. her parents got divorced
   c. her mother left Mayumi
   d. her father got remarried
   e. her grandparents died
   f. she went to college
   g. she got a job
   h. she fell in love with someone
   i. she got engaged
   j. she got married
   k. she disappeared
   l. she died

C. Ms. Suzuki, Ms. Yamaguchi's neighbor, has a one-year-old daughter, Ayako. Listen to Ms. Suzuki and Ms. Yamaguchi's conversation and write in the letters of things that Ayako can do now.

Useful Vocabulary: おむつ *diaper*

Ayako can _____ now.

a. eat anything
b. walk
c. run fast
d. understand what has been said

e. talk a lot
f. write hiragana
g. go to the bathroom by herself
h. read books

D. Ms. Sato, Ms. Yamaguchi's neighbor, has a seven-year-old son, Taro. Listen to her monologue about her son, and answer the following questions.

1. List 4 things Taro can do now. _____

_____

2. List 2 things Taro cannot do yet. _____

_____

3. What does Taro want to be in the future and why? _____

_____

4. Why doesn't his mother approve of Taro's plan? _____

_____

5. What does his mother hope he will be? _____

_____

E. Listen as Professor Yokoi asks her students about problems they had when they first came to Japan. Then fill in the chart in English.

Useful Vocabulary: ふとる *to get fat, gain weight* やせる *to get thin, lose weight*

	PROBLEMS	EFFORT/SOLUTION	RESULT
Kawamura	Couldn't understand conversation with friends.	1.	2.
Gibson	3.	4.	Still can't eat natto.
Curtis	5.	Jogged and ate healthy food.	6.

F. Listen to the morning schedule of Lady Hiroko, and then fill in the blanks to complete the summary.

Lady Hiroko _____ at six o'clock, and _____ for health. For

breakfast, she _____ toast and _____, and _____

tea. Then she _____ the newspaper, and because she _____ English

and French, she also _____ CNN news.

G. Listen as a company secretary talks about the president of Toyoshiba Automobile Company. Then mark each statement true (T) or false (F).

1. _____ The president of Toyoshiba is healthy and energetic.

2. _____ He jogs every morning in the nearby park.

3. _____ His wife cooks a big breakfast for him.

4. _____ He has meetings to attend in the morning.

5. _____ He is a very strict man.

6. _____ He is planning to open a new branch office.

H. Listen to a wedding speech and complete the following statements, filling in the blanks in English.

1. Mr. Yamada was born May _____, 19_____.

2. He _____ from Higashi _____ in 1989 with

_____.

3. He came to the U.S. because _____ in the summer of 1989.

4. Now he is _____.

5. He likes _____.

6. His personality is _____.

Vocabulary and Grammar 5B: Careers and Occupations

A. Choose the right occupation for each description read on the tape.

1. _____   3. _____   5. _____   7. _____   9. _____

2. _____   4. _____   6. _____   8. _____   10. _____

a. きょうし   e. びようし   i. かしゅ
b. けいさつかん   f. だいく   j. さっか
c. がか   g. いしゃ
d. つうやく   h. しゅふ

B. Who would most likely say the following lines? Choose the occupation that best matches each line.

1. _____
2. _____
3. _____
4. _____
5. _____

a. ベルボーイ
b. 運転手
c. ウェーター
d. デパートの店員
e. 医者
f. スーパーのレジ

C. A counselor is conferring with a student. Listen to their conversation and learn what advice the counselor gives to the student. Then mark each statement true (T) or false (F).

The counselor advises the student to:

1. _____ go to bed as early as 7:00.

2. _____ take a light breakfast like yogurt.

3. _____ make many friends.

4. _____ speak out about everything.

5. _____ keep a diary.

6. _____ study hard independently.

7. _____ not depend on the counselor too much.

D. Professor Yokoi lives a busy life. She is a wife, a mother of two children, and teacher of Japanese, and yet she rarely seems to be under stress. Listen as she tells how she manages all this, and circle the best answer for each question.

Useful Vocabulary: 分ける *to divide, to separate*

What does she say about the following things?

1. About bringing work home:
   a. wants to work at home
   b. does not bring home any work
   c. brings back home just a little every day

2. About eating out:
   a. likes to eat out   b. tries not to eat out   c. doesn't like eating out, but does it often

3. About teaching children cooking:
   a. wants them to learn how to cook
   b. wants them to concentrate on studying instead
   c. leaves them in charge of cooking

4. About cleaning and doing laundry:
   a. does it every day   b. does it every other day   c. does nothing on weekdays

5. About going to children's sports games on Saturdays:
   a. it is her husband's job   b. goes when she has time   c. goes with her husband

6. About doing house chores on Sundays:
   a. finishes them all by herself   b. does them with husband's help   c. the whole family does them

7. About activities on Sunday afternoons:
   a. relaxes with family   b. chats with family   c. goes out with family

Vocabulary and Grammar 5C: In the Workplace

A. A juku (cram school) is looking for a new English teacher, and Heather Gibson has applied for the job. Listen as she is interviewed and choose the best answer to each question.

1. As for teaching experience, Gibson _____.
   a. has none   b. has done tutoring   c. was a professor in the U.S.

2. She wants to _____.
   a. teach adults   b. babysit children   c. teach children

3. She got to know about this job _____.
   a. through her friend   b. by the mail   c. by advertisement

4. Gibson came to Japan _____ year(s) ago.
   a. one   b. one and a half   c. two

5. Gibson is asked to teach _____ hours a week.
   a. 3   b. 5   c. 7

6. Gibson is coming to the juku at _____ next Monday.
   a. 4:00   b. 5:00   c. 6:00

B. Listen to a letter Cody Smith wrote to his former teacher, who is coming to Los Angeles soon. Then pick out and circle the questions that Cody Smith asked in the letter.

In the letter Cody Smith is asking his former teacher:

1. If he is busy

2. If he will write him back

3. When he is coming

4. What time his plane arrives

5. If he is going to rent a car

6. What he wants to see in Los Angeles

7. If he plays golf

8. If he is good at sports

9. What kind of food he wants to eat

10. What his phone number is

C. You are in a quiz show. Circle the best answer to each question. You may get some help from your teacher.

1.   a. the national anthem   b. Happy Birthday to You   c. Mary Had a Little Lamb

2.   a. Constitution   b. Thomas Brother's Guide   c. Bible

3.   a. 早くしなさい。   b. いい子ね。   c. たくさん食べなさい。

4.   a. The Seven Samurai   b. Shall We Dance?   c. Totoro

D. Who would say these lines when talking about their jobs? Choose the occupation that best matches each line.

1. _____
2. _____
3. _____
4. _____
5. _____

a. けいさつかん
b. やきゅうせんしゅ
c. かんごふ
d. ゆうびんきょくいん
e. かしゅ
f. きょうし
g. ウェートレス
h. かいしゃいん

E. Listen to Kimura-san, senpai, an alumnus giving a talk to high school students. Then answer the following questions.

Useful Vocabulary: きめる *to decide*, 自ゆう *free(dom)*

1. 木村さんの今の仕事は何ですか。
   a. りゅう学カウンセラー
   b. 会社いん
   c. 学生

2. 木村さんは、高校の時、先生やりょうしんから、どんなことについて言われていましたか。
   a. 人生のゴール
   b. せいせき
   c. クラブかつどう

3. 木村さんの高校生活はどんな生活でしたか。
   a. 楽しかった
   b. つまらなかった
   c. ひまだった

4. 木村さんは高校生の時、どんな生活をしたいと思っていましたか。

   a. アルバイトのたくさんできる生活

   b. あそぶ生活

   c. 自由な生活

5. 木村さんがアメリカへ行ったのは、なぜですか。

   a. お父さんに行かせられたから

   b. 自分が行きたかったから

   c. 友達がいっしょに行こうと言ったから

6. 木村さんの人生を変えたのは何ですか。

   a. アメリカに遊びに行ったこと

   b. じゅけん勉強したこと

   c. 先生のアドバイス

7. 木村さんの友だちは、中学の時と大学の時とでは、どう変わりましたか。

   a. 静かだった → しっかりしていた

   b. 元気だった → つかれていた

   c. よく勉強していた → あまり勉強しなかった

8. 木村さんの友だちは勉強のほかに何をしていましたか。

   a. アルバイト

   b. ボランティアかつどう

   c. both a and b

9. 日本人のりょうしんの多くの人は子どもに何をしてほしいと思っているそうですか。

   a. いい大学へ入って、いいところに就職してほしい。

   b. はやくしあわせな結婚をしてほしい。

   c. 社会のために働いてほしい。

10. このスピーチの中で、木村さんが一番言いたいことは何ですか。

   a. アメリカの教育が一番だ。

   b. 自分のしたいことは自分で考えてきめたほうがいい。

   c. 日本の社会では学歴が大切だ。

Kanji Practice and Exercises

extra study (handwritten in red)

1	校 校	コウ、キョウ school; (printing) proof
	学校：がっこう (school)　小学校：しょうがっこう (elementary school)　中学校：ちゅうがっこう (middle [junior high] school)　高校：こうこう (high school)	

2	卒 卒	ソツ soldier, private; sudden; come to an end; die; graduate
	卒業：そつぎょう (graduation)　卒園：そつえん (graduation from kindergarten)	

3	業 業	ギョウ business, trade, industry; undertaking　ゴウ karma　わざ a work, deed, act, performance, trick
	卒業：そつぎょう (graduation)　*終業式：しゅうぎょうしき (ceremony marking the end of the term)	

4	仕 仕	シ、ジ serve, work for
	仕事：しごと (work)　仕方がない：しかたがない (there's nothing that can be done about it)	

5	就 就	シュウ、ジュ、つ-く settle in; take (a seat/position); depart; study (under a teacher)　つ-ける place, appoint　～に-つ-いて concerning ～, about ～
	就職：しゅうしょく (getting a job)	

6	職	職	ショク employment, job, occupation, office

就職する：しゅうしょくする (to get a job)
職場：しょくば (workplace)
職業：しょくぎょう (profession)

7	退	退	タイ、しりぞ-く retreat　　しりぞ-ける drive away, repel の-く get out of the way, go away の-ける get rid of, remove　　ひ-く retreat; subside

退職する：たいしょくする (to retire)
退学する：たいがくする (to quit school)
退院する：たいいんする (to leave the hospital)
中退する：ちゅうたいする (to quit in the middle)

8	育	育	イク、そだ-てる、はぐく-む raise, rear, bring up そだ-て bringing up, raising　そだ-つ be raised, be brought up, grow up そだ-ち upbringing; growth

教育：きょういく (education)
体育館：たいいくかん (gymnasium)
日本で育ちました：にほんでそだちました (grew up in Japan)

9	若	若	ジャク、ニャク、わか-い young も-しくは or

若い：わかい (young)
若者：わかもの (young person)

10	老	老	ロウ old age お-いる、ふ-ける grow old お-い old age; old man

老人：ろうじん (elderly person)
老いる：おいる (to grow old)

11	愛	愛	アイ love; (as prefix) beloved, favorite　　め-でる love; admire, appreciate いと-しい dear, beloved　　まな- beloved, favorite

動物を愛する：どうぶつをあいする (to love animals)
愛しています：あいしています (love[s])
愛読する：あいどくする (to read with pleasure)

12	恋 恋	レン、こい love こ-う be in love こい-しい dear, beloved			
	恋人：こいびと (lover) 恋愛：れんあい (romantic love)		恋	恋	
13	初 初	ショ、はじ-め beginning はじ-めて for the first time はつ-、うい- first~ 〜そ-める、〜ぞ-める begin to 〜			
	年の初め：としのはじめ (beginning of the year) ✳ 初恋：はつこい (first love) 初夏：しょか (the beginning of summer) 初めて：はじめて (for the first time)		初	初	
14	結 結	ケツ、ケッ、ケチ、むす-ぶ tie, bind; conclude (a contract); bear (fruit) ゆ-わえる bind, tie ゆ-う do up (one's hair)			
	結婚：けっこん (marriage) ✳ 結局：けっきょく (after all)		結	結	
15	婚 婚	コン marriage			
	✳ 婚約する：こんやくする (to become engaged) 結婚する：けっこんする (to get married) ✳ 新婚旅行：しんこんりょこう (honeymoon)		婚	婚	
16	式 式	シキ ceremony, rite; formula, expression (in math); (as suffix) type, style, system			
	結婚式：けっこんしき (marriage ceremony) 卒業式：そつぎょうしき (graduation ceremony) ✳ 洋式：ようしき (Western style)		式	式	
17	研 研	ケン、と-ぐ whet, hone, sharpen; polish; wash (rice)			
	研究：けんきゅう (research)		研	研	

18	究 究	キュウ、きわ-める investigate thoroughly/exhaustively			
	研究室：けんきゅうしつ (professor's office) 研究所：けんきゅうじょ (research institute)		究	究	
19	御 御	ギョ、ゴ、お、おん honorific prefix			
	御研究：ごけんきゅう ([your] research) 御卒業：ごそつぎょう ([your] graduation)		御	御	
20	医 医	イ medicine, healing art; physician			
	医学：いがく (study of medicine) 名医：めいい (famous doctor)		医	医	
21	者 者	シャ、もの person			
	医者：いしゃ (medical doctor) 学者：がくしゃ (scholar) 若者：わかもの (young person)		者	者	
22	師 師	シ teacher, master; army			
	医師：いし (medical doctor) 教師：きょうし (teacher)		師	師	
23	銀 銀	ギン、しろがね silver			
	銀：ぎん (silver) 銀行：ぎんこう (bank) 銀婚式：ぎんこんしき (silver wedding anniversary)		銀	銀	

24	亡 亡	ボウ、モウ dead　　な-くなる die, pass away な-き〜 the late, deceased ほろ-びる perish, come to ruin　　ほろ-ぼす destroy, bring to ruin			
	亡くなる：なくなる (to die [polite]) 死亡する：しぼうする (to die, perish)	亡	亡		
25	忙 忙	ボウ、いそが-しい、せわ-しい busy			
	忙しい：いそがしい (busy)	忙	忙		
26	知 知	チ、し-る (come to) know し-らせ information, news			
	知る：しる (to get to know) 知っている：しっている (knows) 知らせる：しらせる (to inform)	知	知		
27	存 存	ソン、ゾン be, exist			
	存じる：ぞんじる (to know; think [humble]) 存じています：ぞんじています (knows [humble]) 御存知ですか：ごぞんじですか (Do you know) 生存者：せいぞんしゃ (survivor)	存	存		
28	申 申	シン、もう-す say (humble); be named (humble) さる ninth horary sign (monkey)			
	申す：もうす (to say [humble]) 申し上げます：もうしあげます (to say [very 　humble])	申	申		
29	召 召	ショウ summon め-す summon, call for; (honorific) eat, drink, put on, wear, take (a bath/bus), 　buy			
	召す：めす (to summon) 召し上がる：めしあがる (to eat, drink [honorific])	召	召		

30	様 様	ヨウ way, manner; similar, like; condition ～さま Mr./Mrs./Miss/Ms. ～ さま condition　ざま state, predicament, spectacle			
	お父様：おとうさま (your father [honorific]) お母様：おかあさま (your mother [honorific]) 山口ゆり子様：やまぐちゆりこさま (Ms. Yuriko 　Yamaguchi [honorific])				

Kanji Exercises

A. Match each kanji or kanji compound with its closest English equivalent. (Use each letter once.)

1. 愛 _____
2. 医 _____
3. 育 _____
4. 業 _____
5. 銀 _____
6. 結 _____
7. 研究 _____
8. 校 _____
9. 婚 _____

10. 仕 _____
11. 師 _____
12. 式 _____
13. 者 _____
14. 若 _____
15. 就 _____
16. 初 _____
17. 召 _____
18. 職 _____

19. 申 _____
20. 卒 _____
21. 存 _____
22. 退 _____
23. 知 _____
24. 亡 _____
25. 忙 _____
26. 老 _____
27. 様 _____

a. (honorific prefix)　b. eat, drink, wear (honorific)　c. say (humble)　d. bank　e. beginning
f. business　g. busy　h. ceremony　i. die　j. education　k. exist　l. graduate　m. know　n. love
o. marriage　p. medicine　q. Mr./Ms.　r. new　s. occupation　t. old age　u. person　v. raise
w. research　x. retreat　y. school　z. serve　aa. settle in　bb. sharpen　cc. silver　dd. teacher
ee. tie　ff. young

B. Write the hurigana for each kanji or kanji compound.

1. 小学校

　　_____

2. 高校中退

　　_____

3. 卒業式

　　_____

4. 仕事

　　_____

5. 就職

　　_____

6. 退院

　　_____

7. 教育

　　_____

8. 若い

　　_____

9. 苦い

　　_____

10. 老いる

_____

11. 老人

_____

12. 愛

_____

13. 恋愛

_____

14. 初恋

_____

15. 初め

_____

16. 初夏

_____

17. 婚約

_____

18. 結婚

_____

19. 研究

_____

20. 御家族

_____

21. 医者

_____

22. 若者

_____

23. 教師

_____

24. 銀行

_____

25. 亡くなる

_____

26. 死亡

_____

27. 忙しい

_____

28. 知る

_____

29. 御存知ですか。

_____

30. 申し上げる

_____

31. 召し上がる

_____

32. お父様

_____

C. Write the appropriate kanji for the hiragana under the lines.

1. _____ を _____ した _____ に _____ めてヨーロッパへ
       こうこう   そつぎょう   とき   はじ

_____ をしました。
       りょこう

2. _____ が _____ しくて、_____ をするひまもない。
       しごと   いそが   れんあい

3. _____ きな _____ に _____ したい。
    おお   かいしゃ   しゅうしょく

4. おかげ_____ で、_____ になり、_____ _____ いたしました。
         さま   げんき   きのう   たいいん

5. _____ はおもしろい _____ をしていますね。
       たいいくかん   かたち

6. _____ い _____ に、_____ したので、もうすぐ_____ だ。
    わか   とき   けっこん   ぎんこんしき

7. _____、_____でお____しいと____じます。
   まいにち   ごけんきゅう   いそが   ぞん

8. _____は、その_____の____をとり、「_____
   いしゃ   ろうじん   て   あんしん

   しなさい。」と____った。
             い

9. _____さんのお_____が____くなられたことを_____
   やまだ   とうさま   な   ごぞんじ

   ですか。

10. 「どうぞお____し____がり____さい。」
          め   あ   くだ

11. ____はマイク・ジョンソンと____します。_____ _____の
    わたくし   もう   いま   ちゅうがっこう

    _____をしております。どうぞよろしく。
    きょうし

Kanji in Everyday Life

1. Young female clerical workers in Japanese companies have sometimes been referred to as 職場の花, but nowadays many of them find this expression patronizing. Why do you think this is the case?

   _____

   _____

2. When Linda Brown visited the Sugimoto family, she saw that 休校 was written in on one date on the kitchen calendar. What does this mean?

   _____

   _____

3. John Kawamura sees a sign saying 歯科医 on a small building in his neighborhood. What is in the building?

   _____

   _____

4. Mrs. Sano received a letter from a friend in Sapporo, who wrote about the 初雪 in that part of Hokkaido. What time of year do you think Mrs. Sano received this letter?

   _____

   _____

5. One of the national holidays in Japan is 敬老の日. Whom does this holiday honor?

_____

_____

6. When Heather Gibson was visiting her family in Canada, she received a letter from Hitomi Machida in which Hitomi mentioned that she was 多忙. What does that mean?

_____

_____

7. The kanji 未 means "not yet." What is the situation of a person who is described as 未婚? What about a person who is described as 未知?

_____

_____

8. One of the basic chemical elements is called 水銀 in Japanese. Which one do you think it is?

_____

_____

Writing Activities

Vocabulary and Grammar 5A: From Cradle to Grave

A. How old were you when you did each of the following things? Write your age in the blanks. If you have never done something listed, write *X*.

	age		age
ほ育園に入る	_____	大学を卒業する	_____
ようち園に入る	_____	大学院に入学する	_____
小学校に入学する	_____	大学院を卒業する	_____
中学校に入学する	_____	就職する	_____
高校に入学する	_____	退職する	_____
高校を卒業する	_____	結婚する	_____
大学に入学する	_____		

B. Number the events listed in the order that they usually happen in a person's life.

[例] 大学院　　小学校　　高校　　大学　　中学校
　　　　5　　　　1　　　　3　　　　4　　　　2

1. 生まれる　　死ぬ　　年をとる

　　_____　　　_____　　　_____

2. にんしん　　赤ちゃん

　　_____　　　_____

3. 新婚旅行　　プロポーズ　　恋愛　　婚約　　結婚式

　　_____　　　_____　　　_____　　　_____　　　_____

C. When does a person become able to do the following? Write each set of activities in Japanese in the order that people are usually able to do them.

[例] 1. can walk → 歩けるようになります。

1. can talk / can ride a bicycle / can eat by oneself

　a. _____

　b. _____

　c. _____

2. can write kanji / can write hiragana / can read a Japanese newspaper

　a. _____

　b. _____

　c. _____

3. can get married / can go on dates / can go to parties alone

　a. _____

　b. _____

　c. _____

D. In Japan, July 7 is Tanabata, the star festival. On that day children write their wishes on small pieces of paper and hang them as decorations on bamboo plants. Many of the children's wishes include a desire to be able to do something, or do something well. For instance, 「字が上手に書けるようになりたい。」 is a fairly typical wish. A few other wishes are written in English below. Write them in Japanese, as well as two wishes that you might have written yourself as a child.

1. to be able to draw pictures well

    _____

2. to be able to play baseball well

    _____

3. to be able to speak English fluently

    _____

4. to be able to earn good grades (いい点をとる) on tests

    _____

5. to be able to eat carrots

    _____

6. (your wish)

    _____

7. (your wish)

    _____

E. Are you from a strict family or a lenient family? How old were you when you were allowed to do certain things, such as stay at a friend's home, eat as much ice cream as you wanted, take your first part-time job, stay home alone, date, take a trip with friends or alone, and so on? Write five sentences in the 〜させてもらえるようになる construction, following the example.

[例] 私は13さいの時にチョコレートを好きなだけ (as much as I wanted) 食べさせてもらえるようになりました。

1. _____

    _____

2. _____

    _____

3. _____

    _____

4. _____

_____

5. _____

_____

Vocabulary and Grammar 5B: Careers and Occupations

A. Which occupations would you recommend for the people who have made the following statements? You may be able to think of two or three occupations for each person.

1. 毎週日曜日が休める仕事がいいです。

   _____

2. たくさんの人といっしょにする仕事がいいです。

   _____

3. あまり人に会わない仕事がいいです。

   _____

4. 屋外 (outdoors) でする仕事がいいです。

   _____

5. いろいろな国へ行ける仕事がしたいです。

   _____

6. テレビに出たいです。

   _____

7. 有名になりたいです。

   _____

8. いろいろな人をたすける (help) 仕事をしたいです。

   _____

9. お金がたくさんもうかる (to be earned) 仕事がいいです。

   _____

10. 子どもといっしょにいる仕事が好きです。

    _____

B. The following people are describing their daily routines. What do you think their occupations are?

1. 私は毎日コンピュータで本を書いています。_____

2. 私は中学校ですう学を教えています。_____

3. 私は家のデザインをします。_____

4. 私はデパートでくつを売っています。_____

5. 私はレストランでフランス料理を作っています。_____

6. 私はお医者さんといっしょに病気の人のせわ (care) をします。

   _____

7. 私はえいがやテレビで、いろいろなやく (roles) をします。

   _____

8. 私は毎日会社に行きます。_____

9. 私はいろいろな家に手がみを持って行きます。_____

10. 私はえい語の本を日本語にします。_____

11. 私はいろいろな人のかみを切ったり、パーマをかけたりします。

    _____

12. 私は悪い人をつかまえます (catch)。_____

13. 私はやさいやくだものを作ったりします。_____

C. Choose the best completion for each sentence fragment in column A. Use each option in B only once.

A	B
1. _____ お金をためるために、	a. 毎日、学校まで歩くようにします。
2. _____ 毎日、ねる前に	b. なくさないようにしてください。
3. _____ 日本語のれんしゅうの ために、	c. となりの人と話さないようにしてください。
4. _____ けんこうのために、	d. 新しい服を買わないようにしています。
5. _____ しけんの時は、	e. 日本語が上手に話せるようにしたい。
6. _____ このかみは後で ひつよう (necessary) ですから	f. ヘルメットをかぶるようにしましょう。
7. _____ きけん (danger) です から、	g. 歯をみがくようにしています。
8. _____ 日本へ行く前に、	h. 日本語でにっき (diary) をつけるようにしてい ます。

D. What should a person do to avoid catching a cold? Write a few things you can do, using 〜ようにする. The examples are some preventive measures that Japanese people often take. Here are a few possibilities: washing hands, drinking a lot of orange juice, going to bed early, resting well, and not spending time (being) with people who have colds.

> [例] 外から帰ったらうがい (gargle) をするようにします。
> 人がたくさんいる所へ行くときには、マスクをかけるようにします。

1. _____

2. _____

3. _____

E. You are applying for the following jobs. Write what you are doing to maintain or develop your qualifications for each job, using 〜ようにしている.

> [例] スポーツのコーチ：毎日ジョギングやウェート・トレーニングをするようにしています。

1. 学校の先生 _____

2. 医者 _____

3. か手 (singer) _____

4. 歯医者 _____

5. 新聞き者 _____

6. えいがスター _____

7. 通やく _____

8. アナウンサー _____

   (There are no job interviews for the following jobs, but what could these people do to maintain their skills?)

9. 主ふ _____

10. せいじ家 _____

F. The following are some letters that Japanese people have written to an advice columnist. Give three suggestions to each letter writer, using a form of 〜ようにする.

---

1. 私はいつも朝ねぼうして、仕事におくれます。おくれるのがきらいなんですが、朝起きられません。とてもいい目ざましどけいを持っているので、それをセットしてねるのですが、知らない間に止めてしまっているようです。どうしたら仕事におくれないように起きられるでしょうか。

[例] ねる前に、目ざましどけいを二つセットするようにしたらいいです。

1. _____

2. _____

3. _____

---

2. 私は大学生で、今21さいです。高校の時にはガールフレンドがいなかったし、友だちも少なかったので、大学に入ったら友だちをたくさん作ろうとかんがえていました。二年生になって、友だちはできたのですが、ガールフレンドはまだできません。私は頭も顔も悪くないし、せいかく (personality) もしんせつで、やさしいです。どうしたらガールフレンドができるようになるでしょうか。

[例] もっと女子学生に話しかけるようにしたらどうでしょう。

1. _____

2. _____

3. _____

G. Rewrite the following sentences using honorifics. Remember that the honorific forms of some verbs are irregular.

[例] そのしゃしんは、お客さんがとったんですか。→
そのしゃしんは、お客さんがおとりになったんですか。

1. 先生、あの本を読みましたか。

_____

2. 先生はすしがきらいです。

_____

3. そうりだいじん (*prime minister*) は明日はどこにいますか。

   _____

4. 先生はとても元気です。

   _____

5. 先生は3時にうちに帰りました。

   _____

6. 学長は今仕事をしています。

   _____

7. あのお医者さんの書いた本はとてもおもしろいです。

   _____

8. スウェーデンのおう様 (*king*) は、明日は何時にここに来ますか。

   _____

9. 部長、山下さんを知っていますか。

   _____

10. 先生はあのえを見て、「とても好きだ。」と言いました。

    _____

11. 山田社長は図書館へ行きました。

    _____

12. お客さんは何を見ましたか。

    _____

13. お客さん、顔色がちょっと…。何か悪いものでも食べたのでしょうか。

    _____

14. 社長のおくさんは、パリで洋服をたくさん買いました。

    _____

H. The following is a conversation between two employees talking about their boss. Change the appropriate words and phrases to forms that indicate respect for their employer.

A: おはようございます。あれ、山田部長はどうしたんですか。

_____1

B: 病気だそうですよ。さっき、おくさんから電話があって、今日は休むって。

_____2

A: 病気って、どんな病気でしょう。

_____3

B: 熱が39度ぐらいあって、せきが出て、体中が痛いと言っていました。

_____4

A: じゃあ、かぜかもしれませんねえ。

_____5

B: ええ、おくさんもそう言っていました。

_____6

A: もし悪いかぜだったら、明日も休むかもしれませんねえ。

_____7

B: ええ、こまりましたねえ。明日のかいぎ、部長がいなかったら、できませんね。

_____8

A: じゃあ、明日はきっと来ますよ、部長。

_____9

B: そうですね、来てくれるといいですね。

_____10

I. Ms. Tanaka is a professor of English literature at Nagaoka University. Imagine that you are introducing her before she gives a presentation at an academic conference. The basic outline of your introduction follows the information about Ms. Tanaka's life. Be sure to use honorific verbs.

1951 年 12 月 5 日	born in Yamaguchi
1970 年 4 月	entered Kyoto University, studied English
1974 年 3 月	graduated from Kyoto University
1974 年 4 月	entered graduate school
1975 年	went to London, did research on Shakespeare
1977 年	returned to Japan
1979 年 3 月	graduated from graduate school
1979 年 4 月	started teaching at Urawa University
1981 年 7 月	married Susumu Tanaka
1987 年	wrote a book on Shakespeare
1988 年 2 月	published her book
1989 年 4 月	became an assistant professor (じょきょうじゅ)
Now	is teaching English literature at both Narashino and Nagaoka University
	is writing a new book
Next year	is planning to go to the United States

田中先生は今はながおか大学の _____¹ の先生でいらっしゃいます。1951 年に山口で _____²。1970 年には京都大学に

_____³、えい語を勉強 _____⁴。1979 年には大学院を御

卒業 _____⁵ て、うらわ大学でお仕事を _____⁶。

御卒業の前には 1975 年から 1977 年までロンドンでシェークスピアを御研究

_____⁷。1981 年に御結婚 _____⁸。1988 年に初めての本

を _____⁹ てから、1989 年にじょきょうじゅに

_____¹⁰。今、新しい本を _____¹¹。

今はながおか大学とならしの大学で _____¹²。来年

アメリカへ _____¹³ 御よてい (plan) です。

Vocabulary and Grammar 5C: In the Workplace

A. Which Japanese words do the following phrases define? Write the word described by each definition.

1. 仕事におうぼしたとき、会社に行って、いろいろなしつもんをされること。

   _____

2. 仕事がなくなること。 _____

3. どんな学校に行ったか。 _____

4. どんな仕事をしたことがあるか。 _____

5. 仕事をしてもらうお金。 _____

6. 家から会社まで毎日行くこと。 _____

7. 夜おそくまで会社で仕事をすること。 _____

8. 大学生などが短い時間する仕事。 _____

B. Imagine that you are saying the following things to your instructor. Change the appropriate nouns, verbs, and adjectives to the proper humble forms in order to demonstrate your respect.

1. 先生、明日は何時に来ましょうか。

   _____

2. 明日は一日中家にいます。

   _____

3. ここで待っていますから、どうぞごゆっくり。

   _____

4. 先生、この本を借りてもいいですか。

   _____

5. あさってまた電話します。

   _____

6. 母は今出かけていますが、間もなく (soon) 帰って来ます。

   _____

7. 兄にそう言います。

   _____

8. 先生のおくさんをよく知っています。

   _____

9. すみません、明日先生に会いたいんですが。

   _____

C. You are the secretary of a company president. The president tends to imply what he wants you to do rather than give direct orders. If he said the following things, how would you respond?

   おなかがすいたね。→ サンドイッチでもお作りしましょうか。

1. のどがかわいたね。→ _____

2. ちょっと寒いね。→ _____

3. 今日は暑いねえ。→ _____

4. このコーヒーはあんまりあまくないねえ。→ _____

5. これはコピーがいるかもしれないねえ。→ _____

6. 田中さんに手紙を書いた方がいいね。→ _____

7. 部長はどこにいるのかな。→ _____

8. 部長の電話番号は何番かな。→ _____

D. The following is a dialogue between a college professor and Takada, a former student whom she has met by chance while on vacation in Hawaii. Change the underlined parts to either the honorific or the humble form so that Takada is showing proper respect to the professor.

   高田：先生、<u>ひさしぶりですね</u>。<u>元気ですか</u>。

   先生：本とうに。高田さんも元気でやっていますか。

   高田：ええ、おかげさまで。先生、御主人は<u>どうですか</u>。

   先生：ええ、元気ですよ。高田さんは今ニューヨークだと聞きましたよ。

   高田：ええ、三年前から<u>行っています</u>。先生もワシントンに<u>行ったと聞きました</u>。

   先生：新しい大学にかわったんですよ。

   高田：じゃあ、ニューヨークにも<u>来る</u>ことがありますか。

   先生：ええ、毎月一度は行きますよ。たいてい仕事ですけど。

   高田：本とうですか。ニューヨークは<u>どこにとまりますか</u>。

   先生：そうですね、たいていホテルですね。

   高田：じゃあ、今度は家に<u>とまってください</u>。小さい家ですけど、便利な所にありますから。家内も先生に<u>会いたい</u>といつも<u>言っています</u>よ。

   先生：そうですか。じゃあ、いつかおせわになりましょう。

   高田：今度ニューヨークに来るときには、2、3日前に<u>電話してください</u>。くうこうまで<u>むかえに行きます</u>から。

高田：先生、＿＿＿＿＿＿＿＿＿＿＿＿＿＿＿[1] ね。＿＿＿＿＿＿＿＿＿＿[2] か。

先生：本とうに。高田さんも元気でやっていますか。

高田：ええ、おかげさまで。先生、御主人は＿＿＿＿＿＿＿＿＿＿＿[3] か。

先生：ええ、元気ですよ。高田さんは今ニューヨークだと聞きましたよ。

高田：ええ、三年前から＿＿＿＿＿＿＿＿＿[4]。先生もワシントンに

＿＿＿＿＿＿＿＿＿＿＿＿＿＿[5]。

先生：新しい大学にかわったんですよ。

高田：じゃあ、ニューヨークにも ＿＿＿＿＿＿[6] ことがありますか。

先生：ええ、毎月一度は行きますよ。たいてい仕事ですけど。

高田：本とうですか。ニューヨークは＿＿＿＿＿＿＿＿＿＿＿＿＿＿＿[7] か。

先生：そうですね、たいていホテルですね。

高田：じゃあ、今度は家に＿＿＿＿＿＿＿＿＿＿＿＿＿＿[8]。小さい家ですけ
ど、便利な所にありますから。家内も先生に＿＿＿＿＿＿＿＿[9] といつ
も＿＿＿＿＿＿＿[10] よ。

先生：そうですか。じゃあ、いつかおせわになりましょう。

高田：今度ニューヨークに来るときには、2、3日前に

＿＿＿＿＿＿＿＿＿＿＿＿＿＿＿＿[11]。くうこうまで

＿＿＿＿＿＿＿＿＿＿＿＿＿＿＿＿[12] から。

E. Asada and Banno are having the following conversation at Banno's office. Asada is looking for Chisaka, who supposedly came to Banno's office a little while ago. The exact words they use will depend partly on the relationship among the three speakers and their relative statuses. Change the levels of politeness in the dialogue according to the descriptions of the relative status of the three speakers. Remember the following principles:

- Use honorific language when speaking to or referring to someone who ranks above you or when speaking to or referring to an outsider.
- Use humble language when talking to a high-ranking person or an outsider about yourself or people in your group. When speaking to an outsider, use humble language in reference to all in-group members, even if they rank above you within the organization.
- A high-ranking person has the option of using the plain form when speaking to subordinates.

[例] Asada (A), Banno (B), and Chisaka (C) are all colleagues at Sony. They entered the company in the same year and their ages are the same.

A: すみません、千坂さん、いますか。

B: 千坂さんですか。いいえ、ここにはいませんよ。

A: ああ、そうですか。どこですか。

B: さっき、銀行へ行きましたよ。

1. A and B work for Sony, and C is their boss.

   A: _____

   B: _____

   A: _____

   B: _____

2. A and C are colleagues working for Sony. B works for IBM.

   A: _____

   B: _____

   A: _____

   B: _____

3. A and C work for Sony, and C is A's boss. B works for IBM.

   A: _____

   B: _____

   A: _____

   B: _____

4. A works for Sony, and B and C work for IBM. B and C are colleagues.

   A: _____

   B: _____

   A: _____

   B: _____

5. A works for Sony, and B and C work for IBM. C is B's boss.

   A: _____

   B: _____

   A: _____

   B: _____

F. Each of the job titles below is followed by two statements. Circle the statement a person doing each of those jobs would be more likely to make.

[例] くつ屋の店員
    ⓐ お客さんにくつを買ってもらいました。
    b. お客さんにくつを買われました。

1. 車のセールスマン
    a. お客さんに車を買ってもらいました。
    b. お客さんに車を買われました。

2. ウェートレス
    a. ちゅうもんをまちがえて、お客さんにしかってもらいました。
    b. ちゅうもんをまちがえて、お客さんにしかられました。

3. 医者
    a. 夜おそく、病気の人に起こしてもらいました。
    b. 夜おそく、病気の人に起こされます。

4. けいさつかん
    a. よく道を聞いてもらいます。
    b. よく道を聞かれます。

5. か手
    a. お客さんに私のうたを聞いてもらいます。
    b. お客さんに私のうたを聞かれました。

6. スーパーの店員
    a. お客さんにもののねだんをよく聞いてもらいます。
    b. お客さんにもののねだんをよく聞かれます。

7. 社長
    a. 部下にレポートを書いてもらいます。
    b. 部下 (subordinate) にレポートを書かれます。

G. Rewrite the following sentences in the passive form.

1. 有名な作家 (author) がこの本を書きました。

この本は _____

2. あの建ちく家 (architect) がこの建物を建てました。

この建物は _____

3. 田中さんは山本さんをだましました (deceived)。

山本さんは _____

4. 金田さんは私をデートにさそいました (*invited*) 。

   (私は) _____

5. どろぼう(*thief*) が私のさいふ(*wallet*) をぬすみました (*stole*) 。

   (私は) _____

6. 先生はよし子ちゃんのえをほめました (*praised*)。

   よし子ちゃんは _____

7. 弟が私のクッキーを食べてしまいました。

   (私は) _____

8. 先生は昨日ぬきうちテスト (*pop quiz*) をしました。

   (私たちは) _____

9. 昨日は大雨がふりました。
   （おおあめ）

   (私は) _____

10. とても忙しいときに友だちが来ました。

    (私は) _____

H. Younger brothers and sisters are fun, but they can be a pain in the neck, and sometimes get *you* in big trouble. Write a few experiences that you have had, or friends have had, with younger siblings. Imagine things you could suffer from (like siblings eating your snacks, drawing on your homework, playing with your toys, disturbing you [じゃまをする] when you're with your friends, or trying out [着てみる] your new clothes).

[例] 私は人形(*doll*) のうでを弟にとられました。
（にんぎょう）
友だちは妹にしゅくだいをやぶられました (*torn up*)。

1. _____

2. _____

3. _____

I. Japanese teachers can be very mean. For example, they can give you pop quizzes, assign lots of homework, make tests very difficult, and call on you often during class. In what ways have you suffered in Japanese class? Write three sentences using the passive construction.

[例] 一時間に15回もあてられました (*was called on*)。

1. _____

2. _____

3. _____

Chapter 5 Review

A. Complete each of the following sentences in two ways, once by using …ようにする and once by using …ようになる。

[例] さい近、ふとってきたので、→
さい近ふとってきたので、あぶらっぽい *(greasy)* ものを食べないようにしています。
さい近ふとってきたので、このジーンズがはけないようになってしまいました。

1. 旅行に行く前に、

_____

_____

2. 来年までに

_____

_____

3. 外から帰ったら

_____

_____

4. 父はやさいをあまり食べないので、

_____

_____

5. 大学を卒業する前に、

_____

_____

6. 新しいコンピュータを買いましたから、

_____

_____

7. 昨日からとても寒いので

_____

_____

8. あの人はあまり好きじゃないから、

_____

_____

B. Linda Brown has a temporary job as bilingual secretary to the very demanding president of a Japanese company, and she has had to do all sorts of tasks. (As she has discovered, to say that "It's not in my job description," does her no good at all.) The supervisor of clerical workers asked her what she did for the president yesterday. Based on the list, explain in Japanese what she did, using the appropriate humble forms.

[例] 8時半に湯のみ *(tea cup)* をお洗いしました。

8:00   made tea for him

_____ 1

9:00   cleaned his office

_____ 2

10:00 typed a letter

_____ 3

11:00 photocopied a book for him

_____ 4

12:00 went to buy him a box lunch

_____ 5

1:30 wrote a letter for him

_____ 6

3:00 made a phone call for him

_____ 7

4:00 went to mail the letter

_____ 8

C. Ryan Scott had a summer job in the local branch office of a Japanese company. Unfortunately, he wasn't careful in his use of honorific speech. Here are some of the things he said in the course of the summer. Write what he should have said in order to follow the rules of usage, both honorific and humble. Assume that he is talking to or about people who rank above him in his own company. In other words, none of these things were said to outsiders.

[例] 山田さんは図書室へ行きますか。→
山田さんは図書室へいらっしゃいますか。

1. お医者さんは何と言いましたか。

_____

2. 社長はいつ帰りますか。

_____

3. 私は昨夜はうちにいました。

_____

4. どうぞすわってください。

_____

5. 社長のおくさんに会ったことがありません。

_____

6. 何をさがしているんですか。

_____

7. 部長にすいせんじょう (*letter of recommendation*) を書いてほしいです。

_____

8. 部長は熱があるので、休んでいます。

_____

9. 社長はこれから昼御はんを食べる予ていです。

_____

10. 社長、すてきな車ですね。いつ買いましたか。

_____

11. 私はライアン・スコットと言います。

_____

12. か長もあの映画を見ましたか。

_____

D. What are some of the educational and personal qualifications needed for these jobs? What kinds of practical experience provide helpful background?

[例] じゅう医 (veterinarian) →
まず、動物が好きじゃなければだめですね。大学で生物学や化学 (chemistry) をせんこうした方がいいですし、かちく病院 (veterinary clinic) でアルバイトをしたらいいです。大学を卒業してから、じゅう医学校に入学します。

1. 通やく

_____

_____

_____

_____

2. 新聞記者

_____

_____

_____

_____

3. テレビのスポーツ番組(*program*)のアナウンサー

_____

_____

_____

4. 小学校の先生

_____

_____

_____

_____

5. 医者

_____

_____

_____

_____

E. Write a brief chronology of your life, including such milestones as being born, entering and graduating from school, starting your first job, taking a major trip, and anything else you think of as a significant event in your life.

_____

_____

_____

_____

_____

COMMUNICATION AND MEDIA

コミュニケーションとメディア

Listening Comprehension Activities

Vocabulary and Grammar 6A: Telecommunications

A. Listen to the statements and circle the appropriate word for each statement.

Useful Vocabulary: きかい *machine*

1. （こうしゅう電話　ちょうきょり電話　コレクトコール）

2. （ダイヤル　電話ちょう　電話ボックス）

3. （でんごん　プッシュホン　こくさい電話）

4. （ファックス　電話ボックス　るす番電話）

5. （ファックス　ちょうきょり電話　話し中）

6. （いたずら電話　まちがい電話　コレクトコール）

7. （けいたい電話　ポケベル　電ぽう）

B. Listen to the four short conversations between students and a clerk at the information desk. Then, for each situation choose the appropriate information source.

1. Professor Yokoi's telephone number: _____

2. Schedule for buses to Tokyo Station: _____

3. Postage for letter to Germany: _____

4. Directions to friend's house in Shinjuku: _____

a. supermarket in front of school
b. internet
c. first floor of the library
d. ask Mr. Schmidt
e. ask a bus driver at the station

C. Henry Curtis wants to go somewhere over the weekend, but he is not sure he can afford it. Listen as Hitomi Machida suggests that he go to Marine Land in Yokohama. Then mark the following statements either true (T) or false (F).

Useful Vocabulary: イルカ *dolphin*

1. _____ Curtis knows various good places to visit.

2. _____ He can get a brochure for Yokohama Marine Land at a travel agency.

3. _____ There isn't much to do at Yokohama Marine Land.

4. _____ Downtown Yokohama is an enjoyable place.

5. _____ It takes a long time to get to Kamakura from Yokohama by train.

6. _____ Kamakura is a good place to learn about Japanese history.

7. _____ "Tokyo Walk" is an informative magazine about the Tokyo area.

8. _____ "Tokyo Walk" is available at bookstores.

D. Listen to the five problems on the tape and choose the most appropriate suggestion for each problem.

1. _____

2. _____

3. _____

4. _____

5. _____

a. もっと運動すればいいですよ。
b. 電話番号を変えればいいですよ。
c. かけ直したらいいですよ。
d. 日本語の本をたくさん読めばいいでしょうね。
e. もっと安い電話会社に変えればいいじゃないですか。
f. 学校の先生に話してみればいいですよ。

E. Listen to the conversation between John Kawamura and Yoshiko Tanaka. Then write down the things they ask each other to do.

Useful Vocabulary: 文 *sentence*

John asks Yoshiko to read his composition and do the following:

1. _____   3. _____

2. _____

Yoshiko asks John to read her report and do the following:

4. _____

5. _____

F. Tadashi Matsuda, Cody Smith's boss, and his wife have been in the United States for over a week now and they are ready to return to Tokyo tomorrow. Listen as Smith places a call to Matsuda's hotel room. Then indicate whether each of the following statements is true (T) or false (F).

      Useful Vocabulary: しょるい *documents, papers,* はんをおす *to put one's seal to a document*

1. _____ Matsuda did not sleep well last night.

2. _____ Smith has a few things that he wants Matsuda to do.

3. _____ Matsuda will call Harris and ask him to come to the office.

4. _____ Smith originally had no plans for this evening.

5. _____ It was Mrs. Matsuda's idea to invite Smith for dinner.

6. _____ Matsuda asks Smith to choose the restaurant and make reservations.

Vocabulary and Grammar 6B: Post Office

A. Listen to the conversation between Mrs. Suzuki and her son, Taro, and number the following actions in the order that Taro does them to get his letter off.

    ___1__ Write a letter

    _____ Put a stamp on the envelope

    _____ Write the sender's address

    _____ Write the recipient's address

    _____ Write the postal code

    _____ Put the letter into the envelope

    _____ Put the letter in a mailbox

B. Listen as Henry Curtis talks about his progress in Japanese. Then check the true sentences in the following list.

      Useful Vocabulary: ゆめ *dream*

    Curtis:

1. _____ thinks that Japanese class has gotten harder.

2. _____ cannot memorize all the kanji.

3. _____ sometimes does not understand what his teacher says.

4. _____ does not understand the textbook.

5. _____ studies hard at home.

6. _____ never gets help from his friends.

7. _____ watches Japanese TV or movies on weekends.

8. _____ writes letters in Japanese frequently.

9. _____ dreams in Japanese.

10. _____ is very satisfied with his present speaking ability in Japanese.

C. Listen as Professor Yokoi tells John Kawamura about her trip to Osaka, and choose the appropriate answer.

Useful Vocabulary: たいくつする *to get bored,* おべんとう *box lunch,* けっこう *fairly, quite*

1. Kawamura called Professor Yokoi last weekend to _____.
   a. ask about homework
   b. have her meet his parents
   c. give her some fruit from his parents

2. Professor Yokoi went to Osaka in order to _____.
   a. see her sister's family
   b. eat delicious food
   c. meet her sister from Los Angeles

3. She was on the Shinkansen _____.
   a. for three hours   b. alone   c. both a and b

4. She did not get bored on the Shinkansen because _____.
   a. she had someone to talk to
   b. she had things to do
   c. she slept all the way

5. In the train, she had a lunch which _____.
   a. she made at home   b. she bought there   c. her sister made for her

6. She sees her sister's family _____.
   a. once a month   b. once a year   c. every other month

7. She usually gives her sister's family _____.
   a. cookies she bakes
   b. cookies she buys
   c. cookies Kawamura bakes

D. Listen to Satomi Yamaguchi's four co-workers complain about their boss, and write the initial of the person who has/had to do the following jobs.

[Suzuki: S   Yamada: Y   Takada: T   Keiko: K]

1. drive a car for the boss's guest _____

2. make coffee for the boss _____

3. drink sake with the boss _____

4. write letters for the boss _____

5. go buy a present for the boss's wife _____

6. type reports for the boss _____

E. Listen as Henry Curtis tells Masao Hayashi about his first time babysitting. Then complete the following summary by filling in the blanks.

Henry Curtis feels tired today because he didn't _____ well last night. Mrs. Suzuki asked him

to _____, who is nice but _____. Curtis ended up having to

_____ and _____ with the boy. Also, he had to _____

with homework. After they finished the homework, the boy ordered Curtis to

_____. So, Curtis had to _____ and _____.

F. Listen as Masao Hayashi talks about his father. Then choose the best completion for each sentence.

1. Hayashi's father expected a lot from his son because _____.
   a. he himself was a failure   b. Hayashi was his only son   c. Hayashi was a talented boy

2. Hayashi had to learn _____.
   a. judo   b. gardening   c. cleaning a house

3. Hayashi's father _____.
   a. was a gardener   b. liked fishing   c. owned a news agency

4. During the summer, Hayashi had a part-time job because _____.
   a. he had to support his family
   b. he wanted to buy a fishing pole for his father
   c. he was made to get one by his father

5. Hayashi _____ his father for the way he was treated during his childhood.
   a. strongly resents   b. is grateful to   c. doesn't like

Vocabulary and Grammar 6C: Media

A. Listen to the statements and mark them true (T) or false (F) based on the television listings.

今晩のテレビ

	ROPTV	NNHTV	SOSTV
7:00	7:00　7時のニュース 7:25　天気予報 7:30　クイズ「そのな 　　　ぞをとけ」	7:00　わらってあてる 　　　クイズだドン！ 7:30　まんがトラトラ 　　　マン	7:00　大ずもうのみど 　　　ころ、今場所の 　　　3横綱に聞く 7:55　天気予報
8:00	8:00　プロ野球中継 　　　巨人対阪神 　　　甲子園球場から 　　　生中継 　　　（雨天中止の場	8:00　金曜スリーアワ 　　　ードラマシリー 　　　ズ「母の願い、 　　　今日子、強く 　　　生きて！」生まれ 　　　ながらにしてハ 　　　ンディーを背負 　　　う我が子を愛す 　　　る母。主演、榎 　　　通代、遠山薫、 　　　ロバート・クルス	8:00　時代逆 　　　真之助参上「江戸に 　　　さく花散る涙」主演 　　　遠野俊夫、吉田永子
9:00	合は番組に変更 　　　あり） 9:55　天気予報		9:00　金曜洋画の部屋 　　　「ホットランニン 　　　グ」刑事コテロ 　　　がまた殺人犯人 　　　を容赦なく逮捕 　　　主演トミー・リー 　　　ケイト・ジャック 　　　リン・リーチン
10:00	10:00　今週のベスト 　　　ポップス＆ 　　　ベスト演歌	10:45　おいしい旅	
11:00	11:00　ドキュメント 　　　日本の空は今！ 　　　人類の破滅を早 　　　める新しい公害 　　　とは何か	11:00　夜のニュースシ 　　　リーズ　日本の 　　　教育を考える 　　　文部省に聞く	11:00　スポーツダイ 　　　ジェスト　プロ 　　　野球・すもうの 　　　結果

1. _____　2. _____　3. _____　4. _____　5. _____　6. _____　7. _____

B. John Kawamura is interviewing Mr. Matsuda, president of a renowned Japanese company. Listen to the interview, and choose the best completion for each statement.

Useful Vocabulary: さいきん *recently,* せいこうする *to succeed*

1. Mr. Matsuda _____ six hours of sleep a night.
   a. is too busy to get   b. usually gets   c. doesn't need

2. He can sleep well _____.
   a. only in quiet, dark places   b. in his own bed   c. anywhere

3. When he looks at the morning papers, he always reads the _____ sections first.
   a. sports and hobby   b. science and technology   c. economics and politics

4. He goes jogging _____.
   a. whenever he has time   b. if the weather is good   c. every morning no matter what

5. He eats healthy foods _____.
   a. even if he doesn't like them   b. if they taste good   c. if they look good

6. He overcomes stress by _____.
   a. jogging   b. listening to his favorite music   c. both a and b

7. He considers _____ to be the key to success in business.
   a. plenty of exercise and sleep   b. a well-balanced life   c. rich parents

C. Listen as John Kawamura reports to professor Yokoi on what he thought of Mr. Matsuda. Then choose the descriptions about Mr. Matsuda from the list.

Useful Vocabulary: いっしょうけんめい *very hard*

a. bright
b. healthy
c. negative thinking
d. had a hard time when he was young
e. diligent
f. graduated from a famous university

g. knowledgeable
h. saved his company
i. good friend of Professor Yokoi's
j. well-known to the Japanese people
k. knows a lot of famous people

D. Listen as Heather Gibson interviews two students, a male student and a female student, about media. In the chart, mark which student made the following statements.

Useful Vocabulary: でんしメール *e-mail*

問題	男	女
1. 手紙より電話をよく使う。		
2. 外国に友達がいる。		
3. 外国からよく郵便が来る。		
4. 電子メールをよく使う。		
5. ニュースを知るためには、新聞がいいと思う。		
6. 夜、テレビでニュースを見る。		
7. 教育番組をよく見る。		
8. ビデオをよく使う。		
9. 映画館で映画を見るのが好きだ。		
10. マスコミのことをうるさいと思っている。		
11. 週刊誌の記事はうそだと思っている。		
12. 雑誌を買うことがある。		

Kanji Practice and Exercises

1	換 換	カン substitute か-える substitute か-わる be replaced, change over				
	交換手：こうかんしゅ（[telephone] operator） 乗り換える：のりかえる (to transfer from one 　　vehicle to another)		換	換		
2	際 際	サイ time, occasion, when きわ side, edge, verge きわ-どい dangerous, critical, risky; venturous				
	国際：こくさい (international) 交際：こうさい (socializing)		際	際		
3	留 留	リュウ、ル stop; hold fast; detain; keep と-まる／める、とど-まる／める (intr./tr.) stop				
	留学生：りゅうがくせい (international student) 書留：かきとめ (registered mail)　*confirmed* 留守：るす (away from home)		留	留		
4	守 守	シュ、ス、まも-る protect; obey, abide by もり babysitter; (lighthouse) keeper かみ feudal lord				
	留守番電話：るすばんでんわ (answering machine) お守り：おまもり (good luck token) 子守：こもり (taking care of children) *babysitter*		守	守		
5	受 受	ジュ、う-ける receive, catch (a ball), undergo (an operation), take (an exam), 　　sustain (injuries); be well received, be a hit う-ける receiving; receptacle; support, prop; popularity う-かる pass (an exam)				
	試験を受ける：しけんをうける (to take a test) 受話器：じゅわき (telephone receiver)		受	受		

| 6 | 器 器 | キ、うつわ container; apparatus; capacity, ability | | |
| | 受話器：じゅわき (telephone receiver)
食器：しょっき (dishes)
楽器：がっき (musical instrument) | | | |

| 7 | 取 取 | シュ、と-る take
と-れる can be taken; come off | | |
| | クラスを取る：くらすをとる (to take a class)
伝言を受け取る：でんごんをうけとる (to receive
　a message)　聞き取りのテスト：ききとりのてす
　と (a listening comprehension test) | | | |

| 8 | 報 報 | ホウ news, report; reward, retribution
むく-いる reward, retaliate | | |
| | 電報：でんぽう (telegram)
報道：ほうどう (reporting)
天気予報：てんきよほう (weather forecast) | | | |

| 9 | 文 文 | ブン writing, composition, sentence, text, style, literature
モン character, word; design; (ancient unit of money); (unit of length, about
　2.4 cm)
ふみ letter, note　あや design; figure of speech; plan, plot | | |
| | 文：ぶん (sentence, writing) 作文：さくぶん
　(composition)
文学：ぶんがく (literature)
文通：ぶんつう (correspondence) | | | |

| 10 | 打 打 | ダ、チョウ hit, strike
う-つ hit, strike, beat, shoot
ぶ-つ beat, strike | | |
| | 電報を打つ：でんぽうをうつ (to send a telegram)
タイプを打つ：たいぷをうつ (to type)
打ち明ける：うちあける (to reveal a secret) | | | |

| 11 | 調 調 | チョウ investigate; order, harmony; tune, tone
しら-べる investigate, check しら-べ investigation; melody, tune
ととの-える prepare, arrange, put in order
ととの-う be prepared/arranged, be in order | | |
| | ことばを調べる：ことばをしらべる (to look up a
　word)　体の調子がいい：からだのちょうしがい
　い (state of health is good)
調味料：ちょうみりょう (condiments) | | | |

12	英 英	エイ Britain, England, English; brilliant, talented, gifted

英語：えいご (English language)
英国：えいこく (England)
英文：えいぶん (something written in English)

13	映 映	エイ、うつ-す reflect; project; take (a photo) うつ-る be reflected/projected は-える shine, be brilliant

映画：えいが (movie)
反映：はんえい (reflection)

14	画 画	ガ picture, drawing, painting カク stroke (of a kanji) えが-く draw, paint, describe

映画館：えいがかん (movie theater)
まん画：まんが (comic [book])
画家：がか (visual artist; painter)
洋画：ようが (Western-style painting or movie)

15	郵 郵	ユウ mail

郵便：ゆうびん (mail)
郵便局：ゆうびんきょく (post office)
郵便受け：ゆうびんうけ (mailbox for receiving
　　mail)

16	紙 紙	シ、かみ、がみ paper

紙：かみ (paper)
手紙：てがみ (letter)
新聞紙：しんぶんし (newsprint)
和紙：わし (handmade Japanese paper)

17	送 送	ソウ、おく-る send

手紙を送る：てがみをおくる (to send a letter)
郵送する：ゆうそうする (to send by mail)
返送する：へんそうする (to send back)
転送する：てんそうする (to forward)

18	達 達	タツ reach, attain -タチ (plural ending)				
	私達：わた（く）したち (we) 友達：ともだち (friend) 配達する：はいたつする (to deliver) 速達：そくたつ (special delivery)					

19	宅 宅	タク house, home, residence				
	お宅：おたく (your house) 帰宅する：きたくする (to return home) 宅配便：たくはいびん (package delivery service)					

20	重 重	ジュウ、チュウ heavy; serious; lie/pile on top of one another おも-い、おも-たい heavy; serious おも-さ weight おも-み weight, 　importance おも-んじる／んずる attach importance to, honor, respect かさ-なる／ねる lie/pile on top of one another -え -fold, -ply				
	重い：おもい (heavy) 重さ：おもさ (weight) 重病：じゅうびょう (serious illness) 体重：たいじゅう ([body] weight) き重品：きちょうひん (valuables)					

21	刊 刊	カン publish; carve, engrave				
	朝刊：ちょうかん (morning edition) 夕刊： 　ゆうかん (evening edition) 月刊：げっかん (monthly [magazine]) 週刊：しゅうかん (weekly [magazine])					

22	雑 雑	ザツ、ゾウ miscellaneous, a mix ま-ぜる、まじ-える (tr.) mix ま-ざる、ま-じる (intr.) mix, mingle				
	雑誌：ざっし (magazine) 雑音：ざつおん (noise, static) ふく雑：ふくざつ (complicated)					

23	誌 誌	シ write down, chronicle; magazine				
	雑誌：ざっし (magazine) 週刊誌：しゅうかんし (weekly magazine)					

24	記	記	キ write down, note しる-す write/note down			
	記事：きじ (article) 記者：きしゃ (reporter) 日記：にっき (diary) 暗記する：あんきする (to memorize)			記	記	
25	放	放	ホウ、はな-つ set free, release; fire (a gun), emit はな-す set free, release; let go はな-れる get free of ほう-る throw; leave as is			
	放送：ほうそう (to broadcast) 放送局：ほうそうきょく (broadcasting station) 生放送：なまほうそう (live broadcast) 放火：ほうか (arson)			放	放	
26	組	組	ソ、くみ、-ぐみ group, set, crew, class, company く-む put together			
	番組：ばんぐみ ([television or radio] program) 生番組：なまばんぐみ (live program) 乗組員：のりくみいん (crew) 組あい：くみあい (union)			組	組	
27	試	試	シ、こころ-みる、ため-す give it a try, try out, attempt			
	試験：しけん (test) 試作する：しさくする (to make a prototype) 試食する：ししょくする (to try out a food) 試着する：しちゃくする (to try on clothes)			試	試	
28	験	験	ケン effect; testing ゲン beneficial effect しるし sign, indication; effect, benefit			
	試験を受ける：しけんをうける (to take a test) 受験する：じゅけんする (to take a test) 体験：たいけん (experience)			験	験	
29	忘	忘	ボウ、わす-れる forget			
	忘れる：わすれる (to forget) 忘れ物：わすれもの (something accidentally left 　　behind) 忘年会：ぼうねんかい (a year-end party)			忘	忘	

30			コン、こま-る be distressed

困る：こまる (to be distressed) 困っています：こまっています (I'm upset)				

Kanji Exercises

A. Match each kanji or compound with its closet English equivalent. (Use each letter once.)

1. 英_____
2. 映_____
3. 画_____
4. 刊_____
5. 換_____
6. 器_____
7. 記_____
8. 験_____
9. 困_____
10. 際_____

11. 雑誌_____
12. 紙_____
13. 試_____
14. 守_____
15. 受_____
16. 重_____
17. 組_____
18. 送_____
19. 打_____
20. 宅_____

21. 達_____
22. 調_____
23. 文_____
24. 報_____
25. 放_____
26. 忘_____
27. 郵_____
28. 留_____

a. absent   b. be distressed   c. England   d. broadcasting   e. container   f. effect   g. forget
h. group   i. heavy   j. hit   k. house   l. international   m. investigate   n. magazine   o. mail
p. miscellaneous   q. movie   r. occasion   s. occupation   t. painting   u. paper   v. protect
w. publish   x. reach   y. receive   z. reflect   aa. release   bb. report   cc. send   dd. sentence
ee. stop   ff. substitute   gg. try out   hh. write down

B. Write the hurigana for each kanji or kanji compound.

1. 乗り換える

   _____

2. 交換手

   _____

3. 国際

   _____

4. 留学生

   _____

5. 書留

   _____

6. 留守番電話

   _____

7. お守り

   _____

8. 子守

   _____

9. 受け取る

   _____

10. 受験	20. 英語	30. 帰宅
11. 受話器	21. 映画	31. 重い
12. 電報	22. 郵便	32. 重病
13. 天気予報	23. 紙	33. 朝刊
14. 作文	24. 手紙	34. 雑誌
15. 文通	25. 送る	35. 記事
16. 打つ	26. 放送	36. 番組
17. 打電	27. 友達	37. 試験
18. 調べる	28. 配達	38. 忘れる
19. 体の調子	29. 私達	39. 困る

C. Write the appropriate kanji for the hiragana under the lines.

1. ＿＿＿＿＿＿＿＿＿＿ の ＿＿＿＿＿ を ＿＿ さないで ＿＿＿＿ さい。
   るすばんでんわ　　　　でんごん　　　け　　　　　　　　くだ

2. ＿＿＿＿＿、＿＿＿＿＿＿＿＿＿＿ を ＿＿＿ けました。
   せんじつ　　　　しゅうしょくしけん　　　う

3. どんな ＿＿＿＿＿＿ がえんそうできますか。
   がっき

4. つぎの ＿＿＿ で ＿＿＿ り ＿＿＿ えです。
   えき　　　の　　　か

5. この _____ をタイプで _____ った _____ 、_____
      えいぶんてがみ   う   あと   そくたつ

で _____ しておいて _____ さい。
     だ   くだ

6. _____ になりたいので、いろいろ _____ べました。
      しんぶんきしゃ   しら

7. _____ から _____ をしたという _____ を
      ともだち   こくさいけっこん   でんぽう

_____ け _____ った。
     う   と

8. _____ がまだよく _____ からなくて _____ _____ ります。
      にほんご   わ   ときどき   こま

9. _____ を _____ たり、_____ を _____ んだりしました。
      えいが   み   ざっし   よ

10. _____ な _____ をどこかに _____ き _____ れてきたようだ。
      たいせつ   ゆうびん   お   わす

11. _____ は _____ に _____ いない。
      ばんぐみ   なまほうそう   ちが

12. _____ いスーツケースは _____ まで _____ で _____ っておこう。
      おも   いえ   たくはいびん   おく

13. たまに _____ を _____ むことがあります。
          しゅうかんし   よ

Kanji in Everyday Life

1. In the weeks before the New Year's holiday, Japanese people gather in restaurants, clubs, and inns for parties called 忘年会. What is the literal meaning of this term?

   _____

2. One of the oldest surviving works of Japanese literature, compiled in the eighth century, is called 古事記. What do you think this literary work is about?

   _____

3. Linda Brown is taking a course in modern Chinese history at the University of Tokyo, and in her readings there are continual references to the 四人組. To whom does this phrase refer?

   _____

4. Henry Curtis is in a large stationery store in central Tokyo, and he sees a sign indicating the department where 画用紙 is sold. What is 画用紙, and why would someone buy it?

   _____

5. What is a person's 自宅?

   _____

6. In a business letter, the writer discusses terms for 送金. What is that?

   _____

7. You are reading a newspaper account of an airplane that developed mechanical trouble shortly after takeoff and had to return to the airport. Before doing so, however, the pilot had to 放出 some fuel. What does that mean?

   _____

Writing Activities

Vocabulary and Grammar 6A: Telecommunications

A. Many Japanese compound words and phrases contain the kanji 電話. Fill in the blanks with words or phrases that will make each item match the definition.

   [例] 電話を _____ ：電話をすること → 電話を<u>かける</u>

1. 電話を _____ ：話をやめて電話をおくこと

2. _____ 電話：遠い所にする電話

3. _____ 電話：町の中にあって、お金を入れてかける電話

4. _____ ：電話をしたあと電話局にはらうお金

5. _____ 電話：外国にかける電話

6. _____ 電話：家にいないときメッセージをとる電話

7. _____ 電話：話したい人ではなくて、ほかの人の家に電話してしまうこと

8. 電話 _____ ：番号が分からないとき見る本

B. Fill in the blanks with the 〜ば forms of the verbs indicated.

[例] そんなにねむいんですか。こい (strong) コーヒーを _____ (drink)、目がさ
めますよ。→
そんなにねむいんですか。こいコーヒーを<u>飲めば</u>目がさめますよ。

1. かぜをひいたんですか。静かに _____ (rest)、すぐ元気（げん）になりますよ。

2. そのもんだいが分からないんですか。先生に _____ (ask)、教（おし）えてください
ますよ。

3. 部屋が見つからないんですか。私のアパートがもう少し _____ (spacious)、
ルームメートになってもらってもいいんですけどね。

4. そんなに忙（いそが）しいんですか。私が_____ (not sick) お手伝
いするんですけど。

5. アルバイトが忙（いそが）しくて勉強できないんですか。でも、_____
(is a student)、勉強が一番大切（たいせつ）なはずでしょう？

6. とても古いアパートだそうですけど、_____ (inexpensive and
convenient)、私は借りたいですね。

7. この本はとてもむずかしそうに見えますけど、_____ (try reading)、
読めると思います。

8. 山下さんはまだ来ないんですか。でも、いつもおそいから、もう少し
_____ (wait) きっと来ますよ。

9. あ、そのりんごは今買ってきたんです。_____ (not wash)、食べられ
ませんよ。

C. Your university housing office has assigned you a Japanese roommate, who turns out to be pleasant and,
in general, fun to have around. There is just one problem. Your new roommate's parents have always done
everything for him or her. As a result, this new roommate is helpless in many practical matters and often asks
you questions that seem to have obvious answers. Below are some of the questions your roommate has asked.
Give appropriate answers, as in the example.

[例] 電話番号が分からないんですがどうすればいいでしょうか。→
電話ちょうを見ればいいですよ。

1. 友達（だち）の家に電話しましたが、話し中です。どうすればいいですか。

_____

2. 洋服が全部よごれて (*soiled*) いますが、どうすればいいでしょうか。

_____

3. 友達に電話をかけたいんですが、今、レストランにいます。どうすればいいでしょうか。

_____

4. 父と母に手紙を書きたいんですが、ペンのインキがきれてしまったんです。どうすればいいですか。

_____

5. 買い物に行きたいんですが、車がないんです。どうすればいいでしょうか。

_____

6. 私はいつも部屋にいないことが多いです。それで、友達から電話があっても、いつもいません。どうすればいいでしょうか。

_____

7. もう自分の家にいませんから、母のように毎朝起こしてくれる人がいないんです。そのため、朝のじゅ業をよく休んでしまいます。どうすればいいでしょうか。

_____

D. You have been living in Japan for several months. Last week, you went on a trip that you hadn't planned well. As a result, the following things went wrong. What do you think you should have done? Write "I wish" sentences, using ～ばよかった(んだ／んです)(が／けれど／のに).

[例] Since you traveled during a major holiday, every place you went was extremely crowded.

違う日に旅行すればよかったんですが。

1. You found that all of the hotels and inns you wanted to stay in were full, and you ended up staying in a very run-down place.

_____

2. There were no seats available on the trains, so you had to stand or sit on your suitcase most of the way.

_____

3. The bus you had planned to take had been taken out of service, so you had to hire a taxi and pay triple the fare you had planned.

_____

4. A museum (はく物館) you wanted to visit was closed that day.

_____

5. You ran out of cash, but the banks were closed, and you had left your ATM card (キャッシュカード) at home.

_____

E. How do you feel about the following features of Japanese classes? Finish the sentences using 〜ば〜ほど.

[例] テストは少なければ少ないほどいいです。
    or 多ければ多いほどいいです。

1. しゅくだいは _____

2. 試験は _____

3. グループワークやペアワークは _____

4. 先生は _____

5. 学生の人ずう (number of people) は _____

F. Here is a test of your understanding of the three Japanese conditionals. Fill in the blanks with an appropriate verb, using the 〜ば ending whenever possible. If the use of 〜ば is not suitable, decide whether と might work. If neither is appropriate, use 〜たら.

[例] ある
    お金があれば、グリーン車のきっぷが買えます。
    お金があると、いつもすぐ全部使ってしまいます。
    お金があったら、たくさん買っておいてください。

1. 行く

今京都へ_____、きれいなさくらが見られます。

京都へ_____、ぜひ田中さんに会ってきてくださいね。

京都へ_____、雪がふっていました。

2. 作る

このケーキのレシピは、私が_____、いつもしっぱい (failure) する
    んです。

もしこのケーキを_____、私にも少し分けて (share) くださいね。

あのシェフが_____、ぜったいに (absolutely) おいしくできますよ。

3. おもしろい

_____ あの映画を見に行きたいです。

_____ あの映画を見に行ったんですけど。

_____ 教えてください。

4. いる

夜おそくこんな所に一人で_____、あぶないですよ。

昨日家に_____、田中さんがあそびに来た。

日曜日は、家にいるかどうかわかりませんが、もし_____ あそび
   に来てください。

5. 読む

この本、とてもおもしろいから、_____、貸してあげましょう。

この本を_____、日本のことがいろいろわかりました。

この本を_____、日本のことがいろいろわかりますよ。

G. You are working in an office. This morning, five people called and left messages for your colleague, who was in a meeting the whole time. The messages are listed below. Now that your colleague has returned to the office, explain what each of the callers wants to have done.

[例] caller → you: 私にすぐ電話してください。
   you → colleague: すぐ電話してほしいそうですよ。

1. caller → you: 家にすぐ帰ってください。

   you → colleague: _____

2. caller → you: 会ぎ室に来てください。

   you → colleague: _____

3. caller → you: よこい先生に電話してください。

   you → colleague: _____

4. caller → you: お金を返してください。

   you → colleague: _____

5. caller → you: いっしょに仕事をしてください。

   you → colleague: _____

H. How would you feel if your roommate wanted to do the following things? Explain whether you would want your roommate to do each thing, wouldn't want him or her to do it, or don't care either way. Use the constructions 〜てほしい, 〜てほしくない, or 〜ても (〜なくても) いい.

[例] use the phone for hours
何時間も電話を使ってほしくないです。

1. smoke in the room

   _____

2. bring a boyfriend/girlfriend to stay for the weekend

   _____

3. clean the room every week

   _____

4. clean up after having snacks

   _____

5. listen to music late at night

   _____

6. go out every weekend

   _____

7. borrow your clothes

   _____

I. When Linda Brown's neighbor Yayoi Murayama was younger, she thought that her parents were unreasonably strict, controlling, and critical—much more so than her friends' parents. When she turned twenty, the legal age of adulthood in Japan, she declared that she wouldn't put up with certain things anymore. What do you think some of these things were? List five of them, using the 〜ないでほしい or 〜ないでもらいたい forms.

Useful Vocabulary:

門げん	curfew
きめる	to decide on
えらぶ	to choose
ひはんする	criticize
…をぬすみ聞きする	to eavesdrop on
子どもあつかいする	to treat like a child
きんしする	to forbid
…にかんしょうする	to interfere with

1. _____

2. _____

3. _____

4. _____

5. _____

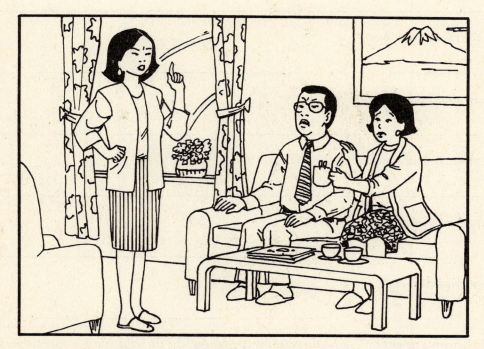

J. After quite a bit of resistance, Yayoi Murayama's parents accepted her requests. However, they also told her there were some things they didn't want her to do any longer. What do you think these things were? Write three of them using もう or これからは〜てほしくない／もらいたくない. Be creative.

[例] (mother speaking) もう私のようふくを着てほしくないわ。自分のようふくは自分で買ってね。

1. _____

2. _____

3. _____

Vocabulary and Grammar 6B: Post Office

A. Fill in the blanks with words that are related to mailing letters and packages and that make sense in the context.

1. 今日は母に手紙を書くことにした。きれいな _____¹ に手紙を書いて、それを _____² に入れた。そして、その上に _____³ を書いて、_____⁴ をはった。そして、アパートの前の _____⁵ に入れた。

2. もうすぐクリスマスなので、外国にいる兄にプレゼントを送ることにした。_____¹ に行って、_____² をはかってもらった。_____³ 便は高いので、_____⁴ で送ることにした。

B. What are some of your daily habits? Answer, and add more information about the following, using variants of the …ことがある construction.

[例] よくラジオを聞きますか。
そうですね、あまり聞きませんが、時々聞くこともあります。
or そうですね、ラジオを聞くことは、ほとんどありません。
or ええ、毎日聞きます。ラジオを聞かないことは全ぜんありません。
or ええ、たいてい聞きますけど、時々聞かないこともあります。

1. 夕食はいつも自分で作りますか。
   _____

2. ご両親によく手紙を書きますか。
   _____

3. 友達とよく電話で話しますか。
   _____

4. よくテレビを見ますか。
   _____

5. 週まつにも家で勉強しますか。
   _____

6. 毎週洗たくしますか。
   _____

C. Complete the sentences with …ことがある or …ことはない.

1. この町はとてもあん全 (safe) で、ドアのかぎをかけるのを忘れても

    _____

2. スミスさんはまじめな学生で、何があってもぜったいに (absolutely)

    _____

3. 私の母はふでぶしょう (bad correspondent) で、手紙を

    _____

4. 私の日本語の先生はとてもやさしい人だから、めったに (rarely)

    _____

5. この車はもう古いので、時々 _____

6. 私のアパートのとなりの部屋に住んでいる人は、忘れっぽい (forgetful) 人で、

    _____

D. Rewrite the following honorific sentences, using the れる／られる honorific forms.

[例] 先生、今朝、新聞をお読みになりましたか。→
先生、今朝、新聞を読まれましたか。

1. これは田中先生がお書きになったご本です。

    _____

2. 社長はゴルフにいらっしゃいましたよ。

    _____

3. 山下部長は三時間前にこちらにいらっしゃいました。

    _____

4. か長、ビールはめし上がりますか。

    _____

5. スミスさんは、アメリカ人ですけど、さしみをよくめし上がります。

    _____

6. 社長がお着きになったら、すぐ電話していただけますか。

    _____

7. 先生、あのプログラム、ごらんになりましたか。

    _____

8. 山下先生は毎日エアロビクスをなさるようですね。

   _____

9. 三田社長はもうお帰りになったようですよ。

   _____

10. 田中課長もあの車をお買いになるそうですね。

    _____

E. You work as an assistant to the company president, Ms. Iseda. One of the department heads, Mr. Ishikawa, calls and tells you that he needs to meet with her tomorrow. Study the president's schedule and explain to Mr. Ishikawa when she will be doing what tomorrow and suggest a good time for the meeting. Use the れる/られる honorific forms.

9:00	arrives at the office
9:00–9:30	makes an international call to New York (国際電話)
9:30–11:30	reads a project report (事業報こく書)
11:30	goes to a lunch meeting (昼食会)
1:30	returns to the office
2:00–3:00	prepares for the 4:00 meeting
3:00–4:00	has appointment with Mr. Okada from the Ministry of Education (文部省)
4:00–5:00	meets with business department (えい業部)
6:00	dinner with visitors from Chicago

[例] 社長は九時に会社に来られます。

1. _____
2. _____
3. _____
4. _____
5. _____
6. _____
7. _____
8. _____

ですから、_____ にアポイントがお取りになれると思います。

F. The following causative-passive statements lack particles. Think who would make whom do what and then fill in the blanks with は, に, or を.

1. 私＿＿＿＿ 上し (superior) ＿＿＿＿ とても長い手紙＿＿＿＿ タイプさせられました。

2. 先生＿＿＿＿ 学生＿＿＿＿ やさしいテスト＿＿＿＿ 作らせられました。

3. 母＿＿＿＿ 弟のせわ (care) ＿＿＿＿ させられました。

4. 先生＿＿＿＿ 作文＿＿＿＿ 書かせられました。

5. 社長＿＿＿＿ ろうどう組あい (labor union) ＿＿＿＿ きゅう料＿＿＿＿ 上げさせられました。

G. Some female workers at the American branch office of a Japanese company are complaining about a male section chief, Mr. Honda, because he abuses his position and makes them do tasks that are not in their job descriptions. What do you think the women are complaining about? Write sentences using the causative-passive construction.

[例]　コーヒーを入れる
　　　私は毎朝コーヒーを入れさせられます。

1. コーヒーカップを洗う

＿＿＿＿＿＿＿＿＿＿＿＿＿＿＿＿＿＿＿＿＿＿＿＿＿＿＿＿＿＿＿＿＿＿＿

2. かたをもむ (massage shoulders)

＿＿＿＿＿＿＿＿＿＿＿＿＿＿＿＿＿＿＿＿＿＿＿＿＿＿＿＿＿＿＿＿＿＿＿

3. くつをみがく

＿＿＿＿＿＿＿＿＿＿＿＿＿＿＿＿＿＿＿＿＿＿＿＿＿＿＿＿＿＿＿＿＿＿＿

4. たばこを買いに行く

＿＿＿＿＿＿＿＿＿＿＿＿＿＿＿＿＿＿＿＿＿＿＿＿＿＿＿＿＿＿＿＿＿＿＿

5. つくえの上をかたづける

＿＿＿＿＿＿＿＿＿＿＿＿＿＿＿＿＿＿＿＿＿＿＿＿＿＿＿＿＿＿＿＿＿＿＿

6. バーにつけ (bill, tab) をはらいに行く

＿＿＿＿＿＿＿＿＿＿＿＿＿＿＿＿＿＿＿＿＿＿＿＿＿＿＿＿＿＿＿＿＿＿＿

H. When it comes to household chores, some couples always agree on a division of labor and others make their partners do everything. Even those couples who have a perfect division of labor sometimes jokingly say one of them is "made to do" such-and-such. What are some of these things? Pretend that you are the complainer. First, using the causative construction, mention five chores that your imaginary spouse makes you do. Then, using the causative-passive as in the example, restate the situation as something that you are made to do. If you can't think of anything, here are some suggestions: doing the dishes, cooking meals, cleaning the house, washing the car, doing laundry, going grocery shopping, and ironing.

[例] 家内は毎日私にさらを洗わせます。
　　　私は家内にさらを洗わせられます。

1. _____
   _____

2. _____
   _____

3. _____
   _____

4. _____
   _____

5. _____
   _____

I. What did you not want to do when you were a child that your parents or other relatives made you do anyway? List four things, using causative-passives.

[例] 私は子どもの時、にんじんがきらいでしたが、いつも母に食べさせられました。

1. _____
   _____

2. _____
   _____

3. _____
   _____

4. _____
   _____

Vocabulary and Grammar 6C: Media

A. Fill in the blanks with question words or 何 + measure words (and perhaps a directional particle) to make "no matter what" sentences appropriate to the situations described.

[例] (an instructor complaining about students)

ここの学生は_____時間があっても、勉強してくれないんです。→
ここに学生はどんなに時間があっても、勉強してくれないんです。

or

(a person with a huge collection of tapes and CDs)

コンパクトディスクは、_____買っても、まんぞく (satisfaction) できません。
→ コンパクトディスクは何まい買っても、まんぞくできません。

1. (a company worker talking about holidays)

日本は、休みの日には_____行ってもこんでいる。仕方がないから、家
で昼ね (nap) でもしよう。

2. (someone who has a poor appetite)

最近、_____食べてもおいしくないんです。一番好きなチョコレートも
まずいんですよ。病気なんでしょうか。

3. (someone trying to locate Yamada)

山田さんは、10日ぐらい前から、_____電話をかけてもいないんです。
旅行中なんでしょうかねえ。

4. (a student doing homework)

このもんだい、とてもむずかしくて、_____聞いてもこたえが分から
ないんです。

5. (to a houseguest)

_____いてくださってもいいんですよ。その部屋はだれも使っていませ
んから。

6. (someone deciding which car to buy)

_____お金があっても、その車は買いたくないですね。新聞によるとす
ぐこわれるそうですから。

7. (a real estate broker talking to a customer)

_____たのんでもだめよ。あの土地 (land) は売るつもりはないって、むか
しから言っていましたから、あのおじいさん。

8. (an instructor talking to students concerning homework and answer keys)

_____ むずかしくても、こたえを見る前に、自分でかんがえてください。

B. Fill in the blanks with 〜て/ でも to complete each statement along the lines indicated by the English cues. Some statements describe the ideal employee from the point of view of an extremely tightfisted and inconsiderate employer. Others describe the ideal employer from the point of view of a lazy and greedy employee.

[例] _____ 、何も言いません。(*salary is low*) →
きゅう料がやすくても、何も言いません。

1. _____、仕事(しごと)を休みません。(*ill*)

2. _____、薬(くすり)を飲んで仕事(しごと)をします。(*has a fever*)

3. _____、早く帰(かえ)らせてくださいます。(*there is work*)

4. _____、朝八時には仕事(しごと)を始めます。(*at the latest*)

5. _____、夜九時までは家に帰(かえ)りません。(*at the earliest*)

6. _____、コンピュータゲームをさせてくださいます。(*busy

times*)

7. _____、気がつきません。(*be late*)

8. どんなに_____、もんく (*complaint*) を言いません。(*made to

work*)

9. _____ 会社に来ます。(*a typhoon comes*)

10. いつ_____、きゅう料を上げてくださいます。(*ask*)

C. Your friend made the following conjectures about his upper-level Japanese class on the first day of classes. Think of reasons why your friend might have had these thoughts, and ask questions to confirm your guess, as in the example.

[例] Friend: このコースはむずかしいに違(ちが)いないですよ。
You: きょ年、A を取った人がいなかったんですね。
or
先生がそう言われたんですか。
or
教か書がむずかしそうなんですか。

1. Friend: このコースの先生はきびしいにちがいないですよ。

You: _____

2. Friend: このコースはしゅくだいがたくさん出るにちがいないですよ。

You: _____

3. Friend: このクラスの学生は、みんな頭がいいにちがいないですよ。

   You: _____

4. Friend: このクラスにはしんせつな学生が多いにちがいないですよ。

   You: _____

D. You are listening to some Japanese tourists' accounts of their trips to the United States. They were impressed by the scenery and famous sights of the various cities, towns, and national parks they visited, but they don't always remember the names of these places. Read each description and help them by guessing the name of the place with …にちがいありません。

[例] この町はカリフォルニアの南部にあって、映画やテレビの中心です。ディズニーランドにも近いです。あ、それはロサンゼルスにちがいありません。

1. この町では、ケイジャン料理を食べながら、ジャズを聞きました。

   _____

2. この町はアメリカの一番古い町の一つです。フリーダムトレールを歩いてから、レッドソックスの試あい (game) を見に行きました。

   _____

3. 毎日のように雨がふりましたが、この町のまわりの山もピュージェットわんのしまじま (islands) もとてもきれいでした。

   _____

4. この国立公園 (national park) ではおんせん (hot springs) を見たり、くま (bears) を見たりしました。

   _____

5. この町はテキサスの大きい町で、せきゆさん業 (petroleum industry) の中心です。

   _____

6. エンパイア・ステート・ビルへ行ったり、ブロードウェイのミュージカルを見たりしました。

   _____

7. すな (sand) の白いビーチであそんだり、しぼりたて (fresh-squeezed) のオレンジジュースを飲んだり、キューバ料理を食べたりしました。

   _____

8. この小さい町はコロラドにありますが、有名な人がそこにべっそうを建てて、冬にはスキーをします。その町の名前はある木のしゅるい (kind) と同じだと思います。

   _____

Chapter 6 Review

A. What kind of advice would you give to your new Japanese coworker, who has just moved to the United States? Respond to the questions with a suggestion ending in 〜ばいいです(よ).

[例] Colleague: 車の運転めんきょを取りたいんですけど。

You: DMV へ行ってテストを受ければいいですよ。

1. Colleague: げん金 (*cash*) をたくさん持って歩きたくないんですけど。

   You: _____

2. Colleague: アパートに一人で住むと高いから、ルームメートをさがしたいんですけど。

   You: _____

3. Colleague: 車を買いたいんだけど、お金が足りないんです。

   You: _____

4. Colleague: かぐや食器をやすく買いたいんですけど。

   You: _____

5. Colleague: アパートに電話をつけたいんですけど。

   You: _____

B. Generally speaking, under what conditions would American college students do the following? Answer using 〜ば structure. If you are not sure, use …かもしれません, …でしょう, …と思います, or …ことがあります.

[例] てつやする (*stay up all night*)
つぎの日に試験があれば、てつやすることがあります。

1. 高い車を買う

   _____

2. キャンパスから遠い所に住む

   _____

3. 夏にアルバイトをする

   _____

4. 週まつずっと、家にいる

   _____

5. ビールを飲みすぎる

_____

C. You are an employee at a company where the work environment is less than desirable: It is hot in the summer and cold in the winter, there is only one restroom for fifty workers, the office gets stuffy because there is little air circulation, noise from office equipment is annoying, there is very little storage space, the walls are very dirty, the lunch break (昼休み) is only twenty minutes long, and there is compulsory overtime (ざん業) nearly every day, among other things. Your coworkers have elected you as their representative, so go to your boss and ask for concrete improvements, using 〜ていただきたいんですが／けれど.

[例] 窓を大きくしていただきたいんですけど…

1. _____

2. _____

3. _____

4. _____

5. _____

D. You are conducting research about people's use of telephones and other means of communication. What kinds of questions would you include on the questionnaire? Write at least five of them.

[例] 手紙を書くことがありますか。

1. _____

2. _____

3. _____

4. _____

5. _____

E. You are the assistant to a department head in a company in Japan. Your boss is very demanding, but he never comes out and says what he wants. Instead, he just drops hints and expects you to read his mind—and you are in trouble if you don't carry out the implied order right away! Write what you must do when your boss makes the following comments. (Since this company is in Japan, your job description is rather vague.)

[例] フライドチキンが食べたいなあ。→
チキンべんとうを買いに行かせられます。

1. のどがかわいたなあ。

_____

2. この花はかれそう (about to wither) だなあ。

_____

3. 今日は暑いなあ。

   _____

4. このコーヒーはあんまりあまくないなあ。

   _____

5. これはコピーがいるかもしれないなあ。

   _____

6. もうすぐむすめのたん生日なんだなあ。

   _____

7. 来週さっぽろへ行かなくちゃならないなあ。どのホテルにとまったらいいかなあ。

   _____

8. 部長の電話番号は何番かなあ。

   _____

9. 田中さんに手紙を書くひま (free time) がないんだなあ。

   _____

10. このいす、窓の前にあればいいかなあ。

   _____

F. When two people complain about each other, it's only fair to listen to both sides. What complaints do you think the following pairs of people might have about each other? Write their complaints using ばかり in the complaint of the higher-status person and the causative-passive in the complaint of the lower-status person.

   [例] 母：むすこはいつもテレビばかり見ているんですよ。
   　　むすこ：いつも母に 勉強させられるんです。

1. (a boss and a subordinate)

   じょうし：この部下はいつも _____

   部下：いつもじょうしに _____

2. (a married couple)

   おじいさん：家内は毎日 _____

   まご：毎日主人に _____

3. (a dog and its owner)

    かい主：うちのいぬはいつも _____

    いぬ：いつもかい主に _____

4. (a student and an instructor)

    先生：学生はいつも _____

    学生：いつも先生に _____

G. Complete the following to construct statements that describe your routine, belief, or general attitude toward life.

    [例] 時間がなくても →
        時間がなくても、新聞を読むようにしています。

1. お金がなくても _____

2. 時間があっても _____

3. 病気になっても _____

4. 忙しくても _____

5. 天気が悪くても _____

6. おそく起きても _____

H. Fill in the blanks with the appropriate conditional forms. If you aren't sure which one to use, review Chapter 7, Book 1, for 〜たら; Chapter 1, Book 2, for と; and Chapter 6, Book 2, for 〜ば. In some cases, more than one form may be used, although perhaps with a different meaning.

1. パーティーに_____（行く）、山田さんに会った。

2. 先生に_____（聞く）わかりますよ。

3. 外が_____（寒い）、家にいます。

4. 電気を_____（消す）、くらくなった。

5. その部屋が_____（静か）、そこでかいぎをし

    ましょう。

6. 今そこに家を_____（建てる）、とても高いで

    すよ。

7. 林さんが_____（来る）、もう心配することは

    ありません。

8. その本が_____（おもしろい）、貸してください。

9. コロナドさんに_____（会う）、よろしくお伝えください。

10. 右へ_____（曲がる）、いぬがとび出して(rush out)きました。

CHAPTER **7**

NATURE AND CULTURE

自然と文化

Listening Comprehension Activities

Vocabulary and Grammar 7A: Geography

A. Listen as Masao Hayashi talks about the place where his parents are living. Then fill in the blanks to complete the summary.

Useful Vocabulary: 気に入る *to get to like*

My parents now live on _____ that is two hours away from Tokyo by

_____. When my father _____ three years ago, they bought the

house, saying, "We don't want live in _____ like Tokyo. We want to live in

_____."

 There are a lot of vegetable fields around the house. There are _____ people, too.

There is a _____ behind the house, and a _____ is there. If you take

a bike, you can go to a _____ where you can fish. The _____ is a

little far by bike, but the beaches are _____.

 My parents like the house very much. I think that living in the country is _____,

but I like to _____ once in a while.

B. Daisuke Yamaguchi was transferred to a branch office in Sapporo, Hokkaido. Listen to him talking to Heather Gibson about the transfer. Then mark the things Daisuke and his mother will be doing starting next month.

 What will Daisuke be doing starting next month?
 a. working hard
 b. writing letters
 c. living alone
 d. cooking for himself
 e. going to convenience stores
 f. showing his mother around
 g. going back and forth between Tokyo and Sapporo

What will his mother be doing starting next month?
a. visiting Daisuke once a month
b. sending parcels to Daisuke
c. relaxing without doing anything for Daisuke
d. taking trips with friends in her spare time
e. working part-time
f. sightseeing in Sapporo

C. Henry Curtis has just moved into a new apartment, and the apartment manager is explaining do's and don'ts. Listen to their conversation, and answer the questions about routines, regulations, and schedules.

What routines, regulations, or schedules cover the following?

1. Garbage: _____

2. Subletting: _____

3. Door lock: _____

4. Rent payment: _____

D. Listen to the statements first and then choose the sentence that best matches each line.

1. _____
2. _____
3. _____
4. _____
5. _____

a. 何かいいことがあったにちがいないよ。
b. よく近くの川でおよいだものだよ。
c. うん、歩くようにしているんだ。
d. 甘いものを食べないように言われたよ。
e. うん、最近よくわかるようになったからね。
f. そうだね。もったいないね。

E. Akemi Mimura has come to an elementary school reunion. Listen to Akemi talking to one of her old classmates, Hiroshi Takahashi. Then, mark (T) for true statements, and (F) for false ones.

1. _____ Mimura has changed a lot in her appearance.

2. _____ There used to be a hill where a golf course exists now.

3. _____ Marine Land was built by the beach last year.

4. _____ Takahashi is in favor of the development of the area.

5. _____ Mimura wants to protect nature.

F. Listen as Mrs. Yamaguchi talks about her perspective as a 60-year-old woman and fill in the blanks to complete each sentence.

Useful Vocabulary: 外食 eating out

What was it like back when Mrs. Yamaguchi was young?

1. Women used to think about _____ at around 20 years old.

2. After getting married, women used to _____.

3. If women worked, leaving their children at nursery schools, it used to be said that

    _____.

4. Men never even _____ the kitchen.

5. They used to eat out _____.

G. Listen to the conversation between Mrs. Suzuki and her 7-year-old son. Then mark each statement true (T) or false (F).

Useful Vocabulary: だって／なぜなら because, やる (= する) to do

1. _____ His mother doesn't know that Taro has not done his homework.

2. _____ Taro doesn't want to start his homework now because he is reading a comic book.

3. _____ Taro's teacher assigns too much homework every day for a student to finish.

4. _____ Taro went to bed last night without finishing his homework.

5. _____ His mother is allowing Taro to watch TV only for 10 more minutes.

Vocabulary and Grammar 7B: Nature and Environment

A. Listen to a monologue by a person who is moving away from urban life, and fill in the blanks to complete the summary.

I have decided to move to _____ next month. Living in a _____ like

Tokyo causes lots of _____, and it is not good for _____ or for me.

When I was _____, I used to play in _____. If I tell my children to

play _____, however, it is dangerous because of _____. If we

continue living like this, our _____ will be harmed.

B. Listen to a monologue about the changes in a town and select the appropriate answer.

1. The town _____ a college town.
   a. used to be   b. has been   c. will be

2. The college has become _____.
   a. famous   b. hard to get in   c. big

3. Around the college, there used to be _____.
   a. big houses   b. cows and horses   c. rice fields

4. The number of _____ has increased in the town.
   a. companies   b. people   c. both a and b

5. The disadvantage of the expansion of the town is _____.
   a. pollution   b. shortage of living space   c. higher cost of living

6. The speaker feels _____ about the changes in the town.
   a. sad   b. happy   c. excited

C. Mrs. Yuriko Yamaguchi is very conscious about conserving energy and recycling things. Listen as her daughter, Satomi Yamaguchi, talks about her mother.

   Useful Vocabulary: むだづかいする *to waste,* すいどう *water service/tap*

   What does Mrs. Yamaguchi tell her family to do?

1. About room lights: _____

2. About tap water: _____

3. About paper plates and napkins: _____

4. About cans, bottles, and newspapers: _____

5. About using automobiles: _____

6. About plastic bags at supermarkets: _____

D. Listen to the four descriptions and identify the animal in each description.

   Useful Vocabulary: はこぶ *to carry*

1. _____   a. うま
                    b. いぬ
2. _____   c. ねこ
                    d. ぶた
3. _____   e. うし
                    f. うさぎ
4. _____

E. Takeshi Mimura is starting a part-time job at a flower shop. This is his first day there. Listen to the shop owner teaching flower names to Mimura. Then match each color with the name of a flower mentioned.

Useful Vocabulary: 温室 *greenhouse*
あんしつ

1. white: _____
2. red: _____
3. yellow: _____
4. purple: _____
5. pink: _____

   a. rose
   b. carnation
   c. plum blossom
   d. cherry blossom
   e. tulip
   f. chrysanthemum
   g. sun flower

F. Listen to the statements first and then choose the sentence that best matches each statement.

1. _____
2. _____
3. _____
4. _____
5. _____

a. ああ、それで、わかい人が多くなったわけですね。
b. ああ、それで、つかれた顔をしているわけですね。
c. ああ、それで、駐車場がいっぱいなわけですね。
d. ああ、それで、楽しそうなわけですね。
e. ああ、それで、動物をかっているわけですね。
f. ああ、それで、さくらの花が早くさいたわけですね。

G. Mrs. Yamaguchi ran into John Kawamura on the street. Listen to their conversation, and fill in the blanks to complete the statements.

1. Kawamura is staying indoors even though it is _____ today.

2. He has to _____ in the library even on Saturday.

3. Even though the class he is taking is only 2 units, there are lots of _____.

4. Even though Mrs. Yamaguchi _____, everybody in her family is eating out tonight.

5. Kawamura feels badly making Mrs. Yamaguchi cook on _____.

H. Ms. Furuta and Mr. Mikami meet at a college reunion held on campus. Listen to their conversation, and choose the most appropriate answer for each blank.

1. When the two were in college, the campus was undergoing _____ development.
a. no   b. a gradual   c. a rapid

2. As a result of the development, the college has _____ now.
a. more students   b. more classrooms   c. beautiful cafeterias   d. more professors

3. Mikami misses the _____ on campus.
a. trees and plants   b. wild animals   c. coffee shops   d. little hill

4. The bad experience Mikami mentions is about _____.
   a. a car accident
   b. hitting and killing an animal
   c. seeing dead animals on the road
   d. the smell of skunks

5. Furuta noticed that more _____ had been built around the campus.
   a. parking lots b. houses c. golf courses d. shops

6. Mikami is suffering from _____ because of the air pollution.
   a. a sore throat b. itchy eyes c. sneezing d. coughing

7. Furuta thinks development _____.
   a. is bad b. is good c. can't be helped d. should be increased

8. Mikami lives in Petaluma because of _____.
   a. a better job b. its convenient location c. its low cost of living d. security

9. The two used to _____ together when they were students.
   a. study b. go camping c. go shopping d. go out for a drink

10. Mikami doesn't like the area around the campus because _____.
   a. the people are conservative
   b. the life is too fast
   c. he easily gets bored
   d. the cost of living is too high

11. Furuta _____ Mikami's living in Petaluma.
   a. makes no comment on b. is rather disappointed with c. understands d. feels happy about

12. Judging from her tone of voice, Furuta will _____ visit Mikami in Petaluma.
   a. definitely b. most likely c. probably not d. never

Vocabulary and Grammar 7C: Culture and Customs

A. A guest is coming tonight and Mrs. Sato is telling her 7-year-old son, Taro, how to behave. Listen to their conversation, and choose the phrase that describes the manners Mrs. Suzuki is explaining to her son. Do not use the same phrase more than once.

Useful Vocabulary: ちゃんと／きちんと *properly*

マナー：

1. お客さまに、げんかんで_____。

2. あいさつする時、_____。

3. おみやげをもらったら、_____。

4. おみやげをすぐにあけるのは、_____。

5. すわる時は、_____。

a. おれいを言う
b. せいざする
c. しつれいだ
d. おじぎする
e. しんじる
f. あいさつする

18	他 他	夕、ほか another, other				
	他に：ほかに (in addition) 他人：たにん (stranger) その他：そのた (and the rest)		他	他		
19	最 最	サイ、もっと-も the most				
	最初：さいしょ (first) 最後：さいご (last) 最近：さいきん (recent) 最高：さいこう (highest, best) 最も古い本：もっともふるいほん (oldest book)		最	最		
20	犬 犬	ケン、いぬ dog				
	犬：いぬ (dog) 犬小屋：いぬごや (doghouse) 番犬：ばんけん (watchdog) 愛犬家：あいけんか (dog lover)		犬	犬		
21	馬 馬	バ、うま、ま horse				
	馬：うま (horse) 乗馬：じょうば (horseback 　riding) 馬車：ばしゃ (horse-drawn vehicle) 高田馬場：たかだのばば (Takadanobaba, an area of 　Tokyo)		馬	馬		
22	虫 虫	チュウ、むし bug, insect				
	虫：むし (insect) 害虫：がいちゅう (harmful insect) 虫歯：むしば (decayed tooth) 弱虫：よわむし (weakling)		虫	虫		
23	頼 頼	ライ、たの-む ask for, request; entrust to たの-もしい reliable, dependable; promising たよ-る rely/depend on				
	頼む：たのむ (to ask for) 信頼：しんらい (trust, confidence) 頼りにならない：たよりにならない (unreliable)		頼	頼		

24	植 植	ショク、う-える plant う-わる be planted				
	植える：うえる (to plant) 植木：うえき (potted plant) 植物：しょくぶつ (plant) 植物園：しょくぶつえん (botanical garden)		植	植		
25	咲 咲	さ-く bloom, blossom				
	花が咲く：はながさく (flowers bloom) 秋咲き：あきざき (autumn-blooming)		咲	咲		
26	必 必	ヒツ certain, sure かなら-ず surely, be sure to without fail, invariably				
	必ず：かならず (for sure) 必死になって：ひっしになって (becoming desperate) 必然：ひつぜん (inevitable)		必	必		
27	要 要	ヨウ main point, principal; necessary, essential い-る need, be necessary かなめ rivet, pivot, main point				
	要ります：いります (needs) 必要：ひつよう (necessary) 重要：じゅうよう (important) 要約：ようやく (summary)		要	要		
28	習 習	シュウ、なら-う learn				
	習う：ならう (learn) 見習う：みならう (learn by example) 学習：がくしゅう (learning) 予習：よしゅう (preparation for class)		習	習		
29	慣 慣	カン、な-れる get used to な-らす accustom to; tame				
	習慣：しゅうかん (habit) 慣習：かんしゅう (custom) 不慣れ：ふなれ (unaccustomed) 慣れる：なれる (to get used to)		慣	慣		

30		レン、ねーる knead; train; polish up ねーれる be mellowed/mature			
練習：れんしゅう (practice) 練習不足：れんしゅうぶそく (lack of practice) 試練：しれん (ordeal)					

Kanji Exercises

A. Match each kanji or kanji compound with its closest English equivalent. (Use each letter once.)

1. 化 _____
2. 界 _____
3. 害 _____
4. 慣 _____
5. 岩 _____
6. 石 _____
7. 球 _____
8. 犬 _____
9. 湖 _____
10. 最 _____

11. 咲 _____
12. 植 _____
13. 州 _____
14. 川 _____
15. 習 _____
16. 世 _____
17. 昔 _____
18. 村 _____
19. 他 _____
20. 虫 _____

21. 島 _____
22. 馬 _____
23. 必 _____
24. 要 _____
25. 頼 _____
26. 林 _____
27. 例 _____
28. 練 _____

a. ball   b. bird   c. bloom   d. boundary   e. insect   f. certain   g. city   h. customs
i. damage   j. dog   k. example   l. get used to   m. horse   n. island   o. knead   p. lake
q. learn   r. long ago   s. necessary   t. other   u. plant   v. request   w. river   x. rock
y. sea   z. society   aa. state   bb. stone   cc. town   dd. the most   ee. tree   ff. village
gg. woods   hh. -ization

B. Write the hurigana for each kanji or kanji compound.

1. 自然

   _____

2. 文化

   _____

3. 国際化

   _____

4. 島々

   _____

5. 半島

   _____

6. 村

   _____

7. 市町村

   _____

8. 湖

   _____

9. 五大湖

   _____

10. 川
_____

11. 小川
_____

12. 本州
_____

13. 九州
_____

14. 四国
_____

15. 北海道
_____

16. 石
_____

17. 岩
_____

18. 岩石
_____

19. 林
_____

20. 森
_____

21. 森林
_____

22. 地球
_____

23. 世界
_____

24. 一世
_____

25. 昔
_____

26. 公害
_____

27. 例
_____

28. 例えば
_____

29. 地方
_____

30. 他に
_____

31. 最初
_____

32. 最後
_____

33. 最も古い
_____

34. 犬
_____

35. 番犬
_____

36. 馬
_____

37. 虫
_____

38. 虫歯
_____

39. 害虫
_____

40. 頼む
_____

41. 信頼
_____

42. 植える
_____

43. 植物園
_____

44. 咲く
_____

45. 必ず
_____

46. 必要
_____

47. 要る
_____

48. 習う
_____

49. 予習
_____

50. 慣れる
_____

51. 習慣
_____

52. 練習不足

　　　_____

C. Write the appropriate kanji for the hiragana under the lines.

1. _____ の _____ を _____ ___ りません。
　　にほん　　　　しゅうかん　　　　ぜんぜん　　 し

2. もっと _____ することが _____ です。
　　　　　こくさいか　　　　　　　　　　ひつよう

3. _____ は _____ 、_____ 、_____ 、
　　にほん　　　　ほんしゅう　　きゅうしゅう　　　ほっかいどう

　　_____ とよばれる _____ つの _____ きな _____ からなっています。
　　しこく　　　　　　　　　よっ　　　　おお　　　　しま

4. _____ には _____ が _____ もながれている。
　　むら　　　　かわ　　　なんぼん

5. _____ に _____ って _____ や _____ の _____ を _____ りぬけた。
　　うま　　　の　　　　はやし　　もり　　　なか　　　とお

6. _____ で _____ も _____ きい _____ の _____ は
　　せかい　　　　もっと　　おお　　　みずうみ　　　なまえ

　　_____ ですか。
　　なん

7. _____ はよくここで _____ の _____ をしたものです。
　　むかし　　　　　　　やきゅう　　　れんしゅう

8. _____ に _____ えたさくらの _____ に _____ が _____ いた。
　　こうえん　　　う　　　　　　　　　き　　　はな　　　さ

9. _____ の _____ もんだいについて _____ そう。
　　ちきゅう　　　こうがい　　　　　　　　　　はな

10. _____ えば、_____ の _____ に _____ んでみたらどうでしょうか。
　　たと　　　　ほか　　　ひと　　　たの

11. _____ が _____ くてねられない。
　　むしば　　　　いた

12. ＿＿＿＿＿に＿＿きな＿＿や＿＿が＿＿がっている。
　　　どうろ　　おお　　　いし　　いわ　　ころ

13. ＿＿＿とねこと、どちらが＿＿きですか。
　　　いぬ　　　　　　　　　　　す

D. Circle the correct kanji for each of the following meanings.

1. old age	老 考 孝		18. dog	太	犬	尤
2. another	池 地 他		19. plant	値	植	直
3. occasion	祭 際 察		20. request	頼	顔	頭
4. island	鳥 馬 島		21. young	苦	答	若
5. testing	駅 駐 験		22. silver	錦	根	銀
6. person	昔 者 音		23. forget	志	忘	忍
7. employment	織 職 識		24. know	知	和	加
8. eat/drink (honorific)	召 告 台		25. serve	仁	伝	仕
9. love	受 窓 愛		26. -zation	北	比	化
10. group	紙 組 練		27. send	咲	達	送
11. example	例 列 烈		28. say (humble)	甲	由	申
12. investigate	調 試 誌		29. take	取	敢	最
13. be distressed	固 困 因		30. ceremony	弐	式	武
14. Britain	英 央 映		31. village	材	村	杓
15. publish	刑 利 刊		32. world	世	他	也
16. lake	潮 瀬 湖		33. necessary	悪	要	妻
17. ball	球 救 珠		34. marriage	結	婚	約

E. Write the appropriate kanji for the hiragana provided under the lines.

1. ＿＿＿＿＿を＿＿＿＿＿して、すぐ＿＿＿＿＿に＿＿＿＿＿した。
　　こうこう　　　　そつぎょう　　　　　　ぎんこう　　　しゅうしょく

2. ＿＿＿のため、＿＿＿＿＿は＿＿＿＿＿を＿＿んだ。
　　ねつ　　　　　　きょう　　　　しごと　　　やす

3. ____は____、____し、____は____きな
　　ちち　　きょねん　　たいしょく　　いま　　　す

　　____を____している。
　　しょくぶつ　　けんきゅう

4. ____い____の____が____より____だと
　　わか　　とき　　きょういく　　なに　　　たいせつ

　　____います。
　　おも

5. ヘミングウェーの「____と____」が____されている
　　　　　　　　　　　ろうじん　　うみ　　えいがか

　かどうか____っていますか。
　　　　　　し

6. ____さんは____の____と____したそうです。
　　やまもと　　　はつこい　　ひと　　けっこん

7. ____する____のために____ねますか。
　　あい　　　ひと　　　　　　し

8. ____が____の____に____さんが
　　わたし　　るす　　とき　　ゆうびんや

　　____を____しに____たようです。
　　でんぽう　　はいたつ　　き

9. ____のみな____もお____のことと____じます。
　　ごかぞく　　　さま　　　げんき　　　　ぞん

10. ____も____と____じように____です。
　　えいこく　　にほん　　おな　　　　しまぐに

11. ____は____で____しい。
　　ことし　　じゅけんべんきょう　いそが

12. ____や____の____で____の
　　しんぶん　　ざっし　　きじ　　せかい

　　____を____る。
　　ようす　　し

13. ____が____きで、____は____や____や
　　しぜん　　す　　　　むかし　　もり　　はやし

　　____や____へ____でよく____かけました。
　　やま　みずうみ　ひとり　　　で

14. ____から____をなくそう。
　　ちきゅう　　こうがい

15. ＿＿＿＿＿＿＿＿がなっていたので、＿＿＿＿＿＿＿＿＿を＿＿＿＿ったら、
    でんわ　　　　　　　　　　　　　　　　じゅわき　　　　　　　　と

    「アメリカのカリフォルニア＿＿＿＿＿からの＿＿＿＿＿＿＿＿＿＿＿＿です。」と
    　　　　　　　　　　　　しゅう　　　　　　　こくさいでんわ

    ＿＿＿＿＿＿＿＿＿＿が＿＿＿＿った。
    こうかんしゅ　　　　　　い

16. ＿＿＿どもの＿＿＿＿れ＿＿＿＿がひどくて＿＿＿＿る。
    こ　　　　　　わす　　　もの　　　　　　　　こま

17. ＿＿＿＿＿＿＿に＿＿＿んでいて、よく＿＿＿＿＿＿になる＿＿＿＿＿＿が
    きんじょ　　　　す　　　　　　　　せわ　　　　　　いしゃ

    ＿＿＿＿＿＿、＿＿＿＿＿＿＿＿＿＿で＿＿＿くなられたそうです。
    さくや　　　　　こうつうじこ　　　　　な

18. さくらの＿＿＿＿が＿＿＿＿くころになると、＿＿＿＿＿＿＿＿＿の
    　　　　はな　　　さ　　　　　　　　　しょうがっこう

    ＿＿＿＿＿＿＿＿を＿＿＿い＿＿＿す。
    にゅうがくしき　　　おも　　だ

19. ＿＿＿は＿＿＿＿＿＿と＿＿＿す＿＿＿＿でございます。
    わたくし　　たなか　　　　　もう　　もの

20. ＿＿＿かな＿＿＿＿＿＿＿＿に＿＿＿っこしたい。
    しず　　　　じゅうたくち　　　　ひ

21. 「＿＿＿＿ししかございませんが、どうぞお＿＿＿＿し＿＿＿がり＿＿＿さい。」
    すこ　　　　　　　　　　　　　　　　　　め　　　あ　　　　くだ

    とその＿＿＿＿の＿＿＿＿＿＿＿は＿＿＿＿った。
    　　　みせ　　　しゅじん　　　　い

22. ＿＿＿くの＿＿＿＿＿＿＿にのぼって、ロッククライミングの＿＿＿＿＿＿をした。
    ちか　　　いわやま　　　　　　　　　　　　　　　　　　　れんしゅう

23. ＿＿＿＿＿＿＿のように、つぎの＿＿＿を＿＿＿＿き＿＿＿＿しなさい。
    れいぶん　　　　　　　　　　　　ぶん　　　か　　　　なお

24. ＿＿＿い＿＿＿＿＿＿を＿＿＿んだので、こしが＿＿＿＿いです。
    おも　　にわいし　　　　はこ　　　　　　　　いた

25. ＿＿＿＿＿＿を＿＿＿つ＿＿＿＿＿＿があると＿＿＿＿いますか。
    でんぽう　　　う　　　ひつよう　　　　　　おも

26. テレビの＿＿＿＿＿＿＿＿＿＿＿＿＿＿に＿＿＿たことがある。
    　　　なまほうそうばんぐみ　　　　　で

27. _____ によって、_____ 、_____ が _____ うので、
    くに   ぶんか   しゅうかん   ちが

    _____ するのは _____ しい。
    りょこう   たの

28. _____ には、まだ _____ や _____ などをかっている _____ がある。
    むら   うし   うま   いえ

29. _____ が _____ こっても、まず _____ に _____ の _____ をかんがえてしまう。
    なに   お   さいしょ   いぬ   あんぜん

30. _____ は _____ で "caterpillar" という。
    けむし ("hair bug")   えいご

31. _____ か _____ に _____ でもあるのですか。
    なに   ほか   しんぱいごと

32. _____ という _____ は _____ な _____ だが、
    きょうし   しょくぎょう   たいへん   しごと

    やっていると _____ しいことも _____ い。
              たの   おお

Kanji in Everyday Life

1. You are browsing through a Japanese magazine and you notice the headline 日本に帰化. The article is about an Italian who is married to a Japanese woman and has lived in Japan for 20 years. What do you think he did?

   _____

2. In what situation do you think the Japanese saying 一石二鳥 is used?

   _____

3. Your host brother, who just started fifth grade this April, showed you a school letter. It says 林間学校のお知らせ and he said he is going to attend this school in the summer. What kind of school is it?

   _____

4. It's winter. You receive a postcard from your Japanese friend who tells you that she is going skiing in Nagano. It says こちらは一面の銀世界です. What kind of world is 銀世界? (Do you remember Nagano where the 1998 Winter Olympics were held?)

   _____

5. You are at a Japanese dentist with your friend who asked you to accompany her. While you are waiting for her to come out, you are looking at a picture poster of a human's teeth whose names are written in Japanese. You notice the kanji compound 犬歯 and there are four of them on the picture. What kind of teeth are 犬歯?

   _____

6. You are reading the sports section in a Japanese newspaper and understand that your favorite singer is going to throw the first ball at 始球式 for the all-star baseball game. What kind of ceremony is 始球式?

   _____

7. Your host father showed you the headline of today's newspaper, saying that it mentioned his best friend. You saw the kanji compound 市会議員出馬表明. You learned that it is election time for the city council members. What do you think your host father's friend is going to do?

   _____

8. As your host mother was driving you to the train station, you recognized your Japanese friend driving another car and there was someone in the passenger seat. You also noticed 中野自動車教習所 written on the side of the car. What do you think your friend was doing in the car?

   _____

Writing Activities

Vocabulary and Grammar 7A: Geography

A. The following sentences were uttered by an American who has been living in Japan for six months. Fill in the blanks with the correct verb form.

1. 来月、北海道へ_____ (travel) ことになりました。

2. 私は五月から日本に住んでいますが、まだなっとうを_____
   (eat) ことがありません。

3. 日本語で手紙を_____ (write) ことができるようになり
   ました。

4. 時々アメリカの家族のことを思い出して、

   _____ (become homesick) ことがあります。

5. もうあまりお金がないので、あと三ヶ月ぐらいでアメリカへ

   _____ (return) ことにしようと思っています。

B. Fill in the blanks with either ことになる or ことにする, whichever is more appropriate in the context.

[例] (a young graduate reporting about his new employment) 来月から日本のき業 (company) で働く ことになりました。

1. (a company employee speaking) この会社では、今月からきゅう料 (salary) は毎月 25日 にはらう ___ことになりました___。

2. (a company owner speaking) この会社では、今月からきゅう料は毎月 25 日にはらう ___ことにします/ました___。

3. (a modest Japanese person speaking) 私、六月に結婚する ___ことになりました___。 *he didn't decide*

4. (a strong-willed person speaking) 最近ちょっとふとり始めたので、毎日2、3 キロ ジョギングする ___ことにしました___。

5. 新しい仕事では、毎月日本にしゅっちょうさせられる ___ことになりました___。 毎月＝まいげつ every month / まいつき

6. (uttered at 10:00 P.M. in an office where everyone has been working overtime together) 今日はもう おそいから、みんな、もう家に帰る ___ことにし___ ましょう。 *let's decide*

C. You are taking a group of twelve-year-olds camping at a beautiful campsite that has all sorts of interesting natural features nearby: a beach, islands, mountains, woods, a lake, a peninsula, and so on. The children want to know which activities are permitted and which are forbidden. Answer their questions to the best of your knowledge, making sure that they enjoy themselves as much as possible, but keeping in mind that you will be held responsible if anything happens to them. (All the children are strong swimmers and in good health.) Use …ことになっている。

[例] あの山にのぼってもいいですか。
いいえ、あの山にのぼってはいけないことになっています。

今日湖 (みずうみ) でおよいでもいいですか。
ええ、今日の午後みんなでおよぐことになっているんですよ。

1. 夜、すなはま (beach) を歩いてもいいですか。

_____

2. 動物にえさをやって (feed) もいいですか。

_____

3. 海で、ボートに乗ってもいいですか。

_____

4. ボートで遠くへ行ってもいいですか。

    _____

5. あの島までおよいで行ってもいいですか。

    _____

6. 今夜、ボートの中でねてもいいですか。

    _____

7. あの山へハイキングに行ってもいいですか。

    _____

8. この小さい魚をつったんですが、食べてもいいですか。

    _____

D. Your ex-boyfriend or ex-girlfriend is getting married in three weeks. You have received an invitation to attend the wedding, but you don't want to go. Think of three plausible reasons why you cannot attend the wedding, using ことになった. Choose the one you like most and circle the number.

   [例] とてもしゅっせき (*attendance*) したかったんですが、おばが入院することになったので、行けません。

1. _____

2. _____

3. _____

E. Fill in the blanks with appropriate expressions, using もの to complete sentences.

   [例] 外国語というのは<u>むずかしいものだ</u>。(*Foreign languages are difficult.*) 勉強しないでいいせいせき (*grades*) を取ろうなどとは、かんがえないでほしい。

1. 日本に行ってもアメリカと同じような生かつをしたがるアメリカ人がいるけれども、日本では日本人のように生かつ_____。(*You should live like a Japanese.*) アメリカと同じことを_____。(*You should not expect* [きたいする] *the same.*)

2. 昨日の夜はスー・グラフトンのミステリーを読んだ。あまりに

   _____ (*since it was so interesting*)、午前三時ごろまで読んでしまった。

3. 親(parent)というものは _____ (nice)。いくらきびしく
   ても、困っているときにはきっとたすけてくれる。

4. フランスのリヨンという町はおいしいレストランで有名だそうだ。ぜひ一度
   _____ (I would like to try going there)。

5. 私達が学生のころには、田中先生は _____ (used to be
   strict)、最近はとてもやさしくなられた。どうしたんだろう。

F. Your Japanese teacher is scolding you for doing or failing to do certain things. Justify your actions using
…ものですから.

[例] 先生：どうしてしゅくだいをしてこなかったんですか。
    あなた：夜12時ごろまでがんばったんですけど、むずかしくて、できなか
    ったものですから。

1. 先生：やかましい(noisy)ですよ。じゅ業中(during class)はしゃべらないで(don't
   talk)ね。

   あなた：_____

2. 先生：起きなさい！教室は昼ねをする所ではないんですよ。

   あなた：_____

3. 先生：教室では食べたり飲んだりするなっていつも言っているでしょう？

   あなた：_____

4. 先生：つくえの上に足をのせるのは、日本ではとってもぎょうぎが悪い(bad
   manners)んですよ。先週もそうせつ明したでしょう？

   あなた：_____

Vocabulary and Grammar 7B: Nature and Environment

A. This evening you need to tell things to several of your friends, but when you phone them, none of them is
home, so you have to leave messages with roommates or family members. Leave your messages in the …よ
うに言ってください form.

[例] You want to meet tomorrow, so you want your friend to phone later. →
    明日会いたいから、後で電話するように言ってくださいませんか。

1. You want her to come over to your house before lunch tomorrow.

   _____

2. You want him to bring his computer with him tomorrow.

   _____

3. You want her to read the newspaper article that is on page 2.

   _____

4. You want him not to forget his homework.

   _____

5. You bought tickets, so you want her not to buy tickets.

   _____

B. What requests, orders, or suggestions would you give to people in the following situations? Answer using …ように言う.

[例] You have just seen some children writing on the wall of a store.
子どもにらく書き (*graffiti*) をしないように言います。

1. You see a man smoking in the nonsmoking section of the airplane.

   _____

2. You're in a waiting room where there is no no-smoking sign. A man sitting nearby is chain-smoking. You normally don't mind having a smoker near you, but have a bad cold today, and the smoke is bothering your throat tremendously.

   _____

3. The deadline for the project you've been working on is 2:00 P.M. It is now 11:30 A.M. Your secretary seems preoccupied today and does not seem to be making much progress in word-processing the necessary documents.

   _____

4. Your friend has been ill for some time, but she has not seen a doctor. You are concerned about her condition.

   _____

5. You are on the train. A child about five years old is traveling with his mother. The child is very noisy and is running around, generally being a nuisance.

   _____

C. Your Japanese friend is coming to the United States for the first time and will be staying with you. He does not know much about American customs, and you are afraid that he may inadvertently do something to inconvenience or annoy your family. Based on the information given, advise him so that he will know what to do. Use …ようにする／〜ないようにする.

    [例] (You know that some people slurp coffee in Japan.)
        コーヒーは音をたてないで (without making noise) 飲むようにしてくださいね。

1. (You know that people wash themselves outside of the bathtub in Japan.)

    _____

    _____

2. (You know that Japanese people close the bathroom door when no one is inside.)

    _____

    _____

3. (You know that in Japan, people may come into other family members' rooms without knocking on the door.)

    _____

    _____

4. (You know that people pick up [持ち上げる] bowls and small plates when they eat.)

    _____

    _____

D. The following sentences tell about things that instructors do. Some concern things that instructors do to achieve a certain result; others concern things that instructors say to their students. Complete each sentence, being aware of the different uses of よう.

    [例] みんなによく聞こえるように大きいこえで話します。
        よくがんばるような学生がいると、ほめます (praise)。
        じゅ業におくれないように言います。

1. みんなによくわかるように _____

    _____

2. 学生たちには毎日勉強するように _____

    _____

3. 学生がしゅくだいを忘れないように _____

_____

4. 教か書を読まないで来るような学生には _____

_____

5. このクラスの学生のように _____

_____

E. Your close friend is in bed with the flu. She lives alone, so you go to her apartment and do several chores for her. When you finish, tell her what you have done and the purpose of each chore, using ように. For example, cook dinner and put it in the refrigerator (so she can eat it later), do laundry (so she has clean clothes to wear the following day), go to the grocery store, bring in the mail and newspaper, buy flowers, or feed the pets (so she doesn't have to feed them later). Use your imagination and come up with good ideas to help your friend out.

[例] きれいなパジャマが着られるように、洗たくしておきました。

1. _____
2. _____
3. _____
4. _____
5. _____

F. Suppose you are a very lenient (so lenient that you are spoiling your students) instructor. What would you say to the students about the following matters? Complete each sentence using 〜なくてもいい.

[例] 朝ねむくて起きられないときは、来なくてもいいですよ。

1. しゅくだいが多くてできないときは、_____
2. ねむくなったときは、_____
3. 試験を受けたくないときは、_____
4. 名前をよばれてもこたえたくないときは、_____
5. このじゅ業とあなたの好きなテレビ番組が重なる (overlap) ときは、_____

_____

6. 英語でこたえたいときは、_____

G. The children of the Tamura family are always complaining about one thing or another. What do you think their parents might say when faced with the following complaints? Answer using either 〜なくてもいい or 〜なくてはいけない.

[例] Child: にんじん、きらいだから、食べたくない。
Parent: きらいでも、体にいいから、食べなくてはいけないよ。

Child: この肉、かたすぎて、食べられない。
Parent: じゃあ、食べなくてもいいよ。

1. Child: もうおなかがいっぱいだから、ぎゅうにゅうは全部飲めない。

   Parent: _____

2. Child: 今日は頭が痛いから、学校に行きたくない。

   Parent: _____

3. Child: この教育番組はつまらないから、見たくない。

   Parent: _____

4. Child: このしゅくだいはむずかしいから、したくない。

   Parent: _____

5. Child: クラスにいじめっ子 (bully) がいるから、学校に行きたくない。

   Parent: _____

6. Child: 今日はあそびたいから、ピアノのれんしゅうはしたくない。

   Parent: _____

H. Choose from the lettered column the appropriate responses to the following phrases.

1. _____ 花に水をやるのを忘れました。

2. _____ このバラはおん室 (greenhouse) で咲きました。

3. _____ 今年は雨がふりませんでした。

4. _____ きくはよくおはか (grave) に持っていく花です。

5. _____ 川の水がよごれています。

6. _____ 山で木をたくさん切っています。

7. _____ 海にさん業はいき物 (industrial waste) をすてています。

8. _____ このへんは工場が多いんです。

9. _____ この紙はもう一度使えますよ。

10. _____ 水が少なくなっているんです。

a. ああ、それで早く咲いたわけですね。
b. ああ、それでかれたわけですね。
c. ああ、それで入院した人にはきくをプレゼントしてはいけないわけですね。
d. ああ、それでのうか (farmers) が困っているわけですね。
e. ああ、それでリサイクルするわけですね。
f. ああ、それでスモッグがひどいわけですね。
g. ああ、それで川のそこ (bottom) が見えないわけですね。
h. ああ、それで魚がみんな死んだわけですね。
i. ああ、それでせつ約しなければいけないわけですね。
j. ああ、それで、鳥や動物がいないわけですね。

I. There are six students in the class whose behavior is somehow problematic. Give a possible reason for such behavior for each.

[例] A: 田中さんは体が弱くて、よくかぜをひくんですよ。
B: それでクラスをよく休むわけですね。

1. A: 山下さんは _____

   B: それでよくクラスにおくれて来るわけですね。

2. A: よし田さんは _____

   B: それでクラスでよくねむっているわけですね。

3. A: カワモトさんは _____

   B: それでよくしゅくだいをしないで来るわけですね。

4. A: すず木さんは _____

   B: それで先生の話を聞いていないわけですね。

5. A: スミスさんは _____

   B: それでいつもクラスでとなりの学生と話しているわけですね。

J. The following state the reasons why the following people have chosen certain professions. Write what careers you think they chose, using …わけです.

[例] 川本さんは子どもが好きだから、小学校の先生になったわけです。

1. 犬山さんはひこうきが好きだから、_____

2. 森田さんは動物が大好きだから、_____

3. 石川さんは映画が好きだから、_____

4. 島田さんはコンピュータが好きだから、_____
   （しまだ）

5. 岩村さんは山が大好きなので、_____
   （いわむら）

Vocabulary and Grammar 7C: Culture and Customs

A. Sometimes you encounter situations that are contrary to your expectations and this disappoints or upsets you. These sorts of situations are often described with …のに constructions. Complete the following sentences with something that makes sense in the context, but feel free to use your imagination. Remember, you're talking about situations that go against your expectations.

[例] 日本人なのに、日本料理がきらいだと言っています。

1. 試験の勉強をがんばったのに、_____
   （しけん）

2. 田中さんはおとなしい人なのに、_____

3. 初めて会ったばかりなのに、_____
   （はじ）

4. おそうしき (funeral) なのに、_____

5. 社長がおじぎをしたのに、_____
   （ちょう）

6. これは日本の雑誌なのに、_____
   （ざっし）

7. 洋食のレストランなのに、_____

8. あの日本人のカップルはアメリカへ行って結婚式をあげたのに、_____
   （けっこんしき）
   _____

B. Professor Arai is talking with another instructor about the students in her second-year Japanese class. She thinks that they are the best students she has had in years, and she offers several examples of their diligence in the face of obstacles. Complete the sentences, telling what you think the students did.

[例] 大雨がふっていたのに、スミスさんは歩いてキャンパスへ来ました。

1. 午前一時をすぎたのに、クラウスさんは _____
   _____

2. しゅくだいが全然ないのに、ユーさんは _____
   （ぜんぜん）
   _____

3. 少しねつがあるのに、ジョンソンさんは _____
   _____

4. 家がキャンパスから遠いのに、キムさんは _____
   _____

5. 昨日はとてもいそがしかったのに、コロナドさんは _____

_____

C. Then Professor Arai starts talking about another class she had years ago. These students had precisely the opposite attitude. They did annoying things and failed to do what they were supposed to despite favorable conditions.

[例] 病気ではないのに、クラスを休みました。

1. _____、

しゅくだいをしませんでした。

2. _____、

その映画を見ませんでした。

3. _____、

教か書を売りました。

4. _____、

クラスでねむりました。

5. _____、

クラスにおくれて来ました。

6. _____、

日本語を使いませんでした。

D. Sometimes parents disappoint their children. The following are some children's reactions to situations in which their parents failed to do something or did something displeasing. Complete each sentence with のに, and then state in English what the parents did to merit that reaction.

[例] 日曜日には海へ連れていってくれるって言ったのに。
(The parents promised to take the child to the beach on Sunday and didn't do it.)

1. 夏休みに _____

_____

2. 今度のたん生日に _____

_____

3. 10 さいになったら _____

_____

4. クリスマスに _____

_____

5. (Make up your own.) _____

_____

E. Write "I wish" sentences, using one of the conditionals + よかったのに for the following situations.

[例] You went on a hike, and it started to rain. You got drenched.
かさかレインコートを持って行けばよかったのに。

1. You received an F in one of your classes.

_____

2. You intended to get up at 6:00 A.M., but it was 8:30 when you woke up.

_____

3. Your good friend asked you what you thought of her new boyfriend. After you told her your opinion, she got very angry.

   _____

4. You wanted to buy a new stereo, but when you found the model you wanted on sale at 50 percent off, you realized that you still didn't have enough money.

   _____

5. For several months, you have had a big crush on an acquaintance of yours, but you haven't done anything about it. You have just heard that that person got engaged last night.

   _____

Chapter 7 Review

A. Suppose you are a gossip columnist for a third-rate magazine. Come up with three gossipy news items that will attract readers. Write the first sentence using …ことになった, followed by another sentence ending in …の話では…そうだ。 (Perhaps some celebrity is getting married, getting divorced, building a mansion, starting a new company, or getting sued [こくそされる].)

> [例] かしゅのヒミコが来月、サムライ・アイスクリーム・バンドのイザナギと
> 結婚_{けっこん}することになった。
> レポーターの本田まさるの話では、ヒミコは ¥30,000,000 のウェディング・
> ドレスを買ったそうだ。

1. _____

   _____

2. _____

   _____

3. _____

   _____

B. If you could find an ideal boyfriend or girlfriend, what would that person be like? Do you have any "nonnegotiable demands"? Tell what you think of each of the following characteristics, using 〜なくても いい, 〜なくてはいけない, or (どちら) でもいいです。

> [例] こくせき(nationality) は（アメリカ、日本、外国)
> a. アメリカ人じゃなくてもいいです。
> b. 日本人でなくてはいけません。
> c. アメリカ人でも、外国人でも、いいです。

1. せは （高い、ひくい）
   _____

2. 体形（たいけい）は （ふとっている、やせている）
   _____

3. 顔は （ハンサム／び人）
   _____

4. きゅう料は （高い、ひくい）
   _____

5. 家は （大きい、小さい）
   _____

6. せいかく (*character, personality*) は （明るい、まじめ）
   _____

7. めがねは （かける）
   _____

8. その他（た）： (*Make up your own.*)
   _____

C. Think of the time when you were in elementary school. What are some of the things you used to do then that you no longer do? What was true then that is no longer true now? Use …ものです.

> [例] よくラジオで →
>   よくラジオでディスコの音楽を聞いたものです。

1. そのころには、1 ドルで
   _____

2. ひまなときには、
   _____

3. りょうしんはいつも
   _____

4. 学校（こう）では
   _____

5. 友だちと

_____

6. (Make up your own)

_____

D. Fill in the blanks with the appropriate Japanese equivalent of the word provided + のに. If the use of のに is not appropriate, use けれど.

[例] 昨日は出かけない<u>つもりだったのに</u>(intended)、食べるものがなくなってしまって、スーパーまで行かなければなりませんでした。

1. 家で勉強_____(wanted to study)、ルームメートがうるさいから、図書館で勉強しました。

2. あまりおなかは_____(not hungry)、昼ごはんの時間ですから何か食べましょう。

3. _____(was tired)、休まないで勉強しました。

4. 「かん字が苦手だ」といつも_____、(are saying) こんなにきれいに書いたんですか。

5. 明日は_____ (busy)、午後デパートのバーゲンセールに行ってみるつもりです。